줄리정 불법 IELTS Speaking

Juli Jung's Immutable Law for IELTS Speaking

2024년 3월 25일 3쇄 인쇄

지은이	줄리정
발행인	홍은경
발행처	SUNNY SUNDAY www.sunnysunday.co.kr
주소	경기도 성남시 분당구 성남대로 343번길 12-2, B 301호
전화	070-8972-0816
성우	Alex Jensen, Crichton Hannah
사진	Ted Kim
삽화	홍진실, 조혜란
디자인·인쇄	디자인온 designon1010@naver.com

ISBN 979-11-953898-4-1 13740

※ 책값은 뒤표지에 있습니다.
※ 잘못된 책은 구입처에서 교환하여 드립니다.
※ 이 책은 저작권법에 의하여 보호를 받는 저작물이므로 무단 전재와 무단 복제를 금합니다.

보이는 Speaking
QR 코드

Academic / General 공통

줄리정 지음

BBC 앵커 출신 영국인 성우가
녹음한 MP3 파일 무료 제공
sunnysunday.co.kr
blog.naver.com/iloveielts

H Publishers Co.

추천의 글

효과적인 아이엘츠 시험 준비의 시작과 끝!

줄리정 선생님을 한번이라도 만나본 사람이라면 그녀의 샘솟는 에너지와 아이엘츠 시험 준비생 개개인에 대한 진심 어린 애정에 깜짝 놀랄 것입니다. 아이엘츠 시험을 면밀히 연구하고 그 간의 온라인·오프라인을 아우르는 전문성과 경험으로 녹여낸 이 책이야말로 효과적인 시험 준비의 시작과 끝이 될 것입니다.

_ **최현경** 주한영국문화원 IELTS 시험센터 팀장

아이엘츠의 보증수표, 7.0의 기적을 일상처럼 일으키는 줄리정 선생님!

줄리정 선생님의 강의를 듣는다는 것은 곧 아이엘츠 보증수표를 거머쥔 것이다. 첫 시험에서 7.0을 획득하는 기적을 일상처럼 일으키는 줄리정 선생님의 노하우와 열정의 집합체인 본 도서 '불법 아이엘츠'가 현재 점수가 몇점이든 단기간에 목표 점수로 이끌어주는 최고의 길잡이가 되리라 확신한다. 시원스쿨랩을 처음 시작할 때 가장 모시고 싶었던 줄리정 선생님께서 본서로 아이엘츠 명가 시원스쿨랩에서 혼신을 다해 강의하신 명품 인강은, 단연코 줄리정 선생님에 대한 과거 수많은 아이엘츠 수험생들의 찬사를 훨씬 뛰어넘는 짙은 감동을 줄 것이다.

_ **양홍걸** 에스제이더블유인터내셔널(시원스쿨) 대표이사

아이엘츠의 여왕, 줄리정이 만든 아이엘츠 고득점을 위한 바이블

Juli has taken the IELTS market by storm with her passion and drive. She has a unique ability to make language learning both fun and practical, and if you do what she says, your English will improve along with your IELTS score! For those reasons, I would certainly recommend her to my Korean friends.

_ **알렉스 젠슨** 前 BBC 앵커, 現 TBS 교통방송 진행자

Special thanks to
Alex Jensen, Crichton Hannah, 김진희, 홍은경, 조혜란, 김성오, 민혜정, 제지윤, 최현경, 장윤정, 김혜지

01 줄리정불법아이엘츠 Speaking 특징

줄리정불법아이엘츠 Speaking은 최근 5년간 아이엘츠 시험 기출문제를 바탕으로 캠브리지 아이엘츠 시리즈에서 자주 나오는 표현과 단어들로 모범 답안을 구성하였다. 기존의 줄리정불법아이엘츠 시리즈와 연관성 있는 구성으로 이미 줄리정의 독자라면 더욱 친숙하고 재미있게 효과적으로 공부할 수 있다.

눈으로만 보는 책이 아니라 듣고 따라 해야 하는 Speaking 책이기 때문에 지적이고 세련된 젊은 영국인 성우의 목소리를 담았다. 현재 TBS e-FM 'This Morning'의 진행자이자 BBC 출신인 영국인 알렉스 젠슨 앵커의 목소리와 동영상을 mp3와 QR 코드를 통해 확인할 수 있다.

발렌티노, 조성진, 증강 현실, 3D 프린팅 등 최신 감각이 반영된 아카데믹하면서도 세련된 답변은 아이엘츠 시험의 고득점을 보장할 뿐만 아니라 학습자의 영어 실력 향상에도 기여할 것이다.

02 줄리정불법아이엘츠 Speaking 학습법

Speaking 시험에서 높은 점수를 받기 위한 가장 중요한 요소는 무엇일까?

흔히들 발음이나 유창함이 Speaking 점수를 결정짓는다고 생각할지 모른다. 하지만 학생들의 실제 시험 점수를 분석해 본 결과, '아이디어와 어휘력'이 뛰어난 학생들이 높은 점수를 받았다. 영어 발음에 사투리가 섞인 부산 출신 학생도, 일본어 발음이 섞인 50대 만학도도, 말의 속도가 아주 느렸던 '고옹~~~~~ 구~울~러~가~유~~~~~~~~~~~' 식의 영어를 구사했던 학생도, 모두 높은 수준의 아이디어와 어휘력으로 6.5 이상을 받았다. 반면 영어권 나라에서 어린 시절부터 5~10년 이상을 보내고 원어민에 가까운 발음을 구사하는 학생들 중에도 '아이디어와 어휘력' 부족으로 Speaking에서 생각보다 높지 않은 점수(5.5~6.0)를 받는 경우도 종종 있다. Speaking 시험은 영어 면접처럼 시험관을 취업하고자 하는 회사의 사장님으로 생각하고 주어진 질문에 대답해야 높은 점수를 받을 수 있다. 또한 part 2, 1~2분 프리젠테이션은 응시자 스스로가 CNN 앵커가 된 느낌으로 유창하고 논리적으로 본인의 의견을 전달하는 것이 중요하다.

IELTS Speaking에는 한국말로도 논리적으로 답변하기 어려운 까다로운 질문들이 많다. 따라서 평소 예상문제 위주로 꾸준하게 브레인스토밍을 하고 유용한 단어와 표현들을 외워서 미리 예상 답변을 마련해 두어야 한다. 예상 문제와 답변을 적은 본인만의 'Speaking Note'를 만들어서 여러 번 소리 내어 연습한 후 녹음해 보자. 본인이 녹음한 파일을 들으면서 장단점을 분석해 보는 것도 좋다.

03 보이는 QR 코드 활용법

줄리정불법아이엘츠 Speaking은 mp3는 물론 시험관의 질문을 동영상으로도 볼 수 있는 QR 코드도 제공한다. 스마트 폰 카메라를 켜고 QR 코드를 인식하면 영국인 시험관이 실제 시험처럼 질문하는 동영상을 무료로 볼 수 있다. 어느 정도 실력이 있는 학생은 학습 전 이 동영상을 보면서 직접 대답해 보고, 이제 막 아이엘츠를 시작한 학생이라면 각 Day가 끝날 때마다 복습 차원으로 활용해 보자.

Contents

Chapter 01

IELTS란?

IELTS 기본 정보
- 1-1. IELTS 시험 종류 … 12
- 1-2. IELTS 시험 응시 방법, 접수, 응시료 … 12
- 1-3. IELTS 시험 장소 … 13
- 1-4. IELTS 시험 당일 준비물 및 입실 절차 … 13
- 1-5. IELTS 시험 시간표 … 14
- 1-6. IELTS 성적 … 14
- 1-7. IELTS 채점 기준 … 15
- 1-8. IELTS vs TOEFL 점수 환산표 … 15

Chapter 02

Speaking

Speaking Tips!
- 1-1. Speaking 시험 주의사항 … 19
- 1-2. 상황별 필수 표현 … 23
- 1-3. Speaking 필수 문법 … 24
- 1-4. 주제별 Vocabulary + Useful Sentence … 30

IELTS Speaking assessment criteria (band descriptors - public version) … 32

Chapter 03

주제별 Speaking 실전문제

Day 1. **Family** 가족 — 35
    Part 1 실전문제 — 36
    Part 2 실전문제 — 40
    Part 3 실전문제 — 44
    불법포인트 정리 — 48

Day 2. **Growing Up** 성장 — 49
    Part 1 실전문제 — 50
    Part 2 실전문제 — 54
    Part 3 실전문제 — 58
    불법포인트 정리 — 62

Day 3. **Health & Food** 건강과 음식 — 63
    Part 1 실전문제 — 64
    Part 2 실전문제 — 68
    Part 3 실전문제 — 72
    불법포인트 정리 — 76

Day 4. **Lifestyles & Leisure Activities** 생활방식과 여가활동 — 77
    Part 1 실전문제 — 78
    Part 2 실진문제 — 82
    Part 3 실전문제 — 86
    불법포인트 정리 — 90

Day 5. **Student Life** 학교(학생) 생활 — 91
    Part 1 실전문제 — 92
    Part 2 실전문제 — 96
    Part 3 실전문제 — 100
    불법포인트 정리 — 104

Day 6. **Communication** 의사소통 — 105
    Part 1 실전문제 — 106
    Part 2 실전문제 — 110
    Part 3 실전문제 — 114
    불법포인트 정리 — 118

Contents

Day 7. **Travelling & Transport** 여행과 교통   119
   Part 1 실전문제   120
   Part 2 실전문제   124
   Part 3 실전문제   128
   불법포인트 정리   132

Day 8. **Past & History** 과거와 역사   133
   Part 1 실전문제   134
   Part 2 실전문제   138
   Part 3 실전문제   142
   불법포인트 정리   146

Day 9. **Natural Environment & Wildlife** 자연환경과 야생동식물   147
   Part 1 실전문제   148
   Part 2 실전문제   152
   Part 3 실전문제   156
   불법포인트 정리   160

Day 10. **Neighbours & Politeness** 이웃과 예의범절   161
   Part 1 실전문제   162
   Part 2 실전문제   166
   Part 3 실전문제   170
   불법포인트 정리   174

Day 11. **Building & Design** 빌딩과 디자인   175
   Part 1 실전문제   176
   Part 2 실전문제   180
   Part 3 실전문제   184
   불법포인트 정리   188

Day 12. **IT(Information Technology)** 정보기술   189
   Part 1 실전문제   190
   Part 2 실전문제   194
   Part 3 실전문제   198
   불법포인트 정리   202

Day 13. **Shopping & Party** 쇼핑과 파티   203
   Part 1 실전문제   204
   Part 2 실전문제   208
   Part 3 실전문제   212
   불법포인트 정리   216

Day 14. **International Relations & Urbanisation** 국제관계와 도시화 — 217
    Part 1 실전문제 — 218
    Part 2 실전문제 — 222
    Part 3 실전문제 — 226
    불법포인트 정리 — 230

Day 15. **Environmental Pollution** 환경오염 — 231
    Part 1 실전문제 — 232
    Part 2 실전문제 — 236
    Part 3 실전문제 — 240
    불법포인트 정리 — 244

Day 16. **The Energy Crisis** 에너지 위기 — 245
    Part 1 실전문제 — 246
    Part 2 실전문제 — 250
    Part 3 실전문제 — 254
    불법포인트 정리 — 258

Day 17. **Economy & Business** 경제와 산업 — 259
    Part 1 실전문제 — 260
    Part 2 실전문제 — 264
    Part 3 실전문제 — 268
    불법포인트 정리 — 272

Day 18. **The Government & Law** 정부와 법 — 273
    Part 1 실전문제 — 274
    Part 2 실전문제 — 278
    Part 3 실전문제 — 282
    불법포인트 정리 — 286

Day 19. **Mass Media, Movie & Play** 대중매체, 영화와 연극 — 287
    Part 1 실전문제 — 288
    Part 2 실전문제 — 292
    Part 3 실전문제 — 296
    불법포인트 정리 — 300

Day 20. **Art** 예술 — 301
    Part 1 실전문제 — 302
    Part 2 실전문제 — 306
    Part 3 실전문제 — 310
    불법포인트 정리 — 314

Chapter
01

IELTS란?

IELTS (International English Language Testing System)

IELTS는 International English Language Testing System의 약자로 국제 공인 영어능력 평가시험이다. IELTS(www.ielts.org)는 미국, 영국, 호주, 캐나다, 뉴질랜드 등 영어권 국가로 유학, 취업, 이민을 희망하는 사람들을 위한 시험으로 영국문화원(British Council), IDP : IELTS Australia와 케임브리지 대학 산하 영어평가 연구소(Cambridge Assessment English)가 공동으로 개발, 관리, 운영하고 있다.

1989년부터 시행되어 현재는 전 세계 140여 개 국 1,600여 개 센터에서 운영되고 있으며 매년 수백만 명의 수험자가 응시하는 큰 규모의 시험이다. 2019년을 기준으로 350만 명 이상이 응시하였으며, 이는 전 세계 TOEFL 응시자보다 많은 숫자다. 미국식 영어를 배우는 우리나라에서는 IELTS 시험이 이제야 활발하게 알려지고 있지만, 전 세계 인구의 3분의 1을 차지하는 중국과 인도에서는 TOEIC, TOEFL 응시자보다 IELTS 응시자가 압도적으로 많다. 국내 응시자 규모 또한 최근 5년 동안 1만명 이상 증가하며 빠르게 성장하고 있다.

IELTS 기본 정보

1-1. IELTS 시험 종류

1) Academic Module

영어권 국가에서의 학사 과정, 혹은 국내외 다양한 국가에서의 석사, 박사 등의 과정에 지원하는 사람들이 준비하는 시험으로 고등교육에 필요한 학문적인 영어 의사소통 능력에 중점을 둔다.

2) General Training Module

영국, 호주, 뉴질랜드, 캐나다 등 영연방 국가로의 이민을 계획하거나 이러한 국가에서 중등교육, 전문 주립대 입학, 직업 연수를 받으려는 사람들을 대상으로 하는 시험으로 그 사회에서 직업을 구하고 생활을 지속하는 데에 필요한 기본적인 영어 의사소통 능력에 중점을 둔다.

※ 이 책 '줄리정불법아이엘츠 Speaking'은 아카데믹과 제너럴 공통이다.

1-2. IELTS 시험 응시 방법, 접수, 응시료

문제지가 주어지고 연필로 답을 적어서 제출하는 지필 시험 방식(IELTS on paper)과, 개별 모니터와 헤드폰으로 문제를 보고 들은 후 마우스와 키보드로 답을 작성하는 컴퓨터 시험 방식(IELTS on computer) 중 하나를 선택할 수 있다. 단, 두 가지 방식 모두 Speaking 시험은 원어민 시험관과 1:1 대면 방식으로 진행되며, 응시하는 국가나 시험장에 따라 실시간 온라인 화상 면접 형태로 Speaking 시험(Video-Call Speaking)을 진행하는 곳도 있다. 지필 시험은 한 달에 4회(토요일 3회/목요일 1회), 컴퓨터 시험은 한 달에 약 50회 진행으로 더 자주 응시할 수 있다. 아이엘츠 시험의 주관사인 영국문화원과 IDP의 접수 사이트를 통해 온라인 접수가 가능하고, 주관사나 시험장별 문제나 난이도의 차이는 없다. 시험 등록 시 허용되는 신분증은 여권이 유일하므로 되도록 유학 기간을 다 포함할 만큼 유효기간이 넉넉히 남은 여권을 꼭 준비하도록 하자. 응시료는 2024년 1월 기준 아래와 같으며, 신용 카드와 계좌 이체의 결제 옵션이 있다.

응시료	Regular IELTS on paper/computer	29만9천원
	IELTS for UKVI on paper/computer	33만3천원
주관사 별 접수사이트	영국문화원 www.britishcouncil.kr/exam/ielts	
	IDP ielts.idp.com/korea	

1-3. IELTS 시험 장소

서울, 경기뿐만 아니라 인천, 대전, 대구, 광주, 부산, 제주 등 거의 전국에서 아이엘츠 시험을 응시할 수 있다. 대학 및 대형 어학원 등을 고사장으로 사용하고 있다.

1-4. IELTS 시험 당일 준비물 및 입실 절차

1) 고사장에서는 아래 명시된 물품만 허용된다.

① 허용 물품

연필/샤프, 지우개, 유효한 여권과 이 여권의 사본 1부 (신분증은 모든 과목의 시험이 끝날 때까지 반드시 지참한다.)

② 금지 물품

허용되는 것 이외 모든 것. 대표적으로, 가방, 커피, 물을 제외한 음료수, 휴대전화, 스마트 기기, 모든 종류의 시계, 블루투스 이어폰, 볼펜, 형광펜, 필통, 무릎 담요, 모자, 목도리, 장갑 등이 있다.

2) 입실 절차 (지필, 컴퓨터 동일)

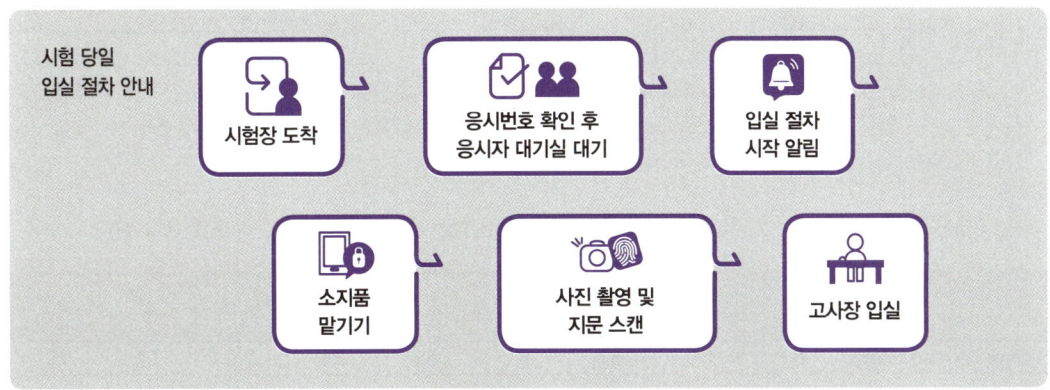

1-5. IELTS 시험 시간표

과 목	시 간 (Briefing부터 Listening까지 휴식 시간 없이 진행된다.)	문제 개수	비 고
Briefing (시험안내)	8:50 ~		답안 작성 시 주의사항 등 시험 전반에 대한 간략한 안내
Writing (쓰기)	9:10 ~ 10:10 (총 1시간)	2개의 Task Task 1은 150 단어 이상 Task 2는 250 단어 이상	점수 비중이 높은 Task 2부터 작성해야 고득점을 받는다.
Reading (읽기)	10:20 ~ 11:20 (총 1시간)	3개의 Passage 각 Passage당 13~14문제 총 40문제	1시간 안에 문제도 풀고 답안지도 작성해야 한다. 시간이 부족하기 때문에 1번부터 순서대로 풀지 말고, 주관식 등 쉬운 문제부터 골라서 먼저 푼다.
Listening (듣기)	11:30 ~ 12:10 (총 40분 : 리코딩 30분 +답안 작성 10분)	4개의 Section 각 Part당 10문제 총 40문제	리코딩이 끝나면 답안 작성을 위한 추가 10분이 주어진다.
Break (휴식)			
Speaking (말하기)	13:00 ~ 18:00 (총 11~14분)	3개의 Part 원어민 시험관과 1:1 인터뷰	추가 접수자는 일요일에 Speaking 시험을 치를 수도 있다.

※ 시험 종료 후에도 답안을 작성하는 응시자들이 매 시험마다 있는데 이러한 행위는 부정행위로 간주되어 실격 처리된다. 따라서 시험관이 시험 종료를 알리면 필기구를 책상에 올려 놓은 후 손을 책상 아래로 내려야 한다.

1-6. IELTS 성적

IELTS의 점수 산출은 각 과목의 점수를 0~9점으로 매기고 0.5점 단위로 채점한다. 0점은 시험에 응시하지 않은 경우이고 9점은 만점이다. 총점은 각 과목의 점수를 더한 후 4로 나누어서 반올림한다.

Listening	Reading	Writing	Speaking	Overall Band Score	CEFR* LEVEL
6.5	7.5	7.0	6.0	7.0	C1

※ CEFR (Common European Framework of Reference) : 유럽 언어의 구사 능력을 표준화 해 둔 공통 기준으로 한 사람이 가진 언어 능력을 6개 등급으로 구분해 두었다. 가장 낮은 A1 부터 A2, B1, B2, C1, C2까지 올라가며, 언어 구사 능력을 상세히 기술해 놓은 Can-Do Statement가 특징이다.

즉, 6.5+7.5+7.0+6.0 = 27이고 이것을 4로 나누면 6.75, 이 점수를 반올림하면 7.0이 된다.

4과목의 점수를 더해서 4로 나눈 평균 값	6.0	6.125	6.25	6.375	6.5	6.625	6.75	6.875	7.0
Overall Band Score	6.0	6.0	6.5	6.5	6.5	6.5	7.0	7.0	7.0

1-7. IELTS 채점 기준

아래의 표는 IELTS 본부 사이트(www.ielts.org)에서 발표한 채점 기준으로 현재의 채점 기준이라고 볼 수 있다. 특히 Academic과 General Training Reading의 맞은 개수에 따른 점수 산정이 다른 것을 눈여겨봐야 하는데 비교적 난이도가 낮다고 여겨지는 General Training이기 때문에 더 많은 문제를 맞혀야 높은 점수를 얻을 수 있다.

Band Score	Listening	Academic Reading	General Training Reading
5	16~22	15~22	23~29
6	23~29	23~29	30~33
7	30~34	30~34	34~37
8	35~39	35~39	38~39

※ 위 과목은 총 40문제가 출제되며, 응시자들이 주로 목표로 하는 점수대만 표기하였다.

1-8. IELTS vs TOEFL 점수 환산표

IELTS	IBT TOEFL
7.5~9.0	113~120
7.0	100
6.5	90~91
6.0	79~80
5.5	69~70
5.0	59~60
4.5	49~50
4.0	39~40
3.5	29~30

Chapter

02

Speaking

- 총 3 Part : Part 1, Part 2, Part 3
- 총 소요시간 : 11 ~ 14분
- 시험 방법 : 원어민 Examiner와 1 : 1 대화

▶▶ 줄리정불법아이엘츠 Speaking 공부 순서

Speaking Tips
(Speaking 시험에서 반드시 숙지할 사항들)

주제별 Speaking 실전문제

Self-Evaluation
학습 전, 실전처럼 영국인 시험관의 질문을 QR 코드나 MP3를 통해 듣고 대답해 보자. 현재 본인의 실력을 알 수 있다.

Brainstorming
질문에 맞는 아카데믹한 아이디어를 떠올린다.

Writing
불법 포인트를 숙지하면서 Sample Answer를 완성한다.

Speaking & Recording
영국인 성우가 녹음한 MP3를 들으며 질문과 대답 모두 10번 이상 따라한다. 자신감이 붙으면 본인의 목소리를 녹음해서 들어본다.

보이는 Speaking QR 코드

영국인 시험관의 질문을 동영상으로 보기!
각 Day가 끝날때 마다 복습 차원으로 활용해보자.

무료 MP3

영국인 성우의 질문과 대답을 MP3로 듣기!
sunnysunday.co.kr
blog.naver.com/iloveielts

Speaking Tips!

1-1. Speaking 시험 주의사항

Writing 시험이 끝난 직후, 각 응시자는 시험관으로부터 본인의 Speaking 시간이 적힌 종이를 받는다. Speaking 시험은 1시부터 진행되고 각 응시자는 원어민 시험관과 1대 1로 11~14분 간 한 방에서 시험을 치른다. 모든 대화는 녹음된다.

1) 일반적인 주의사항

1. 20분 전 대기	Speaking 시험 20분 전에 대기실에 도착한다. 예를 들어 2시에 Speaking 시험을 치른다면 1시 40분까지 대기실에 도착해야 한다.
2. 단정한 복장	반바지와 슬리퍼 차림으로는 좋은 인상을 주기 어렵다. 정장까지는 아니더라도 최대한 단정한 복장으로 신뢰감을 주자.
3. Knock on the Door	시험관이 있는 Speaking 고사장 들어가기 전에 반드시 노크한다. 시험관이 직접 문을 열고 들어오라고 말하는 경우도 있다.
4. 신분증 지참	오전에 치르는 시험뿐만 아니라 오후에 치르는 Speaking 시험에도 신분증이 필요하다. 시험관이 신분증을 보여 달라고 시험 초반부에 요청한다.
5. 자신감 있는 분명한 말투	너무 작거나 기어들어가는 목소리로 대답하면 알아듣기가 어려워서 평가 자체가 어렵고, 추후 재채점 요구 시에도 음질이 떨어져서 평가를 높게 받지 못할 수 있다. 자신감 있는 분명한 목소리로 약간 크게 대답한다.
6. 자연스러운 몸동작	영어권 사람들은 body language 사용에 익숙하다. 너무 경직된 자세보다는 자연스러운 손동작 등을 사용하는 것이 좋다.
7. Eye Contact	시험관의 눈을 보고 대답해야 한다. 간혹 천장, 책상, 창문 등을 보는 학생들이 있는데 이러한 시선처리는 상당히 어색하고 자신감 없어 보이며 무례해 보이기까지 하다. 만약 눈을 보고 말하는 것이 어색하다면 미간, 입, 턱, 목 등에 자연스럽게 시선을 둔다.

8. 문장으로 대답	아무리 간단한 질문이라도 절대로 단답형으로 말하지 않는다. 예를 들어 'What's your name?' 이라고했을때, '정진희' 라고 단답형으로 대답하지 않고, 'My name is 진희정, you can feel free to call me Juli, that's my English name.' 이라고 문장으로 상세하게 대답한다.
9. 한국어 사용 금지	IELTS는 영어 시험이다. 고유명사(영화제목, 한국음식, 도시명…) 등 한국어를 부득이하게 사용할 경우에는 한국어 뒤에 영어로 간단히 설명을 덧붙여 주는 것이 좋다. 예를 들어 '부산' 이라고만 말하기 보다는, '부산, the second biggest city in South Korea' 라고 영어로 설명을 가미한다.
10. 문제 변경 요청 금지	Part 2에서 단 한 번도 생각해보지 못한 어려운 문제를 받았을 때, 간혹 문제를 바꿔 달라고 요청하는 응시자들이 있다. 실제로 시험관이 문제를 바꿔준 경우도 있었지만 이 경우, 높은 점수를 받은 학생은 없었다. 초등학교 때부터 수많은 시험을 치렀지만 시험 문제를 바꿔준 경우가 있었는지를 생각해 보자.
11. 시험관에게 질문금지	'다시 한 번 말씀해 주시겠어요?', '잠깐 생각할 시간을 주시겠어요?' 등과 같이 시험진행과 관련된 질문을 제외한 어떠한 질문도 시험관에게 해서는 안 된다. 예를 들어, '내 취미는 야구이고, 두산 팬인데, 당신도 두산 팬이냐?' 이런 식의 질문은 곤란하다. 또한 시험이 끝나고, '내 점수가 몇 점이냐?' 는 질문도 절대 해서는 안 된다.
12. 말을 중단시켜도 당황하지 말 것	응시자가 대답하는 도중 시험관이 말하는 것을 중단시키는 일이 종종 있다. 이것은 시험관이 시험 시간을 관리하려는 것이지, 응시자의 점수와는 관련이 없다. 당황하지 말자.
13. 지나친 겸손 금지	우리나라에서 겸손은 미덕일 것이다. 하지만 영어권 국가에서 지나친 겸손은 오히려 무능해 보이기까지 하다. 예를 들어, 시험도중 'Sorry, I can't speak English very well.' 이라고 대답하는 학생들이 간혹 있다. 금물이다! IELTS Speaking Test는 응시자의 실제 영어 실력 보다 100배 이상을 보여 줘야 하는 시험이다. 겸손보다는 오히려 잘난 척을 하는 것이 점수에는 이득이다.
14. White Lies are OK	학생들이 자주하는 질문 중의 하나가 '거짓말을 해도 되나요?' 이다. 필자의 답변은 항상 'OK' 다. 하지만 어디까지나 논리적이어야 한다. 예를 들어 운전면허 취득 자격이 안 되는 17세 학생이 본인이 가장 좋아하는 교통 수단을 '자가용' 이라고 말한다면, 논리에 맞지 않다. 하지만 평소 취미는 독서인데, 독서보다는 영화 관련 영어 표현을 더 많이 알고 있다면 내 취미는 영화라고 대답해야 유리하다. 본인이 영어로 많이 알고 있는 분야로 대답을 이끌어가는 것이 고득점 비법이다. 시험관은 경찰관이 아니다!
15. 퇴실 시 인사	시험이 끝나면 'Thank you very much!' 라고 간단한 인사와 함께 퇴실한다. 끝까지 매너있는 모습을 보여주는 것을 잊지 말자.

2) 말할 때 주의사항

1. 국어책 읽기 금지	한 단어씩 또박또박 발음하는 것은 금물이다. 예를 들어 'I would like to have a large house in the future.' 라고 말할 때, '아이 우드 라이크 투 해브 어 라지 하우스 인 더 퓨쳐.' 처럼 한 단어씩 발음을 한다면, 시험관이 알아들을 수 없다. 우리가 Listening을 어려워하는 이유는 영어권 사람들은 한 단어씩 발음하지 않고 연음으로 한꺼번에 발음하기 때문이다. 따라서 '아이드라익트해버 / 라-알지하우스 / 인더퓨-쳐.' 라고 말해야 한다. 특히 large와 future는 각각 [láːrdʒ], [fjúːʃər] 소리가 긴 것(장음)에 유의하자.
2. 축약형으로 말하기	Writing 시험에서 축약형 사용은 금물이지만, Speaking 시험에서는 축약해서 말하는 것이 더 자연스럽다.
3. 주의해야 할 발음	하루 아침에 원어민처럼 영어 발음을 구사할 수는 없지만, 어느 정도 흉내내는 것은 가능하다. 오늘날 영어는 단순한 English가 아닌 Globish(Global + English의 합성어, 영어는 단순한 특정 국가의 언어를 뛰어넘어 세계인의 언어로 사용되고 있음을 나타내는 신조어)로 자리를 잡았기 때문에, 더 이상 특정 국가의 발음을 기준으로 영어를 구사하는 것은 크게 중요하지 않다. 하지만 정확한 입 모양과 혀의 위치 등을 기억해서 연습하는 것은 필수이다. 특히 한국 사람들은 /f/, /r/, /l/ 발음에 서툴다. /f/는 윗니로 아랫입술을 깨물면서 소리 내고, /r/은 혀를 동그랗게 말되 혀 끝이 입 천정에 닿아서는 안 되며, /l/은 혀가 앞니 뒤에 붙어서 소리가 나야 한다. 발음에 자신 없는 학생이라면, 알파벳 발음부터 다시 연습해야 한다. 시험관이 알아들을 수 있는 영어를 구사하자.
4. 리드미컬한 억양	대다수의 학생들은 본인의 영어 발음이 취약한 것은 알고 있지만, 발음보다 억양(intonation)의 **문제**가 더 심각하다는 사실은 잘 모르고 있다. 억양이란 한 문장이 의미에 따라 소리가 올라갔다가 내려갔다가 하는 것을 말한다. 대부분의 한국 학생들은 독해와 문법 위주로 영어를 배우기 때문에 원어민의 억양을 듣고 직접 입으로 소리 내서 말할 기회가 거의 없다. 그래서 갓 고등학교를 졸업한 학생들과 Speaking 모의 고사를 치를 때면, 그들의 단조롭거나 어색한 억양에 웃지 않을 수가 없다. 리드미컬한 억양은 의미를 정확하게 전달하는 데 가장 중요한 요건이다. 잘못된 억양은 오히려 오해와 반감을 살 수도 있다. 따라서 시험뿐만 아니라 실제 영어 사용 시에도 주의를 기울여야 한다. 리드미컬한 억양으로 자연스럽게 말하기 위해서는 많이 들어야 한다. Cambridge IELTS Listening 스크립트를 보면서 (안 보면 더 좋다!) 성우의 억양에 맞춰 반복적으로 소리 내서 읽는 것도 좋은 방법이다.

5. Be Talkative!	Speaking 시험 시간은 11 ~ 14분. 영어 실력을 뽐내기엔 빠듯한 시간이다. 따라서 응시자들은 주어진 시간 안에 최대한 높은 점수를 딸 수 있는 말을 많이 해야 한다. 그러기 위해서는 다양한 아이디어와 말의 속도가 관건인데, Cambridge IELTS 수준의 내용과 성우 정도의 말하기 속도라면 더할 나위가 없다. 풍부한 아이디어를 바탕으로 속도감 있는 대답을 하기 위해선, 평소 Speaking 예상 문제들에 대한 논리적인 답변을 잘 준비해서 어느 정도 입에 붙을 때까지 수십번 반복해야 한다. 원어민 수준의 영어를 구사하는 사람이라 해도 사전 준비 없이는 부족한 아이디어 때문에 Speaking에서 높은 점수를 받기 어렵다.
6. 시제에 맞는 대답	Speaking에서 높은 점수를 받고 싶다면, 올바른 시제 활용에 주의해야 한다. 현재 / 과거 / 미래뿐만 아니라 진행형과 완료형도 적절히 활용해서 상황에 맞게 대답해야 한다. 특히 현재완료를 적절히 사용하면, 높은 점수를 받을 수 있다. 그러기 위해서는 먼저 시험관의 질문이 어떤 시제인지를 정확하게 듣고, 그 대답에 맞는 시제를 선택해서 대답해야 한다. 과거의 경험을 물어본 질문에 대해 현재나 미래 시제를 써서 대답한다면 높은 점수를 기대할 수 없다.
7. No Slang!	wanna, gonna 등의 슬랭을 사용하지 않는다. wanna는 want to나 would like to로 gonna는 going to로 바꿔서 사용한다. 또한 습관적으로 윤호윤호(you know, you know)를 외치거나, thing, something like that, so on 등의 단어들도 가급적 사용하지 않는 것이 좋다. 친구들과의 대화에서 사용하는 말이 아닌, 가급적 공식적이고 격식 있는 말을 사용하자.

요즘 국내 대기업 입사 지원 시, 한국어로 진행하는 면접에도 많은 대학생들은 취업 스터디를 수개월 간 준비한다. 회사에 대한 기본적인 정보, 면접 예상질문 등을 함께 공유하고 모의 인터뷰도 진행한다. 그들이 과연 한국어를 못해서일까? 아무리 모국어라 하더라도 평소 생각해보지 않았던 질문에 대해서는 면접 시험에 통과할 만큼 논리적으로 대답하기 어렵기 때문이다. 그렇기 때문에 외국인 시험관과 영어로 진행하는 IELTS Speaking에는 더 많은, 더 오랜 준비가 필요한 것은 당연하다. 필자가 EBS 프로그램 통역을 할 때 사회자의 cue card를 본 적이 있다. 한국말이라면 자신 있을 그 아나운서의 cue card '안녕하세요. ××× 프로그램 사회자 ○○○ 입니다.' 라고 적힌 것을 보고 깜짝 놀란 적이 있다. 설마 그 아나운서가 '안녕하세요.' 라는 말을 몰라서, 프로그램 이름을 까먹을까 봐, 본인 이름이 생각나지 않아서 적어둔 것은 아닐 것이다. 좀 더 프로페셔널한 자세를 가지고 만에 하나 있을지도 모르는 실수에 대비하고자 만반의 준비를 갖춘 것이다.

1-2. 상황별 필수 표현

1) Say Yes!

질문을 잘못 알아듣거나, 어떻게 답해야 할지 모를 때	1. Could you repeat the question please? 2. Beg your pardon please?
대답이 생각보다 일찍 끝났을 때	1. That's all from me, thank you for your attention. 2. Would you like me to tell you more about it?
질문에 대해 생각할 시간이 필요할 때	1. If you don't mind, could I have a few seconds to think about the question?

Speaking 시험의 examiner는 영국, 호주, 남아공, 미국, 캐나다 등에서 온 native English Speaker 이고 백인만 있는 것이 아니라 흑인, 동양인, 혼혈인 등으로 다양하기 때문에 각 시험관마다 발음과 억양에 다소 차이가 있다. 따라서 만약 영국식 발음에만 익숙한 응시자가 미국인 시험관을 만났다면, 처음에는 당황스럽고 질문을 잘 알아듣지 못하는 경우가 발생할 수 있다. 이 경우 침묵하거나(가장 나쁜 태도!) 본인이 잘못 이해한대로 문제와 상관없는 대답을 한다면 감점 요인이 된다.

따라서 정확히 알아듣지 못한 경우에는 반드시 'Could you repeat the question please?' 이나, 'Beg your pardon please?' 등의 공손하고 완벽한 문장으로 다시 한 번 말해줄 것을 요청해야 한다. 물론 너무 자주 이런 질문을 한다면 이 또한 감점이 될 수 있다. 하지만 정확한 영어 표현으로 한두 번 물어보는 것은 오히려 표현력에서 플러스가 될 수 있다. 여기서 중요한 것은 공손하고 완벽한 문장이다. 만약 'Sorry?' 나 'Pardon?' 이라고 물어본다면 감점까지는 아니더라도 플러스는 될 수 없다. 왜냐하면 위의 표현들은 일단 문장이 아니고 상대방에게 요청 시, 의미를 공손하게 전달하는 Could나 Please를 포함하지 않고 있기 때문이다.

예전에 함께 일하던 글로벌 기업의 호주인 임원은 'Please' 는 불가능을 가능하게 해주는 'magic word' 라고 말했던 적이 있다. 앞으로 상대방에게 어떤 부탁을 할 때, 문장의 앞이나 뒤에 please를 사용하는 것을 잊지 말자!

2) Say No!

내 생각으로는	In my opinion / In my perspective / It seems to me that / I think / As far as I'm concerned / I believe / er.... / um... (음...생각할 때 나타내는 소리)

Speaking 시험에서 본인의 의견을 말하는 것은 당연하다. 따라서 위와 같은 표현들은 '사족' (뱀의 다리를 그리는 것, 불필요한 부분)으로 간주된다. 한두 번 정도 사용하는 것은 괜찮지만 습관처럼 매번 대답할 때마다 사용한다면 감점이 될 수 있다. 위의 사족없이 질문에 바로 답하는 연습을 하자.

1-3. Speaking 필수 문법

1) 현재완료 (have + pp)
현재완료의 질문에는 어떤 시제를 사용해서 대답해야 할까?

앞에서 언급한 바와 같이 Speaking 시험은 시제에 맞춰 대답하는 것이 상당히 중요하다. 시험관이 과거로 물어봤으면 과거로, 현재로 물어봤으면 현재로, 미래로 물어봤으면 미래로 대답해야 하는 것은 잘 알고 있을 것이다. 하지만 현재완료로 물어봤을 땐 어떻게 대답해야 할까?

현재완료란, 과거에서부터 현재까지 연속된 시간을 의미하고 조동사 have/has와 동사의 과거완료형 pp를 결합해서 나타낸다.

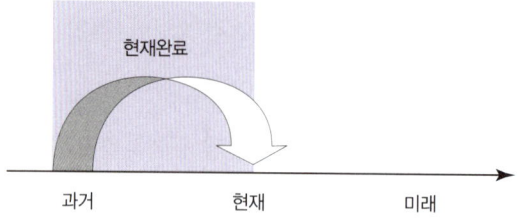

현재완료로 물어본 질문은 그 의도를 잘 파악해서 적절한 시제로 대답해야 한다. 다음 예를 통해 확인해 보자.

> **Have** you ever **received** any training at work?

위의 질문은 have + received, 현재완료 시제를 사용했다. 이에 대해 다음과 같이 대답할 수 있는데

A : Yes, I have. I've been trained how to give a presentation to my clients. (현재완료)
B : Yes, I have. I was trained how to give a presentation to my clients when I first started this job. (과거)

현재완료로 물어본 질문에 대해 현재완료로 대답한 경우는 A이고, 과거로 대답한 경우는 B이다. 얼핏 보면 A가 질문과 시제를 똑같이 맞추었기 때문에 더 좋은 대답이라고 생각할지 모르나 사실상 올바른 대답은 B이다. 시험관의 의도는 직업 훈련을 받은 적이 있는지, 있다면 언제 받았는지를 물어보고자 한 것이기 때문이다.

2) would

would에는 여러가지 용법이 있다. 특히 Speaking은 시험관이 'would you~' 라고 물어보는 질문에 주의해서 대답해야 한다. 'would you ~' 는 'will you' 의 과거형이 아닌, '~ 해주시겠습니까?' 라는 완곡하고 공손한 현재형이다.

> **Would** you say children should be encouraged to do more outdoor activities?

위의 질문은 'Do you think children should be encouraged to do more outdoor activities?' 와 의미가 같고 좀 더 완곡하게 표현한 것이다. 이에 대한 대답은 'Would you' 로 물어봤기 때문에

Yes, I would. They should ~ (긍정)
No, I wouldn't. / Not really. They shouldn't ~ (부정)

라고 'would' 로 대답한다.

다른 예를 살펴보자.

> What **would you** suggest travelers to your hometown see and do?

위의 질문도 마찬가지로 'What do you suggest travelers to your hometown see and do?' 를 완곡하게 표현한 것이다. 이에 대한 대답도 would you로 물어봤기 때문에

I'd suggest they visit the Han River and ~
I'd suggest visiting the Han River and~
I'd recommend they visit the Han River and ~
I'd recommend visiting the Han River and~
I'd encourage them to visit the Han River and ~
* I'd = I would

라고 'would' 로 대답한다.

3) 축약형

Writing 시험에서 축약형 사용은 금물이지만 Speaking 시험에서는 축약해서 말하는 것이 더 자연스럽다. 다음 축약형을 올바르게 발음하도록 하자.

(1) 주어 + be 동사 / 주어 + 조동사의 축약형

주어	be 동사 (am, is, are)	have 조동사 (have, has)	will	would
I	I'm	I've	I'll	I'd
you	you're	you've	you'll	you'd
he	he's	he's	he'll	he'd
she	she's	she's	she'll	she'd
it	it's	it's	it'll	it'd
we	we're	we've	we'll	we'd
they	they're	they've	they'll	they'd

(2) be 동사 + not / 조동사 + not의 축약형

be 동사 (is / was / are / were)	have 조동사 (have, has)	do 조동사 (do, does, did)	will / would can / could should / must
is not = isn't are not = aren't was not = wasn't were not = weren't	have not = haven't has not = hasn't	do not = don't does not = doesn't did not = didn't	will not = won't would not = wouldn't can not (cannot) = can't could not = couldn't should not = shouldn't must not = mustn't

4) 성별에 맞는 대명사 사용

성별에 맞는 대명사를 사용하는 것에 주의하자. 이론적으로는 잘 알고 있으면서도 막상 말로 하면 정말 많은 학생들이 실수를 저지른다. 예를 들어 영어 실력이 상당히 뛰어남에도 불구하고 자신의 부인을 어머니를 he라고 일컫는 경우가 종종 있다. 계속 교정을 해주어도 스스로 신경 써서 고치지 않으면 절대로 극복할 수 없는 부분이다. 사소한 실수로 보일지 모르지만 성별이 수시로 뒤바뀌는 것은 시험관에게 큰 혼란을 줄 수 있다.

다음 문장에서 틀린 곳을 찾아 교정해 보자.

> From now on, I'd like to describe about my mother. He is a middle-aged, extroverted and positive man. In terms of his appearance, he is quite small, about 5 feet and a bit chubby. I always appreciate him because he has devoted his life to take care of me. (×)

mother 는 여자이므로 he → she / man → woman / him → her / his → her 로 바꿔야 한다.

> From now on, I'd like to describe about my mother. **She** is a middle-aged, extroverted and positive **woman**. In terms of **her** appearance, **she** is quite small, about 5 feet and a bit chubby. I always appreciate **her** because **she** has devoted **her** life to take care of me. (○)

middle - aged : 중년의, extroverted : 외향적인 (<-> introverted : 내성적인), positive : 긍정적인
in terms of : ~에 면에서는, 관해서는, appearance : 외모, chubby : 통통한, appreciate : 감사하다
has devoted : 헌신해 왔다 (현재완료), take care of : 돌보다 (= care = look after)

5) 조동사 활용

6.0 이상의 Speaking 점수를 받고 싶다면 조동사의 의미를 정확히 파악하고 적절하게 활용해야 한다. 특히 should have / might have / could have / would have와 같은 완료형 조동사들 다음에 과거완료(pp)가 오는 가정법 과거완료 사용이 중요하다.

가정법 과거완료는 특히 의미 해석에 유의해야 한다. should have pp는 과거에 했다는 것이 아니라, '했어야 했는데' 의 뜻으로 not이 없지만 결과적으로는 '안 했다' 는 뜻이고, shouldn't have pp는 과거에 하지 않았다는 것이 아니라 '하지 말았어야 했는데' 의 뜻으로 not이 있지만 결과적으로는 '했다' 는 뜻이다. 이러한 표현을 잘 활용해서 대답하면 문법과 의미전달 면에서 높은 점수를 받을 수 있다.

(1) should : must 보다 완곡한 표현으로 격식 있는 영어에는 must 대신 should를 많이 쓴다.

should	해야 한다 : 해야 한다고 권유	I should go to the movies. 나는 영화 보러 가야 해.
should not	하면 안 된다 : 하면 안 된다고 권유	I shouldn't go to the movies. 나는 영화 보러 가면 안 돼.
should have pp	했어야 했는데(안 했다) : 하지 못한 것에 대한 후회 가정법 과거완료	I should have gone to the movies. 나는 영화를 보러 갔어야 했어. : 영화 보러 가지 않은 것을 후회
should not have pp	하지 말았어야 했는데(했다) : 한 것에 대한 후회 가정법 과거완료	I shouldn't have gone to the movies. 나는 영화를 보러 가지 말았어야 했어. : 영화 보러 간 것을 후회

(2) might : may의 과거이지만, 과거의 의미보다 may의 완곡한 표현으로 더 자주 사용한다.

might	일지도 모른다	I might go to the movies. 나 영화 보러 갈지도 몰라.
might not	아닐지도 모른다	I mightn't go to the movies. 나 영화 보러 가지 않을지도 몰라.
might have pp	했을지도 몰라(안 했다) : 가정법 과거완료	I might have gone to the movies. 나 영화 보러 갔을지도 몰라.
might not have pp	하지 않았을지도 몰라(했다) : 가정법 과거완료	I mightn't have gone to the movies. 나 영화 보러 가지 않았을지도 몰라.

(3) could : can의 과거이지만, 과거의 의미보다는 can의 완곡한 표현으로 더 자주 쓰인다.

could	할 수 있다.	I could go to the movies. 나 영화 보러 갈 수 있어.
could not	할 수 없다.	I couldn't go to the movies. 나 영화 보러 갈 수 없어.
could have pp	할 수 있었을지도 몰라(못했다). : 가정법 과거완료	I could have gone to the movies. 나 영화 보러 갈 수 있었을지도 몰라.
could not have pp	할 수 없었을지도 몰라(했다). : 가정법 과거완료	I couldn't have gone to the movies. 나 영화 보러 갈 수 없었을지도 몰라.

(4) would : will의 과거이지만, 과거의 의미보다 will의 완곡한 표현으로 더 자주 쓰인다.

would	할 것이다.	I would go to the movies. 나 영화 보러 갈 거야.
would not	하지 않을 것이다.	I wouldn't go to the movies. 나 영화 보러 가지 않을 거야.
would have pp	했을 텐데(안 했다). : 가정법 과거완료	I would have gone to the movies. 나 영화 보러 갔었을 텐데.
would not have pp	하지 않았을 텐데(했다). . 가정법 과거완료	I wouldn't have gone to the movies. 나 영화 보러 가지 않았을 텐데.

1-4. 주제별 Vocabulary + Useful Sentence

시험에 자주 나오는 다음 세 가지 주제에 대한 단어와 유용한 문장을 참고해서 Speaking 답변을 준비해 보자. Speaking 6.5 이상을 달성하기 위한 필수 표현들이다.

1) Hometown / City / Life Style

생활비	the cost of living	The cost of living in my hometown is fairly reasonable compared to other cities.
삶의 속도	the pace of life	As my city has developed remarkably nowadays, the increasingly rapid pace of life has created more problems than it has solved.
치열한 경쟁	the rat race	I've just moved to the countryside because I wanted to get out of the rat race.
현대적 편의시설	modern amenities	One of the best points about living in my town is that it has a lot of modern amenities.
공동체 의식	a sense of community	A sense of community is an intangible yet vital component of a healthy community.
주거용 지역	a residential area	I live in Bundang which is a residential area on the outskirts of Seoul.
상업용 지역	an industrial zone	In my town, fortunately there is no industrial zone, so the pollution isn't too bad.
교외	the suburbs	I prefer to live in the suburbs because it's generally safer and cleaner.
변두리	the outskirts	I live on the outskirts of Busan.
도심지역	the inner city	In my country, most of the inner-city areas are quite safe but some of them can be dangerous late at night.
도심	the heart of the city	I'd like to recommend the Seoul Tower which is located in the heart of the city to overseas visitors.
활기찬	lively bustling vibrant	The younger generation prefers to live in the city center because that area is always bustling until late at night.

2) Transport

대중교통수단	public transport = public transportation	My favorite public transport is the subway because it always arrives on time.
교통수단	transport = transportation	Although there're various forms of transport, I still prefer to travel on foot.
혼잡통행료	a congestion charge	In my perspective, there are a couple of benefits associated with imposing a congestion charge to tackle traffic jams.
교통 혼잡	traffic jams	I used to get annoyed by traffic jams, but now I'm used to them.
사람들이 너무 많아 혼잡한	overcrowded	The buses and subways in my town are usually overcrowded.
버스 노선	a bus route	Fortunately, I live near a convenient bus route.
출퇴근 하다 통학하다	commute	I need my own car to commute to work because I'm tired of other passengers.
출퇴근 시간	the rush hours	I travel during the rush hours, so there is quite a lot of traffic.
왕복하다	to and from	I probably spend about one and a half hours travelling to and from work per day.

3) Environment / wildlife

이산화탄소 배출	carbon dioxide emissions CO₂ emissions	According to the journal, Nature, if carbon dioxide emissions are halved by 2050 compared to 1990, global warming can be stabilized below two degrees.
지구 온난화	global warming	
환경 문제들	environmental issues	There are a few environmental issues which can be solved by the individuals.
온실 효과	the greenhouse effect	A lot of scientists agree that human's activities are making the natural greenhouse effect stronger.
환경세를 부과하다	impose green taxes on impose environmental taxes on	The government should impose green taxes on heavy polluters to preserve our environment.
환경 친화적인	environment-friendly eco-friendly environmentally friendly	Environmentally friendly packaging designs could help to reduce the amount of waste.
대체 에너지	alternative energy	The government needs to develop alternative energy resources such as wind power, solar energy and wave energy.
야생 동식물 보존	wildlife conservation	Wildlife conservation could be the most important role of a zoo.
멸종위기에 처한 동물	endangered animals	Plans to help endangered animals should be developed without delay.
동물 애호가	animal lover	I'm an animal lover so I always try to look after them.

IELTS Speaking assessment criteria (band descriptors – public version)

Band	Fluency and coherence	Lexical resource
9	• Speaks fluently with only rare repetition or self correction ; any hesitation is content-related rather than to find words or grammar • Speaks coherently with fully appropriate cohesive features • Develops topics fully and appropriately	• Uses vocabulary with full flexibility and precision in all topics • Uses idiomatic language naturally and accurately
8	• Speaks fluently with only occasional repetition or selfcorrection ; hesitation is usually content related and only rarely to search for language • Develops topics coherently and appropriately	• Uses a wide vocabulary resource readily and flexibly to convey precise meaning • Uses less common and idiomatic vocabulary skilfully, with occasional inaccuracies • Uses paraphrase effectively as required
7	• Speaks at length without noticeable effort or loss of coherence • May demonstrate language-related hesitation at times, or some repetition and/or self-correction • Uses a range of connectives and discourse markers with some flexibility	• Uses vocabulary resource flexibly to discuss a variety of topics • Uses some less common and idiomatic vocabulary and shows some awareness of style and collocation, with some inappropriate choices • Uses paraphrase effectively
6	• Is willing to speak at length, though may lose coherence at times due to occasional repetition, self-correction or hesitation • Uses a range of connectives and discourse markers but not always appropriately	• Has a wide enough vocabulary to discuss topics at length and make meaning clear in spite of inappropriateness • Generally paraphrases successfully
5	• Usually maintains flow of speech but uses repetition, selfcorrection and/or slow speech to keep going • May over-use certain connectives and discourse markers • Produces simple speech fluently, but more complex communication causes fluency problems	• Manages to talk about familiar and unfamiliar topics but uses vocabulary with limited flexibility • Attempts to use paraphrase but with mixed success
4	• Cannot respond without noticeable pauses and may speak slowly, with frequent repetition and self-correction • Links basic sentences but with repetitious use of simple connectives and some breakdowns in coherence	• Is able to talk about familiar topics but can only convey basic meaning on unfamiliar topics and makes frequent errors in word choice • Rarely attempts paraphrase
3	• Speaks with long pauses • Has limited ability to link simple sentences • Gives only simple responses and is frequently unable to convey basic message	• Uses simple vocabulary to convey personal information • Has insufficient vocabulary for less familiar topics
2	• Pauses lengthily before most words • Little communication possible	• Only produces isolated words or memorised utterances
1	• No communication possible • No rateable language	
0	• Does not attend	

Band	Grammatical range and accuracy	Pronunciation
9	• Uses a full range of structures naturally and appropriately • Produces consistently accurate structures apart from 'slips' characteristic of native speaker speech	• Uses a full range of pronunciation features with precision and subtlety • Sustains flexible use of features throughout • Is effortless to understand
8	• Uses a wide range of structures flexibly • Produces a majority of error-free sentences with only very occasional inappropriateness or basic/unsystematic errors	• Uses a wide range of pronunciation features • Sustains flexible use of features, with only occasional lapses • Is easy to understand throughout; 1 accent has minimal effect on intelligibility
7	• Uses a range of complex structures with some flexibility • Frequently produces error-free sentences, though some grammatical mistakes persist	• Shows all the positive features of band 6 and some, but not all, of the positive features of band 8
6	• Uses a mix of simple and complex structures, but with limited flexibility • May make frequent mistakes with complex structures, though these rarely cause comprehension problems	• Uses a range of pronunciation features with mixed control • Shows some effective use of features but this is not sustained • Can generally be understood throughout, though mispronunciation of individual words or sounds reduces clarity at times
5	• Produces basic sentence forms with reasonable accuracy • Uses a limited range of more complex structures, but these usually contain errors and may cause some comprehension problems	• Shows all the positive features of band 4 and some, but not all, of the positive features of band 6
4	• Produces basic sentence forms and some correct simple sentences but subordinate structures are rare • Errors are frequent and may lead to misunderstanding	• Uses a limited range of pronunciation features • Attempts to control features but lapses are frequent • Mispronunciations are frequent and cause some difficulty for the listener
3	• Attempts basic sentence forms but with limited success, or relies on apparently memorised utterances • Makes numerous errors except in memorised expressions	• Shows some of the features of band 2 and some, but not all, of the positive features of band 4
2	• Cannot produce basic sentence forms	• Speech is often unintelligible
1	• No communication possible • No rateable language	
0	• Does not attend	

Chapter 03

주제별 Sepaking 실전문제

Day 1.	**Family** 가족	35
Day 2.	**Growing Up** 성장	49
Day 3.	**Health & Food** 건강과 음식	63
Day 4.	**Lifestyles & Leisure Activities** 생활방식과 여가활동	77
Day 5.	**Student Life** 학교(학생) 생활	91
Day 6.	**Communication** 의사소통	105
Day 7.	**Travelling & Transport** 여행과 교통	119
Day 8.	**Past & History** 과거와 역사	133
Day 9.	**Natural Environment & Wildlife** 자연환경과 야생동식물	147
Day 10.	**Neighbours & Politeness** 이웃과 예의범절	161
Day 11.	**Building & Design** 빌딩과 디자인	175
Day 12.	**IT(Information Technology)** 정보기술	189
Day 13.	**Shopping & Party** 쇼핑과 파티	203
Day 14.	**International Relations & Urbanisation** 국제관계와 도시화	217
Day 15.	**Environmental Pollution** 환경오염	231
Day 16.	**The Energy Crisis** 에너지 위기	245
Day 17.	**Economy & Business** 경제와 산업	259
Day 18.	**The Government & Law** 정부와 법	273
Day 19.	**Mass Media, Movie & Play** 대중매체, 영화와 연극	287
Day 20.	**Art** 예술	301

Day 01 — Family 가족

PART 1

1) Tell me something about your family.
2) What do you like doing most with your family?
3) Who are you closest to in your family?
4) How much time do you spend with your family?
5) In what way is your family important to you?
6) In what ways have families changed in the last hundred years?
7) Should we rely heavily on our families or is it better to try to be independent?

PART 2

Describe a person in your family who you most admire.

You should say :

　　what their relationship is to you

　　what they have done in their life

　　what they do now

and explain why you admire them so much.

PART 3

1) What characteristics do elder siblings often have?
2) Is it better to grow up in a small family or a large extended family?
3) What role do grandparents play in a family?
4) Which are more important: family or friends?

보이는 Speaking QR 코드

PART 1

1) Tell me something about your family. 당신의 가족에 대해서 말해 보세요.

Brainstorming	Direct Answer	직계 가족, 꽤 작음
	Additional Information	엄마, 아빠, 여동생, 나

✏️ 다음 불법포인트를 참고해서 영어 문장을 완성해 보자. (주어와 시제, 품사와 단복수 등을 고려할 것!)

❶ 나의 직계 가족은 꽤 작습니다.
My _____ is _____ small.
※ 직계 가족 : immediate family / 꽤 : quite(quite[kwait]는 영국 사람들이 습관적으로 사용하는 단어. '조용한'이라는 뜻의 quiet[kwáiət]와 혼동하지 말 것!)

❷ 나의 가족은 어머니, 아버지, 여동생 그리고 나로 구성되어 있습니다.
My family _____ my mother, father, _____ and me.
※ 구성되다 : consist of / 여동생 : younger sister

Q. Tell me something about your family.
A. My immediate family is quite small. My family consists of my mother, father, younger sister and me.

2) What do you like doing most with your family? 당신은 가족과 함께 무엇을 하는 것을 가장 좋아해요?

Brainstorming	Direct Answer	저녁 식사, 일요일 밤에
	Additional Information	매주 저녁 식사를 함

✏️ 다음 불법포인트를 참고해서 영어 문장을 완성해 보자. (주어와 시제, 품사와 단복수 등을 고려할 것!)

❶ 가족과 함께 하는, 내가 가장 좋아하는 것은 일요일 밤 그들과 저녁 식사를 하는 것입니다.
_____ to do with my family is to _____ with them _____ .
※ 내가 가장 좋아하는 것 : my favourite thing / 저녁식사를 하다 : have dinner
일요일 밤에 : on Sunday nights(전치사 on에 주의!)

❷ 우리는 매주 함께 그것을 합니다.
We _____ together _____ .
※ 그것을 하다 : do that(=have dinner, 같은 말의 반복을 피하기 위해 사용한 표현) / 매주 : every week

Q. What do you like doing most with your family?
A. My favourite thing to do with my family is to have dinner with them on Sunday nights. We do that together every week.

3) Who are you closest to in your family? 당신의 가족 중에 가장 가까운 사람은 누구예요?

Brainstorming	Direct Answer	사촌, 은경
	Additional Information	나보다 3살 어림, 매우 활발하고 재미있음

✏️ 다음 **불법포인트**를 참고해서 영어 문장을 완성해 보자. (주어와 시제, 품사와 단복수 등을 고려할 것!)

> ❶ 나는 은경이라(고 불리)는 나의 사촌과 가장 가깝습니다.
> I'm _____ to my _____ , _____ Eunkyung.
> ※ 가장 가까운 : closest / 사촌 : cousin / ~라고 불리는 : called
>
> ❷ 그녀는 나보다 3살이 더 어리고 매우 활발하고 재미있습니다.
> She is three years _____ than me and is very _____ and funny.
> ※ 더 어린 : younger(young의 비교급은 more young이나 more younger가 아닌 것에 주의!) / 활발한 : outgoing

Q. Who are you closest to in your family?
A. I'm closest to my cousin, called Eunkyung. She is three years younger than me and is very outgoing and funny.

4) How much time do you spend with your family? 당신의 가족과 얼마나 많은 시간을 보내요?

Brainstorming	Direct Answer	꽤 많은 시간
	Additional Information	매일 저녁 : 저녁 식사, TV 쇼 시청, 보드 게임

✏️ 다음 **불법포인트**를 참고해서 영어 문장을 완성해 보자. (주어와 시제, 품사와 단복수 등을 고려할 것!)

> ❶ 나는 나의 가족과 꽤 많은 시간을 보냅니다.
> I spend _____ with my family.
> ※ 꽤 많은 시간 : quite a lot of time
>
> ❷ 우리는 보통 함께 저녁 식사를 하고, 텔레비전 쇼를 시청하거나 보드게임을 하면서 매일 밤을 보냅니다.
> We usually _____ every evening together, eating dinner and watching television shows or _____ .
> ※ (시간)을 보내다 : spend / 보드게임을 하다 : play board games

Q. How much time do you spend with your family?
A. I spend quite a lot of time with my family. We usually spend every evening together, eating dinner and watching television shows or playing board games.

5) In what way is your family important to you? 어떤 점에서 당신의 가족이 당신에게 중요해요?

Brainstorming	Direct Answer	나를 항상 지지함
	Additional Information	영국으로 대학 가는 것을 결심했을 때 나를 격려해줌

✏️ 다음 불법포인트를 참고해서 영어 문장을 완성해 보자. (주어와 시제, 품사와 단복수 등을 고려할 것!)

❶ 그들이 항상 나를 지지한다는 점에서요.
_____ they are always there to _____ me.
※ ~라는 점에서 : in that / 지지하다 : support

❷ 내가 영국으로 대학 진학을 결정했을 때, 그들은 매우 격려해 주셨습니다.
When I decided to _____ in the UK, they were very _____ .
※ 대학에 진학하다 : go to university / 격려하다 : encourage

Q. In what way is your family important to you?
A. In that they are always there to support me. When I decided to go to university in the UK, they were very encouraging.

6) In what ways have families changed in the last hundred years?
어떤 점에서 지난 백 년 동안 가족들은 변했나요?

Brainstorming	Direct Answer	그들이 그랬던 것처럼 가깝지 않음
	Additional Information	서로 떨어져 사는 게 일반적임

✏️ 다음 불법포인트를 참고해서 영어 문장을 완성해 보자. (주어와 시제, 품사와 단복수 등을 고려할 것!)

❶ 대부분의 경우에, 가족들은 그들이 과거에 그랬던 것처럼 가깝지 않습니다.
In most cases, families are not as _____ as they _____ .
※ 가까운 : close([kləus]라고 발음하는 것에 주의! 동사인 [kləuz]와 스펠링은 같지만 발음은 다르다.)
(과거에) 그랬던 것처럼 : used to be

❷ 요즘은 서로 떨어져 사는 것이 가족들에게 일반적입니다.
_____ , it is normal for families to _____ each other.
※ 요즘은 : nowadays(스펠링 주의!) / 떨어져 살다 : live apart from

Q. In what ways have families changed in the last hundred years?
A. In most cases, families are not as close as they used to be. Nowadays, it is normal for families to live apart from each other.

7) Should we rely heavily on our families or is it better to try to be independent?
우리는 가족들에게 상당히 의존해야 할까요? 아니면 독립하려고 노력하는 것이 더 나은가요?

Brainstorming	Direct Answer	독립하는 게 더 나음
	Additional Information	지나치게 의존하면 짐이 됨

✏️ 다음 불법포인트를 참고해서 영어 문장을 완성해 보자. (주어와 시제, 품사와 단복수 등을 고려할 것!)

❶ 독립하는 것이 더 낫습니다.
It is _____ to _____ .
※ 더 나은 : better(good의 비교급, good-better-best를 꼭 기억하자!) / 독립하다 : be independent

❷ 만약 당신이 가족에게 너무 지나치게 의존한다면, 당신은 결국 짐이 될지도 모르기 때문 입니다.
Since you might _____ being a _____ if you _____ too heavily _____ your family.
※ 결국 (어떤 처지에) 처하게 되다 : end up ~ing / 짐, 부담 : burden / 의존하다 : rely on

Q. Should we rely heavily on our families or is it better to try to be independent?
A. It is better to be independent. Since you might end up being a burden if you rely too heavily on your family.

PART 2

Describe a person in your family who you most admire.

You should say :
    what their relationship is to you
    what they have done in their life
    what they do now
and explain why you admire them so much.

당신의 가족 중에 당신이 가장 존경하는 사람을 묘사하세요.

당신은 반드시 말해야 합니다.
    그 사람과 어떤 관계인지
    그 사람은 그의 삶에서 무엇을 해왔는지
    그 사람이 지금은 무엇을 하는지
그리고 당신이 그 사람을 왜 그렇게 많이 존경하는지 설명하세요.

※ a person, 한 사람에 대해 묘사하는 문제인데, 하위 질문에는 모두 복수를 의미하는 their, they, them이라고 물어보는 것에 당황해 할지도 모른다. 여기에서 they는 복수를 의미하는 복수대명사가 아니고, 어떤 사람의 성별을 언급하고 싶지 않거나 모를 때 he나 she 대신에 쓰는 '그 사람'이라는 단수의 의미이다.

주어지는 1분을 어떻게 활용할 것인가? (How to Use Your 1 Minute Preparation Time)

1. 질문 파악 인물 묘사에 초점을 맞추는 문제이다.	내가 영어로 잘 설명할 수 있는 사람을 떠올린다.
2. 묘사 대상 결정하기 영어로 가장 자신있게 묘사할 수 있는 사람을 떠올린다.	평소 연습했던 '인물들' 중에서 영어로 가장 자신 있게 묘사할 수 있는 사람이 우리 가족 중의 한 명이라고 가정하고 스토리를 만들자.
3. 하위 질문 확인 + 스토리 작성 하위 질문의 개수를 확인하고, 각각에 대한 답을 적는다.	sub-questions는 3개처럼 보이지만, 마지막 문장의 'and explain why you admire them so much'를 포함해서 4개이다. 반드시 4개의 질문에 모두 답하되, 답의 길이는 똑같지 않아도 상관없다.
4. 주제 관련 아카데믹 표현 사용 평소 인물과 관련해서 학습한 아카데믹한 표현들을 떠올린다.	admire, my older sister, the eldest, a real animal lover, my lovely sister, a passionate activist, passionate, considerate, a selfless person
5. 주의해야 할 문법 문제의 시제 및 인칭 대명사 등을 확인한다.	문제는 현재형으로 나와 있지만, 내용에 따라 과거나 미래 시제가 답변에 사용될 수도 있다. 또한 인물을 칭하는 명사를 다양하게 사용해야 한다. 여기 sample answer에서처럼 누나 or 언니를 선정했다면, my older sister, Taehee, she, my lovely sister 등으로 다양하게 표현해 보자.

Brainstorming

Sub-question 1 what their relationship is to you	태희, 언니(누나), 첫째
Sub-question 2 what they have done in their life	동물 애호가, 아픈 동물들 입양, 동물 보호소에서 자원봉사, 우리가 아이였을 때 날개 부러진 새를 발견, 침실에 둥지를 만들어 먹이를 주면서 돌봄
Sub-question 3 what they do now	수의사가 되기 위해 공부하고 있음, 동물 권리를 위한 운동가
Sub-question 4 and explain why you admire them so much	동물을 소중히 아낌, 열정적이고 사려 깊음, 나도 이타적인 사람이 되고 싶게 함

✏️ 다음 불법포인트를 참고해서 영어 문장을 완성해 보자. (주어와 시제, 품사와 단복수 등을 고려할 것!)

❶ 지금 나는 내 가족 중에서 내가 가장 존경하는 누군가를 소개하려고 합니다.
Now, I'm going to _____ someone I most _____ in my family.
※ 소개하다 : introduce / 존경하다 : admire

❷ 내가 언급하는 사람은 '태희'라는 나의 언니(누나)입니다. 나는 세 명의 여자 형제들이 있습니다. 진희와 영희, 둘은 나보다 더 어리고, 태희는 첫째입니다.
The person who I'm _____ is my older sister, called Taehee. I have three sisters, Two are younger than me, Jinhee and Younghee, and Taehee is _____ .
※ 언급하다 : refer to / 첫째 : the eldest

❸ 그녀는 진정한 동물 애호가이고 그녀는 아픈 동물들을 입양해서 건강을 되찾게 했을 뿐만 아니라 동물보호소에서 자원봉사를 많이 했습니다. 나는 우리가 아이였을 때 집 밖의 진입로에서 날개가 부러진 새를 그녀가 발견한 것을 기억합니다. 그녀는 이 새를 집안으로 가져왔고 그녀의 침실에 둥지를 만들었습니다. 나의 사랑스러운 언니(누나)는 날마다 먹이를 주는 것에 신경 썼고, 2주 후 새를 놓아주기 전에 새의 날개가 아물 때까지 다정하게 새를 돌봤습니다.
She is _____ and has done a lot of _____ at animal _____ as well as adopting sick animals which she has _____ . I remember when we were children, she found _____ outside our house, on the driveway. She brought it into the house and made a _____ for it in her bedroom. My lovely sister was careful to _____ it every day and gently _____ the bird until its wing had healed before setting it free after _____ .
※ 진정한 동물 애호가 : a real animal lover / 자원봉사 : volunteer work / 보호소 : shelter
간호해서 건강을 되찾다 : nurse back to health / 날개가 부러진 새 : a bird with a broken wing / 둥지 : nest
먹이다 : feed / 돌보다 : look after / 2주 : a couple of weeks

❹ 지금, 태희는 동물들을 돌보는데 그녀의 인생을 헌신하기 위해서 수의사가 되기 위해 공부를 하고 있습니다. 그녀는 동물 권리를 위한 열정적인 운동가입니다.
Now, Taehee is studying to be a _____ so that she can _____ her life to looking after animals. She is _____ for _____ .
※ 수의사 : vet(veterinarian의 약어) / 헌신하다 : dedicate / 열정적인 운동가 : a passionate activist
동물의 권리 : animal rights

❺ 나는 그녀가 스스로 방어하거나 말할 수 없는 동물들을 매우 소중히 돌보는 점을 존경합니다. 그녀가 얼마나 열정적이고 사려 깊은지 보는 것은 감동적입니다. 그것은 나를 그녀처럼 좀 더 이타적인 사람이 되고 싶게 만듭니다.
I admire how much she cares for animals that cannot _____ or speak for themselves. It is inspiring to see how _____ and _____ she is. It makes me want to be a more _____ , like she is.
※ 방어하다 : defend / 열정적인 : passionate / 사려 깊은 : considerate / 이타적인 사람 : selfless person

Sample Answer

> Describe a person in your family who you most admire.
>
> You should say:
>   what their relationship is to you
>   what they have done in their life
>   what they do now
> and explain why you admire them so much.

Now, I'm going to introduce someone I most admire in my family.

The person who I'm referring to is my older sister, called Taehee. I have three sisters. Two are younger than me, Jinhee and Younghee, and Taehee is the eldest.

She is a real animal lover and has done a lot of volunteer work at animal shelters as well as adopting sick animals which she has nursed back to health. I remember when we were children, she found a bird with a broken wing outside our house, on the driveway. She brought it into the house and made a nest for it in her bedroom. My lovely sister was careful to feed it every day and gently looked after the bird until its wing had healed before setting it free after a couple of weeks.

Now, Taehee is studying to be a vet so that she can dedicate her life to looking after animals. She is a passionate activist for animal rights.

I admire how much she cares for animals that cannot defend or speak for themselves. It is inspiring to see how passionate and considerate she is. It makes me want to be a more selfless person, like she is.

That's all from me, thank you very much for your attention.

PART 3

1) What characteristics do elder siblings often have?
　손위 형제자매들은 종종 어떤 특징을 가지고 있나요?

Brainstorming	Direct Answer	권위적, 성숙함
	Supporting Sentence 1	부모 같은 역할, 보호하려 함
	Supporting Sentence 2	남동생이나 여동생이 버릇없게 굴면 화를 냄

✏️ 다음 불법포인트를 참고해서 영어 문장을 완성해 보자. (주어와 시제, 품사와 단복수 등을 고려할 것!)

❶ 손위 형제자매들은 종종 매우 권위적이고 성숙합니다.
_____ are often very bossy and _____ .
※ 손위 형제자매 : elder sibling / 성숙한 : mature

❷ 그들은 때때로 부모 같은 역할을 맡고 매우 보호하려고 할 수 있습니다.
They sometimes _____ being like a parent and can be very _____ .
※ 역할을 맡다 : assume a role of / 보호하려고 하는 : protective

❸ 나는 만약 그들의 남동생이나 여동생이 버릇없게 굴면 손위 형제자매들은 또한 화를 잘 낼 수 있다고 생각합니다.
I think that elder siblings often also _____ if they think their younger brother or sister is being _____ .
※ 화를 잘 내다 : have a hot temper / 버릇없는 : spoiled

Q. What characteristics do elder siblings often have?
A. Elder siblings are often very bossy and mature. They sometimes assume the role of being like a parent and can be very protective. I think that elder siblings often also have a hot temper if they think their younger brother or sister is being spoiled.

2) Is it better to grow up in a small family or a large extended family?
소가족에서 자라는 것이 더 좋은가요? 대가족에서 자라는 것이 더 좋은가요?

Brainstorming	Direct Answer	대가족
	Supporting Sentence 1	강력한 지지망과 정서적 안정
	Supporting Sentence 2	더 재미있고 파티처럼 될 수 있음
	Supporting Sentence 3	소규모 모임은 어색해 질 가능성이 있음

✏️ 다음 불법포인트를 참고해서 영어 문장을 완성해 보자. (주어와 시제, 품사와 단복수 등을 고려할 것!)

❶ 확실히 대가족에서 자라는 것이 훨씬 더 좋습니다.
Definitely, it is better to _____ with a large extended family.
※ 자라다 : grow up

❷ 이것은 만약 당신이 당신을 사랑하는 사람들을 많이 갖고 있다면, 당신은 강력한 지지망과 많은 정서적 안정을 갖기 때문입니다.
This is because you have _____ and a lot of _____ if you have a lot of people who love you.
※ 강력한 지지망 : a strong support network / 정서적 안정 : emotional stability

❸ 만약 가족 모임에 많은 사람들이 있다면 더 재미있고, 가족 모임은 파티처럼 될 수 있습니다.
_____ are also more fun if there are a lot of people there, and they can even be like a party.
※ 가족 모임 : family gathering

❹ 만약 논쟁이나 갈등이 있다면 때때로 소규모 모임은 어색해질 가능성이 있습니다.
Sometimes small gatherings have the potential to be _____ if there are _____ or _____ .
※ 어색한 : awkward / 논쟁 : argument / 갈등 : conflict

Q. Is it better to grow up in a small family or a large extended family?

A. Definitely, it is better to grow up with a large extended family. This is because you have a strong support network and a lot of emotional stability if you have a lot of people who love you. Family gatherings are also more fun if there are a lot of people there, and they can even be like a party. Sometimes small gatherings have the potential to be awkward if there are arguments or conflicts.

3) What role do grandparents play in a family?
집안에서 조부모는 어떤 역할을 하나요?

Brainstorming	Direct Answer	손주의 응석을 받아주는 것
	Supporting Sentence 1	어린 친척들을 양육하고 돌보는 것을 거듦
	Supporting Sentence 2	충고와 지원을 하면서 손주들과 긴밀한 유대감을 발전시킴

✏️ 다음 불법포인트를 참고해서 영어 문장을 완성해 보자. (주어와 시제, 품사와 단복수 등을 고려할 것!)

❶ 조부모의 주된 역할은 손주들의 어린 시절에 그들의 응석을 받아주는 것입니다.
The main role of grandparents is to _____ their _____ throughout their _____ !
※ 응석을 받아주다 : spoil / 손주 : grandchildren / 어린 시절 : childhood

❷ 조부모는 그들의 어린 친척들을 양육하고 돌보는 것을 거들기 위해서 존재해야 합니다.
Grandparents should be there to _____ their young relatives and to help look after them.
※ 양육하다 : nurture

❸ 아이들이 성장함에 따라, 그들은 조언과 지원을 제공하는 역할을 하는 조부모님과 매우 긴밀한 유대감을 발전시킬 수 있습니다.
As children grow up, they can develop a very close _____ with their grandparents, whose role is to offer _____ .
※ 유대 : bond / 조언과 지원 : advice and support

Q. What role do grandparents play in a family?
A. The main role of grandparents is to spoil their grandchildren throughout their childhood! Grandparents should be there to nurture their young relatives and to help look after them. As children grow up, they can develop a very close bond with their grandparents, whose role is to offer advice and support.

4) **Which are more important : family or friends?**
어느 것이 더 중요한가요 : 가족 또는 친구들?

Brainstorming	Direct Answer	가족
	Supporting Sentence 1	부모님과의 유대가 친구들과의 관계보다 강하고 안정적
	Supporting Sentence 2	나의 양육에 중요한 역할
	Supporting Sentence 3	부모님을 존경, 정말 감사함

✎ 다음 불법포인트를 참고해서 영어 문장을 완성해 보자. (주어와 시제, 품사와 단복수 등을 고려할 것!)

❶ 비록 우정이 나에게 매우 특별하지만 나는 가족이 더 중요하다고 생각합니다.
Although _____ are very special to me, I think family is more important.
※ 우정 : friendships

❷ 나의 형제자매들과의 유대관계는 깨지지 않고 내가 가진 나의 부모님과의 긴밀한 유대는 친구들과의 관계보다 더 강하고 더 안정적입니다.
My _____ with my siblings are _____ and the _____ I have with my parents is stronger and more _____ than my relationships with friends.
※ 유대관계 : tie / 깨지지 않는 : unbreakable / 긴밀한 유대 : close bond / 안정적인 : stable

❸ 나의 가족은 나의 양육에 중요한 역할을 했고 나를 지금의 나로 만들었습니다.
My family have _____ my _____ and have made me the person that I am today.
※ ~에서 중요한 역할을 하다 : play a vital role in / 양육 : upbringing

❹ 나는 그런 이유로 나의 부모님을 존경하고 그들에게 정말 감사합니다.
I respect my parents for that and _____ them.
※ ~에게 정말 감사하다 : be so grateful to

Q. Which are more important : family or friends?
A. Although friendships are very special to me, I think family is more important. My ties with my siblings are unbreakable and the close bond I have with my parents is stronger and more stable than my relationships with friends. My family have played a vital role in my upbringing and have made me the person that I am today. I respect my parents for that and am so grateful to them.

Day 1 Family 불법포인트 정리

직계 가족	immediate family	둥지	nest
꽤	quite	먹이다	feed
구성되다	consist of	돌보다	look after
여동생	younger sister	2주	a couple of weeks
내가 가장 좋아하는 것	my favourite thing	수의사	vet / veterinarian
저녁식사를 하다	have dinner	헌신하다	dedicate
일요일 밤에	on Sunday nights	열정적인 운동가	a passionate activist
그것을 하다	do that	동물의 권리	animal rights
매주	every week	방어하다	defend
가장 가까운	closest	열정적인	passionate
사촌	cousin	사려 깊은	considerate
~라고 불리는	called	이타적인 사람	selfless person
더 어린	younger	손위 형제자매	elder sibling
활발한	outgoing	성숙한	mature
꽤 많은 시간	quite a lot of time	역할을 맡다	assume a role of
(시간)을 보내다	spend	보호하려고 하는	protective
보드게임을 하다	play board games	화를 잘 내다	have a hot temper
~라는 점에서	in that	버릇없는	spoiled
지지하다	support	자라다	grow up
대학에 진학하다	go to university	강력한 지지망	a strong support network
격려하다	encourage	정서적 안정	emotional stability
가까운	close	가족 모임	family gathering
(과거에) 그랬던 것처럼	used to be	어색한	awkward
요즘은	nowadays	논쟁	argument
떨어져 살다	live apart from	갈등	conflict
더 나은	better	응석을 받아주다	spoil
독립하다	be independent	손주	grandchildren
결국 (어떤 처지에) 처하게 되다	end up ~ing	어린 시절	childhood
짐, 부담	burden	양육하다	nurture
의존하다	rely on	유대	bond
소개하다	introduce	조언과 지원	advice and support
존경하다	admire	우정	friendships
언급하다	refer to	유대관계	tie
첫째	the eldest	깨지지 않는	unbreakable
진정한 동물 애호가	a real animal lover	긴밀한 유대	close bond
자원 봉사	volunteer work	안정적인	stable
보호소	shelter	~에서 중요한 역할을 하다	play a vital role in
간호해서 건강을 되찾다	nurse back to health	양육	upbringing
날개가 부러진 새	a bird with a broken wing	~에게 정말 감사하다	be so grateful to

Day 02 — Growing Up 성장

PART 1

1) Can you tell me something about your hometown?
2) Can you tell me about some famous scenic spots in your hometown?
3) What do you remember most about growing up?
4) What kind of child were you?
5) Did you ever get into trouble at home or school?
6) Do you miss anything about your childhood?
7) Do you still have a friend from your childhood?

PART 2

Describe a happy childhood event you still remember.

You should say:
　　when it happened
　　who was involved in the event
　　how you felt at the time
and explain why you remember this particular occasion.

PART 3

1) Do children find it easy to make friends?
2) Is it better for children to have a few close friends, or many?
3) Has the image of childhood changed in your country?
4) Do you think children should be treated the same as adults?

보이는 Speaking QR 코드

PART 1

1) Can you tell me something about your hometown? 당신의 고향에 대해서 말해 줄 수 있어요?

Brainstorming	Direct Answer	서울
	Additional Information	대한민국 수도, 인구 밀도 높음

✏️ 다음 불법포인트를 참고해서 영어 문장을 완성해 보자. (주어와 시제, 품사와 단복수 등을 고려할 것!)

❶ 나의 고향은 서울입니다.
My _____ is Seoul.
※ 고향 : hometown

❷ 이곳은 대한민국의 수도이고 세계에서 가장 인구 밀도가 높은 도시들 중 하나입니다.
It is the _____ of Korea and is one of the most _____ in the world.
※ 수도 : capital / 인구 밀도가 높은 도시들 : densely populated cities(one of the 다음에 셀 수 있는 명사가 올 경우, 복수로 쓰는 것에 주의!)

Q. Can you tell me something about your hometown?
A. My hometown is Seoul. It is the capital of Korea and is one of the most densely populated cities in the world.

2) Can you tell me about some famous scenic spots in your hometown?
당신은 고향의 유명한 명승지에 대해 말해 줄 수 있어요?

Brainstorming	Direct Answer	N서울타워, 랜드마크
	Additional Information	멋진 풍경이 보임

✏️ 다음 불법포인트를 참고해서 영어 문장을 완성해 보자. (주어와 시제, 품사와 단복수 등을 고려할 것!)

❶ N서울타워는 서울에 있는 유명한 랜드마크입니다.
N Seoul Tower is a famous _____ in Seoul.
※ 랜드마크 : landmark(멀리서 보고 위치 파악에 도움이 되는 대형 건물 같은 것)

❷ 탑 꼭대기에서는 도시 전체의 멋진 풍경이 보입니다.
From _____ , there is a wonderful view of the whole city.
※ 탑 꼭대기 : the top of the tower(정관사 the 사용에 주의)

Q. Can you tell me about some famous scenic spots in your hometown?
A. N Seoul Tower is a famous landmark in Seoul. From the top of the tower, there is a wonderful view of the whole city.

3) **What do you remember most about growing up?** 당신이 자라면서 가장 기억나는 것은 무엇이에요?

Brainstorming	Direct Answer	조부모님과 많은 시간을 보냄
	Additional Information	바닷가나 시골로 당일치기 여행을 갔음

✏️ 다음 불법포인트를 참고해서 영어 문장을 완성해 보자. (주어와 시제, 품사와 단복수 등을 고려할 것!)

❶ 나는 조부모님과 함께 많은 시간을 보낸 것을 기억합니다.
I remember spending _____ with my grandparents.
※ 많은 시간 : a lot of time(a lot of의 '많은'이라는 뜻으로 셀 수 있는 명사뿐만 아니라 셀 수 없는 명사 앞에도 쓴다.)

❷ 내가 아이였을 때 우리는 바닷가나 시골로 당일치기 여행을 많이 가곤 했습니다.
We _____ take _____ to the beach or to the countryside a lot when I was a child.
※ ~하곤 했다 : used to / 당일 여행 : daytrip

Q. **What do you remember most about growing up?**
A. I remember spending a lot of time with my grandparents. We used to take daytrips to the beach or to the countryside a lot when I was a child.

4) **What kind of child were you?** 당신은 어떤 아이였어요?

Brainstorming	Direct Answer	버릇없는 아이
	Additional Information	숙제를 제때 끝내지 않음, 내 마음대로 안되면 떼를 씀

✏️ 다음 불법포인트를 참고해서 영어 문장을 완성해 보자. (주어와 시제, 품사와 단복수 등을 고려할 것!)

❶ 나는 매우 버릇없는 아이였습니다.
I was a very _____ child.
※ 버릇없는 : naughty

❷ 나는 제때에 한번도 숙제를 끝내지 않았고 내 마음대로 안되면 떼를 쓰곤 했습니다.
I never finished my homework _____ and used to _____ if I didn't _____ .
※ 제때에, 정각에 : on time / 떼를 쓰다 : throw a tantrum / 자기 마음대로 하다 : get one's own way

Q. **What kind of child were you?**
A. I was a very naughty child. I never finished my homework on time and used to throw a tantrum if I didn't get my own way.

5) Did you ever get into trouble at home or school?
당신은 집이나 학교에서 문제를 일으킨 적이 있었어요?

Brainstorming	Direct Answer	네, 정기적으로
	Additional Information	반항적, 선생님께 야단을 맞음

✏️ 다음 불법포인트를 참고해서 영어 문장을 완성해 보자. (주어와 시제, 품사와 단복수 등을 고려할 것!)

❶ 네, 꽤 정기적으로!
Yes, quite _____ !
※ 정기적으로 : regularly

❷ 내가 더 어렸을 때 나는 반항적이었고, 들은 대로 하는 것을 좋아하지 않아서 선생님들께서 나를 자주 야단치셨습니다.
I was _____ when I was younger and didn't like to do as I was told so my teachers often _____ me.
※ 반항적인 : rebellious / 야단치다 : scold

Q. Did you ever get into trouble at home or school?
A. Yes, quite regularly! I was rebellious when I was younger and didn't like to do as I was told so my teachers often scolded me.

6) Do you miss anything about your childhood? 당신은 어린 시절에 대해 그리운 것이 있나요?

Brainstorming	Direct Answer	친구들과 가족과 시간을 많이 보낼 수 있었던 것
	Additional Information	지금은 일을 너무 많이 해서 그들을 볼 시간이 없음

✏️ 다음 불법포인트를 참고해서 영어 문장을 완성해 보자. (주어와 시제, 품사와 단복수 등을 고려할 것!)

❶ 나는 친구들과 가족과 함께 많은 시간을 보낼 수 있었던 것이 그립습니다.
I miss _____ spend a lot of time with my friends and family.
※ 할 수 있다 : be able to

❷ 지금 나는 일을 너무 많이 해서 그들을 볼 만큼 많은 시간이 없습니다.
Now, I work so much that I don't have _____ time to see them.
※ ~할 만큼 많은 : as much

Q. Do you miss anything about your childhood?
A. I miss being able to spend a lot of time with my friends and family. Now, I work so much that I don't have as much time to see them.

7) **Do you still have a friend from your childhood?** 당신은 어린 시절의 친구가 아직도 있어요?

Brainstorming	Direct Answer	중학교 때 친구들
	Additional Information	모두 서울에 삶, 한 달에 한 번 만나 저녁을 먹음

✏️ 다음 **불법포인트**를 참고해서 영어 문장을 완성해 보자. (주어와 시제, 품사와 단복수 등을 고려할 것!)

❶ 네, 나는 중학교에서 만났던 몇 명의 친구들과 아직도 매우 가깝습니다.
Yes, I am still _____ with a few friends I had at middle school.
※ 매우 가까운 : very close

❷ 우리 모두는 아직도 서울에서 살고 있고 한 달에 한 번 저녁 식사를 하러 만나려고 노력합니다.
We all still live in Seoul and try to _____ _____ for dinner.
※ 만나다 : meet up(meet up과 meet 모두 '만나다'라는 뜻이지만 meet up이 좀 더 캐주얼한 표현이다.)
  한 달에 한 번 : once a month

Q. Do you still have a friend from your childhood?
A. Yes, I am still very close with a few friends I had at middle school. We all still live in Seoul and try to meet up once a month for dinner.

PART 2

Describe a happy childhood event you still remember.

You should say:
- when it happened
- who was involved in the event
- how you felt at the time

and explain why you remember this particular occasion.

당신이 여전히 기억하는 행복한 어린 시절의 행사에 대해 묘사하세요.

당신은 반드시 말해야 합니다.
- 그 일이 언제 일어났는지
- 행사에 누가 참여했는지
- 그때 당신은 어떻게 느꼈는지

그리고 당신이 이 특별한 행사를 왜 기억하는지 설명하세요.

※ event와 occasion 모두 '행사'를 의미하는 동의어이다. 행사라고 해서 대단한 이벤트를 떠올리려고 애쓰지 말고, 생일이나 졸업식 등과 같이 주변에서 흔히 발생하는 소재를 떠올리자. 과거 시제에 주의하면서 말하기!

주어지는 1분을 어떻게 활용할 것인가? (How to Use Your 1 Minute Preparation Time)

1. 질문 파악 행사 묘사에 초점을 맞추는 문제이다.	내가 영어로 잘 설명할 수 있는 행사를 떠올린다.
2. 묘사 대상 결정하기 영어로 가장 자신 있게 묘사할 수 있는 행사를 떠올린다.	평소 연습했던 '행사들' 중에서 영어로 가장 자신 있게 묘사할 수 있는 행사가 어릴 적에 있었다고 가정하고 스토리를 만들자.
3. 하위 질문 확인 + 스토리 작성 하위 질문의 개수를 확인하고, 각각에 대한 답을 적는다.	sub-questions는 3개처럼 보이지만, 마지막 문장의 'explain why you remember this particular occasion'을 포함해서 4개이다. 반드시 4개의 질문에 모두 답하되, 답의 길이는 똑같지 않아도 상관없다.
4. 주제 관련 아카데믹 표현 사용 평소 행사와 관련해서 학습한 아카데믹한 표현들을 떠올린다.	a happy memory, the childhood event, my 10th birthday party, party food, games, wish me a happy birthday, one of the fondest memories
5. 주의해야 할 문법 문제의 시제 및 인칭 대명사 등을 확인한다.	어린 시절에 있었던 행사를 묘사하는 문제로 답변에는 과거 시제가 주를 이룬다. 시제는 스피킹에서 가장 중요한 문법이기 때문에 시험관에게 받은 브레인스토밍 노트에 '과거 시제 주의'라고 크게 써놓자!

Brainstorming

Sub-question 1 when it happened	10살 생일 파티, 여름 방학 중, 주말
Sub-question 2 who was involved in the event	토요일 : 부모님과 친구들과 놀이공원에 감, 집으로 돌아와 파티음식과 게임을 즐김 일요일 : 친척들과의 파티, 조부모님, 이모들, 삼촌들, 사촌들이 참석함
Sub-question 3 how you felt at the time	모든 사람들이 내 생일을 축하해준 것이 특별함, 대부분의 가족들은 서울에서 멀리 삶, 그들을 보는 것은 나에게 많은 의미가 있음
Sub-question 4 and explain why you remember this particular occasion	내가 사랑하는 모든 사람이 한 장소에 함께 있었음

✏️ 다음 **불법포인트**를 참고해서 영어 문장을 완성해 보자. (주어와 시제, 품사와 단복수 등을 고려할 것!)

❶ 지금 나는 어린 시절의 행복한 기억에 대해서 이야기하려고 합니다.
Now, I'm going to talk about a happy memory from my _____.
※ 어린 시절 : childhood

❷ 내가 선택한 어린 시절의 행사는 10살 생일 파티입니다. 여름 방학 중에 주말이었던 것으로 기억합니다.
The childhood event that I have chosen is my 10th birthday party. I remember it was a weekend in the summer, during the _____.
※ 학교 방학 : school holidays

❸ 어느 토요일에 부모님께서는 시 외곽 지역의 놀이공원으로 나와 내 친구들을 데리고 갔습니다. 우리는 롤러코스터와 다른 놀이기구들을 타면서 하루를 보냈습니다. 그 후에 우리는 나의 집으로 돌아갔습니다. 그리고 어머니는 나와 친구들이 즐길 약간의 잔치 음식과 게임들을 준비하셨습니다. 그 후 일요일에 나는 나의 모든 친척들과 또 다른 파티를 했습니다. 나의 조부모님, 이모들과 삼촌들 그리고 모든 사촌이 내 생일을 위해 오셨습니다.
One Saturday, my parents took me and a group of my friends to _____ just outside of the city. We spent the day going on roller-coasters and trying all the different _____. After that, we went back to my house and my mum had prepared some party food and games for me and my friends to enjoy. Then on the Sunday, I had another party with all of my _____. My grandparents, aunts and uncles and all of my cousins came for the day.
※ 놀이공원 : an amusement park / 놀이기구 : ride / 친척 : relative

❹ 나는 모든 사람들이 나에게 생일을 축하해주기 위해 그러한 노력을 한 것이 정말 특별하다고 느꼈습니다. 대부분의 나의 가족들은 서울에 있는 나의 집에서 멀리 삽니다. 그래서 그들을 보는 것은 나에게 많은 의미가 있었습니다.
I felt so special that everyone had _____ such _____ to _____. Most of my family members _____ from my home in Seoul, so to see them really meant a lot to me.
※ 노력하다 : make an effort / 나에게 생일을 축하해주다 : wish me a happy birthday / 멀리 살다 : live far away

❺ 이것은 내 유년시절의 가장 좋아하는 기억들 중 하나인데, 내가 사랑하는 모든 사람들이 한 장소에 함께 있었던 몇 번 안되는 기억 중의 하나이기 때문입니다.
It is one of the _____ memories from my childhood because it was one of the few times when all my loved ones were gathered together in one place.
※ 가장 좋아하는 : fondest

Sample Answer

> Describe a happy childhood event you still remember.
>
> You should say:
> when it happened
> who was involved in the event
> how you felt at the time
> and explain why you remember this particular occasion.

Now, I'm going to talk about a happy memory from my childhood.

The childhood event that I have chosen is my 10th birthday party. I remember it was a weekend in the summer, during the school holidays.

One Saturday, my parents took me and a group of my friends to an amusement park just outside of the city. We spent the day going on roller-coasters and trying all the different rides. After that, we went back to my house and my mum had prepared some party food and games for me and my friends to enjoy. Then on the Sunday, I had another party with all of my relatives. My grandparents, aunts and uncles and all of my cousins came for the day.

I felt so special that everyone had made such an effort to wish me a happy birthday. Most of my family members live far away from my home in Seoul, so to see them really meant a lot to me.

It is one of the fondest memories from my childhood because it was one of the few times when all my loved ones were gathered together in one place.

That's all from me, thank you very much for your attention.

PART 3

1) Do children find it easy to make friends?
아이들은 친구를 사귀는 것이 쉽다고 생각해요?

Brainstorming	Direct Answer	어색함이 적어서 더 쉬움
	Supporting Sentence 1	더 용감하고 더 개방적이고 비슷한 흥미들을 발견함
	Supporting Sentence 2	수줍어하는 아이들도 있지만 수줍은 어른보다는 친구를 사귀기 쉬움

✏️ 다음 불법포인트를 참고해서 영어 문장을 완성해 보자. (주어와 시제, 품사와 단복수 등을 고려할 것!)

❶ 아이들은 어른들보다 어색함이 더 적기 때문에 친구들을 사귀는 것이 더 쉽습니다.
Since children have less _____ than adults, it is easier for them to
_____ .
※ 어색함 : inhibition / 친구들을 사귀다 : make friends

❷ 어색함이 없다는 것은 그들이 더 용감하고 다른 아이들에게 이야기하는 데 더 개방적이고 비슷한 흥미들을 발견한다는 것을 의미합니다.
Having a lack of inhibitions means that they are _____ and are _____ to talking with other children and finding similar interests.
※ 더 용감한 : braver / 더 개방적인 : more open

❸ 물론, 몇몇 아이들은 수줍음을 겪어서 친구들을 사귀는 데 어려울 수 있지만, 수줍은 성인보다 수줍은 아이들이 친구를 사귀는 것이 여전히 더 쉽습니다.
Of course, some children do suffer from _____ so it can be difficult for them to make friends but it is still easier for shy children to make friends than shy adults.
※ 수줍음 : shyness

Q. Do children find it easy to make friends?
A. Since children have less inhibitions than adults, it is easier for them to make friends. Having a lack of inhibitions means that they are braver and are more open to talking with other children and finding similar interests. Of course, some children do suffer from shyness so it can be difficult for them to make friends but it is still easier for shy children to make friends than shy adults.

2) Is it better for children to have a few close friends, or many?
아이들에게는 친한 친구 몇 명이 있는 것이 더 나아요 아니면 친구가 많은 것이 더 나아요?

Brainstorming	Direct Answer	많은 친구들이 있는 것이 더 나음
	Supporting Sentence 1	또래 친구들로부터 배우고, 다양한 사람들과 섞이는 것이 중요함
	Supporting Sentence 2	개방적이고 사려 깊을 가능성이 더 높음

✏️ 다음 **불법포인트**를 참고해서 영어 문장을 완성해 보자. (주어와 시제, 품사와 단복수 등을 고려할 것!)

❶ 아이들에게는 많은 친구들이 있는 것이 더 낫습니다.
It is _____ for them to have many friends.
※ 더 나은 : better

❷ 나는 사람들은 나이가 들면서 보통 가까운 친구들로 구성된 소규모를 더 좋아하지만 아이들에게는 또래 친구들로부터 배우고 다른 유형의 사람들과 섞이는 것이 중요하다고 생각합니다.
I think people usually develop a preference for a small group of _____ as they _____ , but it is important for children to learn from their _____ and _____ different types of people.
※ 친한 친구들 : close friends / 나이가 들다 : get older / 또래 친구들 : peers / 섞이다 : mix with

❸ 그러므로 많은 친구들을 가진 아이들은 개방적이고 사려 깊을 가능성이 더 높습니다.
Therefore, children who have many friends _____ be _____ and _____ .
※ ~일 가능성이 더 높다 : be more likely to / 개방적인 : open-minded / 사려 깊은 : considerate

Q. Is it better for children to have a few close friends, or many?
A. It is better for them to have many friends. I think people usually develop a preference for a small group of close friends as they get older, but it is important for children to learn from their peers and mix with different types of people. Therefore, children who have many friends are more likely to be open-minded and considerate.

3) Has the image of childhood changed in your country?
당신의 나라에서는 어린 시절의 이미지가 바뀌었나요?

Brainstorming	Direct Answer	많이 변함
	Supporting Sentence 1	아이들에게 더 많은 압박
	Supporting Sentence 2	놀 시간이 더 적음, 영어와 수학을 잘하는데 초점이 맞춰짐

✏️ 다음 불법포인트를 참고해서 영어 문장을 완성해 보자. (주어와 시제, 품사와 단복수 등을 고려할 것!)

❶ 어린 시절의 이미지는 나의 부모님 세대 이후로 많이 변해왔습니다.
The image of childhood has changed a lot since my _____ .
※ 부모님 세대 : parents' generation

❷ 요즘은 아이들에게 우등생이 되고 열심히 공부하라는 더 많은 압박이 있습니다.
There is more pressure on children nowadays to be _____ and work hard.
※ 우등생 : high achiever

❸ 아이들은 놀 시간이 더 적고, 영어와 수학 같은 특정한 과목들을 뛰어나게 잘하기 위한 교육과 학습에 초점이 더 많이 맞춰진 것처럼 보입니다.
It _____ there is less time for children to play and more focus placed on education and on learning to _____ in specific subjects such as English and mathematics.
※ ~처럼 보이다 : seem like / 뛰어나게 잘 하다 : excel

Q. Has the image of childhood changed in your country?

A. The image of childhood has changed a lot since my parents' generation. There is more pressure on children nowadays to be high achievers and work hard. It seems like there is less time for children to play and more focus placed on education and on learning to excel in specific subjects such as English and mathematics.

4) Do you think children should be treated the same as adults?
당신은 아이들을 어른들과 똑같이 대해야 한다고 생각해요?

Brainstorming	Direct Answer	똑같이 대해서는 안됨
	Supporting Sentence 1	더 많은 보살핌이 필요함
	Supporting Sentence 2	적절한 행동에 대한 이해 부족, 성숙한 생각을 하는 사람이 아님
	Supporting Sentence 3	어른처럼 대하는 건 불공평함

✏️ 다음 문법포인트를 참고해서 영어 문장을 완성해 보자. (주어와 시제, 품사와 단복수 등을 고려할 것!)

❶ 아니요, 아이들을 어른들과 똑같이 대해서는 안됩니다.
No, children should not be treated _____ adults.
※ ~와 똑같이 : the same as

❷ 아이들은 어른들보다 훨씬 더 많은 보살핌이 필요합니다.
Children need much more _____ than adults.
※ 보살핌 : nurturing

❸ 아이들은 또한 적절한 행동에 대한 이해가 부족하고 아직 성숙한 생각을 하는 사람들이 아닙니다.
Children also have less understanding of _____ and are not yet _____ thinkers.
※ 적절한 행동 : appropriate behaviour / 성숙한 : mature

❹ 어른처럼 아이를 대하고 어른과 같은 기대를 갖는 것은 불공평할 것입니다.
It would be _____ to treat a child like an adult and have the same _____ of them.
※ 불공평한 : unfair / 기대 : expectation

Q. Do you think children should be treated the same as adults?
A. No, children should not be treated the same as adults. Children need much more nurturing than adults. Children also have less understanding of appropriate behaviour and are not yet mature thinkers. It would be unfair to treat a child like an adult and have the same expectations of them.

Day 2 Growing Up 불법포인트 정리

고향	hometown	나에게 생일을 축하해주다	wish me a happy birthday
수도	capital	멀리 살다	live far away
인구 밀도가 높은 도시들	densely populated cities	가장 좋아하는	fondest
랜드마크	landmark	어색함	inhibition
탑 꼭대기	the top of the tower	친구들을 사귀다	make friends
많은 시간	a lot of time	더 용감한	braver
~하곤 했다	used to	더 개방적인	more open
당일 여행	daytrip	수줍음	shyness
버릇없는	naughty	더 나은	better
제때에, 정각에	on time	친한 친구들	close friends
떼를 쓰다	throw a tantrum	나이가 들다	get older
자기 마음대로 하다	get one's own way	또래 친구들	peers
정기적으로	regularly	섞이다	mix with
반항적인	rebellious	~일 가능성이 더 높다	be more likely to
야단치다	scold	개방적인	open-minded
할 수 있다	be able to	사려 깊은	considerate
~할 만큼 많은	as much	부모님 세대	parents' generation
매우 가까운	very close	우등생	high achiever
만나다	meet up	~처럼 보이다	seem like
한 달에 한 번	once a month	뛰어나게 잘 하다	excel
어린 시절	childhood	~와 똑같이	the same as
학교 방학	school holidays	보살핌	nurturing
놀이공원	an amusement park	적절한 행동	appropriate behaviour
놀이기구	ride	성숙한	mature
친척	relative	불공평한	unfair
노력하다	make an effort	기대	expectation

Day 03 — Health & Food 건강과 음식

PART 1

1) Do you enjoy cooking? [Why/Why not?]
2) What type of things can you cook? [Why?]
3) What kinds of food are popular in your country?
4) Do you prefer to eat with other people or on your own? [Why?]
5) Are you good at sports?
6) What is the most popular sport in your country?
7) What do you do to keep fit?

PART 2

Talk about a sport that interests you but you have never tried.

You should say :
    where it is usually played
    what kinds of people usually play it
    why it interests you
and say if you think you will ever do this sport or not, and why.

PART 3

1) Why do you think sport is important?
2) Do you think famous sportspeople are good role models for children?
3) Do you agree that sports stars earn too much money?
4) Who is your favourite sports star?

보이는 Speaking QR 코드

PART 1

1) Do you enjoy cooking? [Why/Why not?] 당신은 요리하는 것이 즐거워요? [왜?/왜 아닌지?]

Brainstorming	Direct Answer	즐기지 않음
	Additional Information	너무 많은 인내심 요구, 항상 모든 것을 태움

✏️ 다음 불법포인트를 참고해서 영어 문장을 완성해 보자. (주어와 시제, 품사와 단복수 등을 고려할 것!)

❶ 아니요, 나는 요리하는 것을 즐기지 않습니다.
No, I don't enjoy _____ .
※ 요리하는 것 : cooking(enjoy 다음에 동명사(V+ing)를 쓰는 것에 주의!)

❷ 이것은 너무 많은 인내심을 요구하고 나는 항상 결국 모든 것을 태웁니다.
It requires too much _____ and I always _____ burning everything.
※ 인내심 : patience / 결국 어떠한 상황에 처하게 되다 : end up ~ing

Q. Do you enjoy cooking? [Why/Why not?]
A. No, I don't enjoy cooking. It requires too much patience and I always end up burning everything.

2) What type of things can you cook? [Why?] 당신은 어떤 종류의 음식을 요리할 수 있어요? [왜?]

Brainstorming	Direct Answer	해산물 요리, 화이트 와인 소스 홍합 요리
	Additional Information	건강에 관심 있고, 해산물 요리는 가벼운 저녁으로 완벽한 선택

✏️ 다음 불법포인트를 참고해서 영어 문장을 완성해 보자. (주어와 시제, 품사와 단복수 등을 고려할 것!)

❶ 나는 해산물 요리, 특히 화이트 와인 소스 홍합 요리를 잘합니다.
I _____ cooking seafood, especially _____ in white wine sauce.
※ ~을 잘하다 : be good at / 홍합 : mussel

❷ 이것은 나는 건강에 관심이 있고, 해산물 요리는 건강한 주중의 가벼운 저녁으로 완벽한 선택이기 때문입니다.
This is because I _____ health and seafood is the perfect choice for a healthy midweek _____ .
※ ~에 관심 있다 : be interested in / 가벼운 저녁 : supper(dinner라고 쓴 학생들이 많을 것이다. 하지만 dinner의 원래의 뜻은 '푸짐한 식사'로 시간대와는 상관이 없다. 명절 때 점심을 가장 푸짐하게 먹는다면 점심을 dinner라고도 말한다. supper는 만찬이라는 뜻도 있지만 현대 영어에서는 자기 전에 먹는 가벼운 식사를 의미한다.)

Q. What type of things can you cook? [Why?]
A. I am good at cooking seafood, especially mussels in white wine sauce. This is because I am interested in health and seafood is the perfect choice for a healthy midweek supper.

3) **What kinds of food are popular in your country?** 당신의 나라에서는 어떤 종류의 음식이 인기 있나요?

Brainstorming	Direct Answer	비빔밥
	Additional Information	모든 재료 미리 준비됨, 뜨거운 밥 위에 재료를 더함

✏️ 다음 불법포인트를 참고해서 영어 문장을 완성해 보자. (주어와 시제, 품사와 단복수 등을 고려할 것!)

❶ 비빔밥은 한국의 가장 대표적인 음식입니다. '비빔'은 '섞인'을 의미하고, '밥'은 한국인들의 주식인 '쌀'을 의미합니다.
Bibimbap is _____ of Korean. 'Bibim' means 'mixed' and 'bap' means 'rice', a _____ for most Koreans.
※ 가장 대표적인 음식 : the most representative food / 주식 : food staple

❷ 모든 재료들은 미리 준비되어 있어서 사람들은 뜨거운 (스팀으로 찐) 밥 위에 그것들을 더할 수 있습니다.
All of the _____ are prepared _____ so people can add them on top of _____ .
※ 재료 : ingredient / 미리 : in advance / 뜨거운 스팀으로 찐 밥 : hot steamed rice

Q. **What kinds of food are popular in your country?**
A. Bibimbap is the most representative food of Korea. 'Bibim' means 'mixed' and 'bap' means 'rice', a food staple for most Koreans. All of the ingredients are prepared in advance so people can add them on top of hot steamed rice.

4) **Do you prefer to eat with other people or on your own? [Why?]**
당신은 다른 사람들과 먹는 것을 더 좋아해요? 아니면 혼자 먹는 것을 더 좋아해요? [왜?]

Brainstorming	Direct Answer	다른 사람들과 먹는 것을 더 좋아함
	Additional Information	외식, 먹는 동안 친구나 가족과 어울리는 것을 즐김

✏️ 다음 불법포인트를 참고해서 영어 문장을 완성해 보자. (주어와 시제, 품사와 단복수 등을 고려할 것!)

❶ 나는 다른 사람들과 먹는 것을 더 좋아합니다.
I _____ to eat with other people.   ※ ~을 더 좋아하다 : prefer

❷ 나는 보통 외식을 하고, 먹는 동안 친구들이나 가족과 어울리는 것을 즐깁니다.
I usually _____ at restaurants and enjoy _____ friends or family while I eat.
※ 외식하다 : dine out(=eat out) / ~와 어울리다 : socialise with

Q. **Do you prefer to eat with other people or on your own? [Why?]**
A. I prefer to eat with other people. I usually dine out at restaurants and enjoy socialising with friends or family while I eat.

5) Are you good at sports? 당신은 스포츠를 잘 하나요?

Brainstorming	Direct Answer	수영 같은 개인 스포츠는 잘함
	Additional Information	축구나 농구 같은 단체 스포츠는 잘해 본 적이 없음

✏️ 다음 불법포인트를 참고해서 영어 문장을 완성해 보자. (주어와 시제, 품사와 단복수 등을 고려할 것!)

❶ 네, 나는 수영과 같은 개인 스포츠는 잘합니다.
Yes, I am good at _____ such as swimming.
※ 개인 스포츠 : individual sports

❷ 하지만 축구나 농구 같은 단체 스포츠는 결코 잘해 본 적이 없습니다.
But I have never been very good at _____ like football or basketball.
※ 단체 스포츠 : group sports

Q. Are you good at sports?
A. Yes, I am good at individual sports such as swimming. But I have never been very good at group sports like football or basketball.

6) What is the most popular sport in your country?
당신의 나라에서 가장 인기 있는 스포츠는 뭐예요?

Brainstorming	Direct Answer	야구
	Additional Information	집에서 게임을 보면서 치킨과 맥주를 즐김

✏️ 다음 불법포인트를 참고해서 영어 문장을 완성해 보자. (주어와 시제, 품사와 단복수 등을 고려할 것!)

❶ 야구는 한국에서 가장 인기 있는 스포츠입니다.
Baseball is _____ in Korea.
※ 가장 인기 있는 스포츠 : the most popular sport

❷ 나는 종종 집에서 게임들을 보면서 후라이드 치킨과 맥주를 즐깁니다.
I often enjoy fried chicken and beer while I watch games _____ .
※ 집에서 : at home

Q. What is the most popular sport in your country?
A. Baseball is the most popular sport in Korea. I often enjoy fried chicken and beer while I watch games at home.

7) What do you do to keep fit? 당신은 건강을 유지하기 위해서 무엇을 하나요?

Brainstorming	Direct Answer	일주일에 3번 조깅이나 수영을 함
	Additional Information	균형 잡힌 식사

✏️ 다음 문법포인트를 참고해서 영어 문장을 완성해 보자. (주어와 시제, 품사와 단복수 등을 고려할 것!)

❶ 나는 적어도 일주일에 3번씩 조깅이나 수영 같은 운동을 규칙적으로 합니다.
I do _____ like jogging or swimming at least _____ .
※ 규칙적인 운동 : regular exercise / 일주일에 세 번 : three times a week

❷ 또한 나는 붉은 고기는 적게 먹지만 통곡물과 야채, 과일은 더 많이 먹는 균형이 잘 잡힌 식사를 하려고 노력합니다.
Also, I try to eat _____ which means eating less red meat but having more _____ , vegetables and fruit.
※ 균형이 잘 잡힌 식사 : a well-balanced diet / 통곡물 : whole grain

Q. What do you do to keep fit?
A. I do regular exercise like jogging or swimming at least three times a week. Also, I try to eat a well-balanced diet which means eating less red meat but having more whole grains, vegetables and fruit.

PART 2

Talk about a sport that interests you but you have never tried.

You should say :

    where it is usually played

    what kinds of people usually play it

    why it interests you

and say if you think you will ever do this sport or not, and why.

결코 해 본적은 없지만 당신에게 흥미로운 스포츠에 대해 이야기하세요.

당신은 반드시 말해야 합니다.
    어디에서 보통 이 스포츠를 하는지
    어떤 유형의 사람들이 보통 이 스포츠를 하는지
    왜 이 스포츠가 당신에게 흥미로운지
그리고 당신이 이 스포츠를 할 것이라고 생각하는지 아닌지 그리고 왜 그런지 말하세요.

※ 내가 영어로 잘 묘사할 수 있는 스포츠를 떠올린다. 내가 실제로는 이 스포츠를 즐기고 있다고 하더라도 한 번도 해보지 않은 것처럼 스토리를 만들어 가는 것이 중요하다.

주어지는 1분을 어떻게 활용할 것인가? (How to Use Your 1 Minute Preparation Time)

1. 질문 파악 스포츠 묘사에 초점을 맞추는 문제이다.	내가 영어로 잘 설명할 수 있는 스포츠를 떠올린다.
2. 묘사 대상 결정하기 영어로 가장 자신 있게 묘사할 수 있는 스포츠를 떠올린다.	평소 연습했던 스포츠 중에서 영어로 가장 자신 있게 묘사할 수 있는 스포츠를 한 번도 해 본 적 없지만 흥미로운 스포츠로 가정하고 스토리를 만들자.
3. 하위 질문 확인 + 스토리 작성 하위 질문의 개수를 확인하고, 각각에 대한 답을 적는다.	sub-questions는 3개처럼 보이지만, 마지막 문장의 'and say if you think you will ever do this sport or not, and why'를 포함해서 4개이다. 반드시 4개의 질문에 모두 답하되, 답의 길이는 똑같지 않아도 상관없다.
4. 주제 관련 아카데믹 표현 사용 평소 스포츠와 관련해서 학습한 아카데믹한 표현들을 떠올린다.	ice skating, ice rink, artificially made, professionally, very physically fit, good balance and strong core muscles, just for fun, fitness levels, a good activity, such a beautiful, graceful activity, exceptional skill, proper training, team sports, the socialising aspect, in the Olympics
5. 주의해야 할 문법 문제의 시제 및 인칭 대명사 등을 확인한다.	이 문제에서 sport는 셀 수 있는 명사이다. 따라서 단수로 쓸 때는 a sport 혹은 the sport라고 쓰고, 복수로 쓸 때는 sports라고 쓰는 것에 주의하자!

Brainstorming

Sub-question 1 where it is usually played	아이스 스케이팅, 아이스 링크
Sub-question 2 what kinds of people usually play it	전문적으로 하는 사람 - 어리고 신체적으로 건강한 사람 재미로 하는 사람 - 모든 연령, 모든 건강 수준 여자 친구 혹은 남자 친구와의 데이트로 좋음
Sub-question 3 why it interests you	아름답고, 우아한 스포츠로 보임
Sub-question 4 and say if you think you will ever do this sport or not, and why	적절한 훈련을 받는 것이 아닌, 친구와 재미로 하고 싶음, 나의 균형감각은 형편없음, 올림픽에서 아이스 스케이트 선수를 보는 것을 즐김

✏️ **다음 불법포인트를 참고해서 영어 문장을 완성해 보자. (주어와 시제, 품사와 단복수 등을 고려할 것!)**

❶ 지금 나는 결코 해 본 적이 없는 스포츠를 묘사하고 싶습니다.
Now, I would like to _____ that I have never tried.
※ 스포츠를 묘사하다 : describe a sport(sport는 셀 수 있는 명사, 단수로 쓸 때는 a sport라고 표현하는 것에 주의!)

❷ 내가 선택한 스포츠는 아이스 스케이팅입니다. 아이스 스케이팅은 보통 인공적으로 만들어진 아이스 링크에서 합니다. 그래서 이것은 추울 때인 겨울뿐만 아니라 연중 아무 때나 할 수 있습니다.
_____ is ice skating. Ice skating is done on an ice rink which is usually _____ . So it can be done _____ , not just in the winter when it is cold.
※ 내가 선택한 스포츠 : the sport which I've chosen(앞 문장에서는 처음으로 sport를 언급했기 때문에 a sport, 이 문장에서는 앞에서 언급한 sport를 다시 언급하기 때문에 the sport이다.) / 인공적으로 만들어진 : artificially made
연중 아무 때나 : at any time of the year

❸ 아이스 스케이팅을 전문적으로 하는 사람들의 유형은 보통 어리고 그들은 좋은 균형과 강한 코어 근육을 지녀야 하기 때문에 신체적으로 매우 건강합니다. 하지만, 단지 재미로 아이스 스케이팅을 하는 사람들의 유형은 모든 연령 대와 건강 수준이 될 수 있습니다. 많은 사람들이 여자 친구나 남자 친구와 데이트 할 때 하기 좋은 활동이라고 생각합니다.
The kind of people who do it _____ are usually young and very _____ since they need to have good balance and _____ . However, the kind of people who go ice skating _____ can be of all ages and fitness levels. Many people consider it to be a good activity to do when they _____ with a girlfriend or boyfriend.
※ 전문적으로 : professionally / 신체적으로 건강한 : physically fit / 강한 코어 근육 : strong core muscle(코어 근육은 우리 몸의 중심을 잡아주는 근육으로 척추와 복부, 엉덩이까지 포함한다.) / 단지 재미로 : just for fun
데이트하다 : be on a date

❹ 이것은 내가 관심있는 스포츠인데 아이스 스케이팅은 또한 특출한 기량을 요구하는 아름답고 우아한 활동처럼 보이기 때문입니다.
It's a sport that I'm interested in because it _____ such a beautiful, _____ activity that also requires _____ .
※ ~처럼 보이다 : look like / 우아한 : graceful / 특출한 기량 : exceptional skill

❺ 나는 아이스 스케이팅을 시도해 보고 싶지만 실제로 적절한 훈련을 받는 것이 아니라 내 친구들과 함께 단지 재미로 아이스 링크에 갈 것입니다. 내 균형 감각은 형편없고 나는 어울리는 면에서 팀 스포츠에 참여하는 것을 더 좋아합니다. 하지만 나는 여전히 올림픽에서 아이스 스케이팅 선수들을 보는 것을 즐깁니다.
I would like to try the sport but I think I would only go to an ice rink for fun with my friends _____ actually getting _____ . _____ is terrible and I prefer _____ team sports for the socialising aspect. However, I still enjoy watching ice skaters _____ .
※ ~이 아니라 : as opposed to / 적절한 훈련 : proper training / 내 균형 감각 : my sense of balance
참여하다 : take part in(=attend / participate in) / 올림픽에서 : in the Olympics(Olympics의 첫 글자를 대문자로 쓰는 것에 주의!)

Sample Answer

Talk about a sport that interests you but you have never tried.

You should say:
   where it is usually played
   what kinds of people usually play it
   why it interests you
and say if you think you will ever do this sport or not, and why.

Now, I would like to describe a sport that I have never tried.

The sport which I've chosen is ice skating. Ice skating is done on an ice rink which is usually artificially made. So it can be done at any time of the year, not just in the winter when it is cold.

The kind of people who do it professionally are usually young and very physically fit since they need to have good balance and strong core muscles. However, the kind of people who go ice skating just for fun can be of all ages and fitness levels. Many people consider it to be a good activity to do when they are on a date with a girlfriend or boyfriend.

It's a sport that I'm interested in because it looks like such a beautiful, graceful activity that also requires exceptional skill.

I would like to try the sport but I think I would only go to an ice rink for fun with my friends as opposed to actually getting proper training. My sense of balance is terrible and I prefer taking part in team sports for the socialising aspect. However, I still enjoy watching ice skaters in the Olympics.

That's all from me, thank you very much for your attention.

PART 3

1) Why do you think sport is important?
당신은 왜 스포츠가 중요하다고 생각해요?

Brainstorming	Direct Answer	스포츠가 운동하는 좋은 방법을 제공
	Supporting Sentence 1	건강을 유지하기 위해서는 균형 잡힌 식단과 규칙적인 운동이 필요함
	Supporting Sentence 2	친구들과 팀 게임에 참여할 수 있어 재미있음

✏️ 다음 불법포인트를 참고해서 영어 문장을 완성해 보자. (주어와 시제, 품사와 단복수 등을 고려할 것!)

❶ 다양한 종류의 스포츠가 필수적인 이유는 스포츠가 운동하는 좋은 방법을 제공하기 때문입니다.
The main reason that various kinds of sport are _____ is because they offer good ways to exercise.
※ 필수적인 : integral(important를 반복하기 보다는 integral, significant, essential 등과 같은 동의어를 활용하자!)

❷ 건강을 유지하기 위해서 균형이 잘 잡힌 식단을 유지하고 규칙적인 운동을 하는 것이 필요합니다.
In order to _____ , it is necessary to _____ and to _____ .
※ 건강을 유지하다 : stay healthy(=keep fit) / 균형이 잘 잡힌 식단을 유지하다 : maintain a well-balanced diet
규칙적인 운동을 하다 : do regular exercise

❸ 나는 스포츠 활동들은 또한 재미있다고 생각하는데 사람들은 만약 그들이 원하면 친구들과 팀 게임에 참여할 수 있기 때문입니다.
I think that sporting activities can be fun too, because people can _____ team games with friends if they want to.
※ 참여하다 : participate in(=attend / take part in)

Q. Why do you think sport is important?
A. The main reason that various kinds of sport are integral is because they offer good ways to exercise. In order to stay healthy, it is necessary to maintain a well-balanced diet and to do regular exercise. I think that sporting activities can be fun too, because people can participate in team games with friends if they want to.

2) Do you think famous sportspeople are good role models for children?
당신은 유명한 운동선수들이 아이들에게 좋은 롤모델이라고 생각해요?

Brainstorming	Direct Answer	좋은 롤모델
	Supporting Sentence 1	건강한 신체와 생활방식의 이미지를 대표함
	Supporting Sentence 2	야외 활동을 하도록 격려해서 아이들은 운동을 시작하고 경쟁심을 가짐
	Supporting Sentence 3	꿈을 실현시킬 수 있는 훌륭한 삶을 사는 데 도움

✏️ 다음 불법포인트를 참고해서 영어 문장을 완성해 보자. (주어와 시제, 품사와 단복수 등을 고려할 것!)

❶ 네, 나는 대부분의 유명한 스포츠 스타들은 아이들에게 좋은 롤모델이라는 것에 동의합니다.
Yes, I would agree that most _____ are good role models for children.
※ 유명한 스포츠 스타 : famous sports star

❷ 그들은 건강한 신체와 생활방식의 이미지를 대표합니다.
They _____ a healthy body and lifestyle image.
※ 대표하다 : represent

❸ 운동 선수들은 아이들에게 좀 더 많은 야외 활동에 참여하도록 격려할 수 있어서 아이들은 운동을 시작하고 경쟁심을 발달시킵니다.
_____ can encourage children to take part in more _____ , so that youngsters start doing exercise and develop _____ .
※ 운동 선수 : athlete / 야외 활동 : outdoor activity / 경쟁심 : a sense of competition

❹ 이러한 영감은 아이들이 꿈을 실현시킬 수 있는 훌륭한 삶을 사는데 도움을 줍니다.
This _____ helps to lead children to an excellent life in which they can _____ .
※ 영감 : inspiration / 꿈을 실현시키다 : fulfil one's dream(fulfil은 영국식, fulfill은 미국식 스펠링)

Q. Do you think famous sportspeople are good role models for children?
A. Yes, I would agree that most famous sports stars are good role models for children. They represent a healthy body and lifestyle image. Athletes can encourage children to take part in more outdoor activities, so that youngsters start doing exercise and develop a sense of competition. This inspiration helps to lead children to an excellent life in which they can fulfil their dreams.

3) Do you agree that sports stars earn too much money?
당신은 스포츠 스타들이 너무나 많은 돈을 번다는 것에 동의해요?

Brainstorming	Direct Answer	너무 많은 돈을 벌고 액수는 충격적
	Supporting Sentence 1	연봉은 사회 기여도에 기초해야 함
	Supporting Sentence 2	간호사나 소방관은 많이 벌지 못하는데 운동 선수가 엄청 많이 버는 것은 불공평

✏️ 다음 불법포인트를 참고해서 영어 문장을 완성해 보자. (주어와 시제, 품사와 단복수 등을 고려할 것!)

❶ 네, 스포츠 스타들은 너무나 많은 돈을 벌고, 그들 중 일부가 버는 액수는 충격적입니다.
Yes, sports stars do earn too much money and the amount that some of them make is _____ .
※ 충격적인 : shocking

❷ 나는 연봉은 직업이 사회에 제공한 기여에 기초해야 한다고 생각합니다.
I believe that salaries should be based on the _____ jobs offer to society.
※ 기여 : contribution

❸ 간호사나 소방관은 비록 그들이 생명을 구하더라도 많은 돈을 벌지 못하지만 오직 그들의 팬들을 즐겁게 해주는 운동 선수들이 엄청 많은 돈을 버는 것은 공평하지 않다고 생각합니다.
It is unfair that nurses and firefighters don't make much money even though they save lives, but sportspeople who only _____ their fans make _____ _____ .
※ 즐겁게 해주다 : entertain / 엄청 많은 돈 : a huge amount of money

Q. Do you agree that sports stars earn too much money?
A. Yes, sports stars do earn too much money and the amount that some of them make is shocking. I believe that salaries should be based on the contribution jobs offer to society. It is unfair that nurses and firefighters don't make much money even though they save lives, but sportspeople who only entertain their fans make a huge amount of money.

4) Who is your favourite sports star?
당신이 가장 좋아하는 스포츠 스타는 누구예요?

Brainstorming	Direct Answer	데이비드 베컴
	Supporting Sentence 1	가난한 집에서 태어났지만 성공하기 위해서 열심히 운동함
	Supporting Sentence 2	가정적인 남자

✏️ 다음 불법포인트를 참고해서 영어 문장을 완성해 보자. (주어와 시제, 품사와 단복수 등을 고려할 것!)

❶ 내가 가장 좋아하는 스포츠 스타는 데이비드 베컴인데 그는 놀라운 축구 선수일뿐만 아니라 좋은 롤모델이기 때문입니다.
My favourite sports star is David Beckham because he is a good role model _____ an amazing football player.
※ ~뿐만 아니라 : as well as

❷ 그는 가난한 집안에서 태어났지만 성공을 이루기 위해서 열심히 운동했습니다.
He _____ but _____ to achieve his success.
※ 가난한 집에서 태어나다 : come from humble beginnings / 열심히 운동하다 : work hard(운동선수가 일하는 것은 운동하는 것, 학생이 일하는 것은 공부하는 것으로 해석한다.)

❸ 나는 또한 그가 아내를 돌보고 4명의 아이들과 놀아주는 가정적인 남자라는 점을 존경합니다.
I also respect that he is _____ who _____ his wife and plays with his four children.
※ 가정적인 남자 : a family man / 돌보다 : look after(=care / take care of)

Q. Who is your favourite sports star?
A. My favourite sports star is David Beckham because he is a good role model as well as an amazing football player. He came from humble beginnings but worked hard to achieve his success. I also respect that he is a family man who looks after his wife and plays with his four children.

Day 3 Health & Food 불법포인트 정리

요리하는 것	cooking	데이트하다	be on a date
인내심	patience	~처럼 보이다	look like
결국 어떠한 상황에 처하게 되다	end up ~ing	우아한	graceful
~을 잘하다	be good at	특출한 기량	exceptional skill
홍합	mussel	~이 아니라	as opposed to
~에 관심 있다	be interested in	적절한 훈련	proper training
가벼운 저녁	supper	내 균형 감각	my sense of balance
가장 대표적인 음식	the most representative food	참여하다	take part in / attend / participate in
주식	food staple	올림픽에서	in the Olympics
재료	ingredient	필수적인	integral / important / significant / essential
미리	in advance	건강을 유지하다	stay healthy / keep fit
뜨거운 스팀으로 찐 밥	hot steamed rice	균형이 잘 잡힌 식단을 유지하다	maintain a well-balanced diet
~을 더 좋아하다	prefer	참여하다	participate in / attend / take part in
외식하다	dine out / eat out	규칙적인 운동을 하다	do regular exercise
~와 어울리다	socialise with	유명한 스포츠 스타	famous sports star
개인 스포츠	individual sports	대표하다	represent
단체 스포츠	group sports	운동 선수	athlete
가장 인기 있는 스포츠	the most popular sport	야외 활동	outdoor activity
집에서	at home	경쟁심	a sense of competition
규칙적인 운동	regular exercise	영감	inspiration
일주일에 세 번	three times a week	꿈을 실현시키다	fulfil one's dream
균형이 잘 잡힌 식사	a well-balanced diet	충격적인	shocking
통곡물	whole grain	기여	contribution
스포츠를 묘사하다	describe a sport	즐겁게 해주다	entertain
내가 선택한 스포츠	the sport which I've chosen	엄청 많은 돈	a huge amount of money
인공적으로 만들어진	artificially made	~뿐만 아니라	as well as
연중 아무 때나	at any time of the year	가난한 집에서 태어나다	come from humble beginnings
전문적으로	professionally	열심히 운동하다 / 열심히 공부하다	work hard
신체적으로 건강한	physically fit	가정적인 남자	a family man
강한 코어 근육	strong core muscle	돌보다	look after / care / take care of
단지 재미로	just for fun		

Day 04 Lifestyles & Leisure Activities
생활방식과 여가활동

PART 1

1) What do you do in your free time?
2) Do you have a busy social life?
3) What would you like to change about your lifestyle?
4) Is being late acceptable in your culture? [Why/Why not?]
5) Are you ever late for appointments? [Why/Why not?]
6) What type of excuses do you think are alright for lateness?
7) How do you feel when someone is late for an appointment with you?

PART 2

Describe a hobby you want to take up when you are much older.

You should say:
   what the hobby is
   what special equipment is needed, if any
   when you want to take it up
and explain why this is a suitable hobby for older people.

PART 3

1) Do you agree that we learn best from our mistakes?
2) Can we gain life experience from books and movies?
3) Are the types of leisure activities that are popular today the same as those that were popular when your parents were young?
4) What types of leisure activities may become more popular in the future?

보이는 Speaking QR 코드

PART 1

1) What do you do in your free time? 당신은 여가 시간에 무엇을 하나요?

Brainstorming	Direct Answer	영화 보기, 갤러리나 전시회 방문함
	Additional Information	스트레스 해소에 도움을 줌

✏️ 다음 불법포인트를 참고해서 영어 문장을 완성해 보자. (주어와 시제, 품사와 단복수 등을 고려할 것!)

❶ 여가 시간에 나는 친구들과 영화를 보러 가거나 갤러리나 전시회를 방문하는 것을 즐깁니다.

In my free time, I enjoy _____ with my friends or visiting art galleries and _____ .

※ 영화 보러 가다 : go to the cinema(=go to the movies) / 전시회 : exhibition

❷ 이러한 활동들은 스트레스를 해소하는데 도움을 줍니다.

These activities help _____ .

※ 스트레스를 해소하다 : relieve stress

Q. What do you do in your free time?

A. In my free time, I enjoy going to the cinema with my friends or visiting art galleries and exhibitions. These activities help relieve stress.

2) Do you have a busy social life? 당신은 바쁜 사회 생활을 하나요?

Brainstorming	Direct Answer	바쁨
	Additional Information	평일 밤에는 집에 있지만 주말에는 친구들을 많이 만남

✏️ 다음 불법포인트를 참고해서 영어 문장을 완성해 보자. (주어와 시제, 품사와 단복수 등을 고려할 것!)

❶ 네, 꽤 바쁩니다.

Yes, it is _____ busy.

※ 꽤 : quite(quite[kwait]는 영국 사람들이 습관적으로 사용하는 단어, '조용한'이라는 뜻의 quiet[kwáiət]와 혼동하지 말 것!)

❷ 나는 보통 평일 밤에는 일로 피곤하기 때문에 집에 머물지만, 주말에는 내가 할 수 있는 한 많이 친구들을 만나는 것을 좋아합니다.

I usually _____ during _____ because I am tired from work, but _____ I like to meet up with my friends _____ .

※ 집에 머물다 : stay at home / 평일 밤 : weeknight / 주말에 : on the weekend / 내가 할 수 있는 한 많이 : as much as I can

Q. Do you have a busy social life?

A. Yes, it is quite busy. I usually stay at home during weeknights because I am tired from work, but on the weekend I like to meet up with my friends as much as I can.

3) **What would you like to change about your lifestyle?** 당신의 생활 양식에 대해 무엇을 바꾸고 싶어요?

Brainstorming	Direct Answer	주당 40시간만 일하고 싶음
	Additional Information	현재 밤늦게까지 일해서 피곤함

✏️ 다음 **불법포인트**를 참고해서 영어 문장을 완성해 보자. (주어와 시제, 품사와 단복수 등을 고려할 것!)

❶ 나는 오직 주당 40시간만 일하고 싶습니다.
I would like to work only _____ .
※ 주당 40 시간 : 40 hours a week

❷ 현재 나는 밤늦게까지 사무실에 있어야 해서 대부분의 근무 시간에 피곤함을 느낍니다.
Currently, I have to stay at the office _____ so I _____ most of the time.
※ 밤 늦게까지 : until late at night / 피곤함을 느끼다 : feel tired

Q. **What would you like to change about your lifestyle?**
A. I would like to work only 40 hours a week. Currently, I have to stay at the office until late at night so I feel tired most of the time.

4) **Is being late acceptable in your culture? [Why/Why not?]**
당신의 문화에서는 늦는 것이 허용되요? [왜?/왜 아닌지?]

Brainstorming	Direct Answer	약간 무례함
	Additional Information	늦는 것은 불가피함으로 심한 모욕은 아님

✏️ 다음 **불법포인트**를 참고해서 영어 문장을 완성해 보자. (주어와 시제, 품사와 단복수 등을 고려할 것!)

❶ 늦는 것은 약간 무례한 것으로 간주되어서 사람들은 시간을 엄수하려고 합니다.
Being late _____ be a little bit _____ so people try to be _____ .
※ ~로 간주되다 : be considered to / 무례한 : rude / 시간을 엄수하는 : punctual

❷ 하지만 사람들이 때때로 약간 늦는 것은 불가피해서 이것은 심한 모욕이 아닙니다.
However, it is _____ that people will sometimes be slightly late so it is not _____ .
※ 불가피한 : inevitable / 심각한 모욕 : a serious insult

Q. **Is being late acceptable in your culture? [Why/Why not?]**
A. Being late is considered to be a little bit rude so people try to be punctual. However, it is inevitable that people will sometimes be slightly late so it is not a serious insult.

5) Are you ever late for appointments? [Why/Why not?] 당신은 약속에 늦은 적이 있어요? [왜?/왜 아닌지?]

Brainstorming	Direct Answer	교통 상황이 나쁠 때 가끔 늦음
	Additional Information	5 ~ 10분 정도여서 용인되는 수준임

✏️ 다음 불법포인트를 참고해서 영어 문장을 완성해 보자. (주어와 시제, 품사와 단복수 등을 고려할 것!)

❶ 나는 친구들을 만나기로 약속을 했을 때 교통 상황이 나쁜 경우 가끔씩 늦습니다.
Occasionally I am late when I have _____ friends if the traffic is bad.
※ 만나기로 약속을 하다 : arrange to meet

❷ 하지만 보통 대략 5분 또는 10분 정도여서 늦는 게 허용되는 수준입니다.
Although it is usually only by about 5 or 10 minutes so it is _____ of being late.
※ 허용되는 수준 : an acceptable level

Q. Are you ever late for appointments? [Why/Why not?]
A. Occasionally I am late when I have arranged to meet friends if the traffic is bad. Although it is usually only by about 5 or 10 minutes so it is an acceptable level of being late.

6) What type of excuses do you think are alright for lateness?
당신은 어떤 형태의 핑계가 늦는 것에 있어 괜찮다고 생각해요?

Brainstorming	Direct Answer	교통 체증, 급한 집안 일
	Additional Information	서울의 출퇴근 시간 교통 체증은 악명 높음

✏️ 다음 불법포인트를 참고해서 영어 문장을 완성해 보자. (주어와 시제, 품사와 단복수 등을 고려할 것!)

❶ 교통 체증이나 급한 집안일 때문에 늦는 것은 허용되는 핑계입니다.
Being late because of _____ or _____ are acceptable excuses.
※ 교통 체증 : a traffic jam(=traffic congestion) / 급한 집안일 : family emergency

❷ 특히 서울에서 출퇴근 시간 동안 교통 체증은 악명이 높습니다.
Especially _____ is _____ during the rush hours in Seoul.
※ 교통 체증 : traffic congestion(셀 수 없는 명사임에 주의!) / 악명 높은 : notorious

Q. What type of excuses do you think are alright for lateness?
A. Being late because of a traffic jam or family emergencies are acceptable excuses. Especially traffic congestion is notorious during the rush hours in Seoul.

7) How do you feel when someone is late for an appointment with you?
누군가 당신과의 약속에 늦을 때 당신은 기분이 어떤가요?

Brainstorming	Direct Answer	몇 분 늦으면 신경 쓰지 않음
	Additional Information	30분 이상 늦으면 짜증남

✏️ 다음 **불법포인트**를 참고해서 영어 문장을 완성해 보자. (주어와 시제, 품사와 단복수 등을 고려할 것!)

❶ 만약 그들이 단지 몇 분 늦는다면 나는 신경 쓰지 않습니다.
If they are only a few minutes late, I don't _____ .
※ 신경 쓰다 : mind

❷ 하지만 누군가 매우 늦으면, 30분 이상 늦으면, 내 시간이 낭비된다는 것에 짜증이 납니다.
But if someone is very late, more than _____ , then I _____ that my time is being wasted.
※ 30분 : half an hour(30 minutes라고도 할 수 있지만, half an hour이라고도 표현해 보자!) / 짜증나다 : feel annoyed

Q. How do you feel when someone is late for an appointment with you?
A. If they are only a few minutes late, I don't mind. But if someone is very late, more than half an hour, then I feel annoyed that my time is being wasted.

PART 2

Describe a hobby you want to take up when you are much older.

You should say:
- what the hobby is
- what special equipment is needed, if any
- when you want to take it up

and explain why this is a suitable hobby for older people.

당신이 훨씬 더 나이가 들어서 시작하고 싶은 취미에 대해 묘사하세요.

당신은 반드시 말해야 합니다.
- 그 취미가 무엇인지
- 만약에 있다면 어떤 특별한 용품이 필요한지
- 언제 취미를 시작하길 원하는지

그리고 왜 이것이 나이든 사람들에게 적합한 취미인지 설명하세요.

※ 내가 영어로 잘 묘사할 수 있는 취미를 떠올린다. 내가 실제로는 이 취미를 즐기고 있다고 하더라도 아직 시작해보지 않은 것처럼 스토리를 만들어 가는 것이 중요하다.

주어지는 1분을 어떻게 활용할 것인가? (How to Use Your 1 Minute Preparation Time)

1. 질문 파악 취미 묘사에 초점을 맞추는 문제이다.	내가 영어로 잘 설명할 수 있는 취미를 떠올린다.
2. 묘사 대상 결정하기 영어로 가장 자신 있게 묘사할 수 있는 취미를 떠올린다.	평소 연습했던 취미 중에서 영어로 가장 자신 있게 묘사할 수 있는 취미를 아직 해보지는 않았지만 노인이 되어 시작할 취미라고 가정하고 스토리를 만들자.
3. 하위 질문 확인 + 스토리 작성 하위 질문의 개수를 확인하고, 각각에 대한 답을 적는다.	sub-questions는 3개처럼 보이지만, 마지막 문장의 'and explain why this is a suitable hobby for older people'를 포함해서 4개이다. 반드시 4개의 질문에 모두 답하되, 답의 길이는 똑같지 않아도 상관없다.
4. 주제 관련 아카데믹 표현 사용 평소 취미와 관련해서 학습한 아카데믹한 표현들을 떠올린다.	a hobby, scrapbooking, equipment, creative, collect, reminisce, a suitable hobby, a particularly good hobby, amateur, a creative outlet
5. 주의해야 할 문법 문제의 시제 및 인칭 대명사 등을 확인한다.	이 문제에서 hobby는 셀 수 있는 명사이다. 따라서 단수로 쓸 때는 a hobby 혹은 the hobby라고 쓰고, 복수로 쓸 때는 hobbies라고 쓰는 것에 주의하자!

Brainstorming

Sub-question 1 what the hobby is	스크랩북 만들기
Sub-question 2 what special equipment is needed, if any	기의 필요 없음. 공책, 풀, 개인 사진들
Sub-question 3 when you want to take it up	아이들의 어린 시절 순간들을 수집하고 기록하며 아이가 성장했을 때 그것들을 추억할 수 있음
Sub-question 4 and explain why this is a suitable hobby for older people	건강할 필요가 없음. 창의적이어서 노인성 치매의 위험을 낮춤

✏️ 다음 **불법포인트**를 참고해서 영어 문장을 완성해 보자. (주어와 시제, 품사와 단복수 등을 고려할 것!)

❶ 지금 나는 나이가 더 들어서 시작하기 원하는 취미에 대해 이야기하고 싶습니다.
Now, I _____ a hobby I want to start when I'm older.
※ ~에 대해 이야기하고 싶다 : would like to talk about

❷ 내가 선택한 취미는 스크랩북 만들기입니다.
The hobby which I've chosen is _____ .
※ 스크랩북 만들기 : scrapbooking

❸ 이 취미는 공책, 풀, 개인 사진들 같은 약간의 용품만 필요합니다. 나는 창의적인 것을 즐기기 때문에, 나는 또한 이 책을 예쁘게 만들기 위해 금색 은색 반짝이와 형광펜과 같은 미술 재료들이 필요할 것입니다.
Very little _____ is needed for this hobby, just a notebook, glue and personal photographs. Since I enjoy being creative, I would also need _____ such as gold and silver _____ and highlighter pens to make the book look pretty.
※ 용품 : equipment / 미술 재료 : art materials / 반짝이 : glitter

❹ 스크랩북 만들기의 주된 목적은 기억들을 기록하는 것입니다. 나는 아마도 내가 아이들을 가졌을 때 이것을 시작할 것이고 그 결과 그들의 어린 시절 동안의 순간들을 모으고 기록할 수 있을 것입니다. 그 후 우리는 아이들이 더 나이가 들었을 때 추억할 수 있을 것입니다.
The main purpose of scrapbooking is to _____ memories. I would probably start doing it when I have children so that I could _____ and document moments during their childhood. Then we would be able to _____ when they are older.
※ 기록하다 : document / 수집하다 : collect / (행복했던 시절을) 추억하다 : reminisce

❺ 스크랩북 만들기는 어떤 나이의 사람들에게도 적절한 취미지만, 이것은 특히 나이든 사람들에게 좋은 취미인데 어떤 진정한 신체적인 건강을 요구하지 않기 때문입니다. 이 취미는 창의력을 발산하는 수단이므로 나이든 사람들의 노인성 치매 위험을 낮출 수 있습니다.
Scrapbooking is a suitable hobby for people of any age, but a particularly good one for older people because it does not require any real physical fitness. Since this hobby is _____ , it can reduce the risk of _____ in older people.
※ 창의력을 발산하는 수단 : a creative outlet / 노인성 치매 : Alzheimer's disease(알츠하이머병은 치매를 일으키는 가장 흔한 퇴행성 뇌질환으로, 1907년 독일의 정신과 의사인 알로이스 알츠하이머(Alois Alzheimer) 박사에 의해 최초로 보고되었다.)

Sample Answer

> Describe a hobby you want to take up when you are much older.
>
> You should say:
> - what the hobby is
> - what special equipment is needed, if any
> - when you want to take it up
> - and explain why this is a suitable hobby for older people.

Now, I would like to talk about a hobby I want to start when I'm older.

The hobby which I've chosen is scrapbooking.

Very little equipment is needed for this hobby, just a notebook, glue and personal photographs. Since I enjoy being creative, I would also need art materials such as gold and silver glitter and highlighter pens to make the book look pretty.

The main purpose of scrapbooking is to document memories. I would probably start doing it when I have children so that I could collect and document moments during their childhood. Then we would be able to reminisce when they are older.

Scrapbooking is a suitable hobby for people of any age, but a particularly good one for older people because it does not require any real physical fitness. Since this hobby is a creative outlet, it can reduce the risk of Alzheimer's disease in older people.

That's all from me, thank you very much for your attention.

PART 3

1) Do you agree that we learn best from our mistakes?
당신은 우리가 실수로부터 가장 잘 배운다는 것에 동의해요?

Brainstorming	Direct Answer	동의
	Supporting Sentence 1	실수를 반복하지 않는 것이 중요함
	Supporting Sentence 2	다른 사람들의 실수로부터 배우는 것도 가능함
	Supporting Sentence 3	친구들의 실수를 보면 그것을 인식하고 같은 실수를 하지 않는 것이 중요함

✏️ 다음 불법포인트를 참고해서 영어 문장을 완성해 보자. (주어와 시제, 품사와 단복수 등을 고려할 것!)

❶ 어느 정도 나는 우리가 실수로부터 가장 잘 배운다는 것에 동의합니다.
_____ , I agree that we learn best from our mistakes.
※ 어느 정도 : to a degree

❷ 만약 우리가 실수를 한다면, 우리는 실수를 반복하지 않는 것이 중요합니다.
If we _____ , it is important that we don't _____ it.
※ 실수하다 : make a mistake / 반복하다 : repeat

❸ 나는 또한 다른 사람들의 실수로부터 배우는 것도 가능하다고 생각합니다.
I think that it is _____ to learn from other people's mistakes as well.
※ 가능한 : possible

❹ 만약 사람들이 그들의 친구가 실수하는 것을 본다면 그것을 인식하고 같은 실수를 하지 않는 것이 유익할 수 있습니다.
If people see their friend make a mistake, it can be beneficial to _____ it and not do the same thing.
※ 인식하다 : recognise

Q. Do you agree that we learn best from our mistakes?
A. To a degree, I agree that we learn best from our mistakes. If we make a mistake, it is important that we don't repeat it. I think that it is possible to learn from other people's mistakes as well. If people see their friend make a mistake, it can be beneficial to recognise it and not do the same thing.

2) Can we gain life experience from books and movies?
우리는 책과 영화에서 인생 경험을 얻을 수 있나요?

Brainstorming	Direct Answer	장르에 따라 다름
	Supporting Sentence 1	실제 상황들에 대한 영화나 책들에서는 배울 수 있음
	Supporting Sentence 2	공상과학이나 판타지는 진지하게 받아들여서는 안됨

✏️ 다음 불법포인트를 참고해서 영어 문장을 완성해 보자. (주어와 시제, 품사와 단복수 등을 고려할 것!)

❶ 이것은 한 사람이 어떤 장르의 책과 영화를 읽거나 보는 것을 즐기냐에 달려 있습니다.
It _____ which genre of books and films a person enjoys reading or watching.
※ 달려 있다 : depend

❷ 사람들이 배울 수 있는 실제 상황들에 대한 영화나 책은 많습니다.
There are a lot of books and movies about _____ which they could learn from.
※ 실제 상황 : real life situation

❸ 하지만 공상과학이나 판타지와 같은 장르는 순전히 오락을 위해서이고 너무 진지하게 받아들여져서는 안됩니다.
However, genres such as _____ or fantasy are purely for _____ and should not be taken too seriously.
※ 공상과학 : science fiction / 오락 : entertainment

Q. Can we gain life experience from books and movies?
A. It depends which genre of books and films a person enjoys reading or watching. There are a lot of books and movies about real life situations which they could learn from. However, genres such as science fiction or fantasy are purely for entertainment and should not be taken too seriously.

3) Are the types of leisure activities that are popular today the same as those that were popular when your parents were young?

오늘날 인기 있는 여가 활동의 종류들이 당신의 부모님이 젊었을 때 인기 있었던 것과 같은가요?

Brainstorming	Direct Answer	많은 면에서 같음
	Supporting Sentence 1	인기 있는 여가 활동들은 지금도 사교 중심
	Supporting Sentence 2	팀 스포츠, 영화 관람, 음악 콘서트

✏️ 다음 불법포인트를 참고해서 영어 문장을 완성해 보자. (주어와 시제, 품사와 단복수 등을 고려할 것!)

❶ 많은 면에서 네, 그렇습니다.
_____ , yes they are.
※ 많은 면에서 : in many ways

❷ 지금 인기 있는 여가 활동들이 사교 중심으로 돌아가는 것은 부모님이 젊었을 때 그랬던 것과 같습니다.
Popular leisure activities _____ socialising which is the same now as it was when my parents were young too.
※ ~를 중심으로 돌아가다 : revolve around

❸ 때로는 축구나 배드민턴 같은 팀 스포츠를 하면서 어울릴 수 있는 반면 다른 때에는 가족 혹은 친구들과 영화를 보러 가거나 음악 콘서트를 즐기는 것을 포함할지도 모릅니다.
Sometimes it could be socialising while playing a team sport such as football or badminton, while other times it might involve _____ or enjoying music concerts with family or friends.
※ 영화 보러 가다 : go to the cinema(=go to the movies)

Q. Are the types of leisure activities that are popular today the same as those that were popular when your parents were young?

A. In many ways, yes they are. Popular leisure activities revolve around socialising which is the same now as it was when my parents were young too. Sometimes it could be socialising while playing a team sport such as football or badminton, while other times it might involve going to the cinema or enjoying music concerts with family or friends.

4) What types of leisure activities may become more popular in the future?
어떤 종류의 여가 활동들이 미래에는 더 인기가 있을까요?

Brainstorming	Direct Answer	기술과 함께 보내는 여가 시간
	Supporting Sentence 1	이미 현대 기술에 사로잡혀 있음
	Supporting Sentence 2	미래에는 더 많은 기술 관련 취미들이 있을 것임

✏️ 다음 **불법포인트**를 참고해서 영어 문장을 완성해 보자. (주어와 시제, 품사와 단복수 등을 고려할 것!)

❶ 미래에는 사람들과 어울리는 대신에 기술과 함께 여가 시간을 보내는 것에 더 흥미가 있을 것입니다.
In the future, there may be more interest in spending leisure time with technology _____ with people.
※ ~ 대신에 : instead of

❷ 나는 이미 사람들이 컴퓨터와 스마트폰 같은 현대 기술에 사로잡혀 가고 있다고 생각합니다.
I think that people are already _____ modern technology, such as computers and smartphones.
※ 사로잡히게 되다 : become obsessed with

❸ 하지만 미래에는 지금 우리가 소유하고 있는 것보다 더 많은 기술 관련 취미들에 대한 선택들이 있을 것입니다.
But in the future, there will be even more choices of _____ hobbies than what we have now.
※ 기술 관련한 : technology-related

Q. What types of leisure activities may become more popular in the future?
A. In the future, there may be more interest in spending leisure time with technology instead of with people. I think that people are already becoming obsessed with modern technology, such as computers and smartphones. But in the future, there will be even more choices of technology-related hobbies than what we have now.

Day 4 Lifestyles & Leisure Activities 불법포인트 정리

영화 보러 가다	go to the cinema / go to the movies	~에 대해 이야기하고 싶다	would like to talk about
전시회	exhibition	스크랩북 만들기	scrapbooking
스트레스를 해소하다	relieve stress	용품	equipment
꽤	quite	미술 재료	art materials
집에 머물다	stay at home	반짝이	glitter
평일 밤	weeknight	기록하다	document
주말에	on the weekend	수집하다	collect
내가 할 수 있는 한 많이	as much as I can	(행복했던 시절을) 추억하다	reminisce
주당 40 시간	40 hours a week	창의력을 발산하는 수단	a creative outlet
밤 늦게까지	until late at night	노인성 치매	Alzheimer's disease
피곤함을 느끼다	feel tired	어느 정도	to a degree
~로 간주되다	be considered to	실수하다	make a mistake
무례한	rude	반복하다	repeat
시간을 엄수하는	punctual	가능한	possible
불가피한	inevitable	인식하다	recognise
심각한 모욕	a serious insult	달려 있다	depend
만나기로 약속을 하다	arrange to meet	실제 상황	real life situation
허용되는 수준	an acceptable level	공상과학	science fiction
교통 체증	a traffic jam / traffic congestion	오락	entertainment
급한 집안일	family emergency	많은 면에서	in many ways
악명 높은	notorious	~를 중심으로 돌아가다	revolve around
신경 쓰다	mind	~ 대신에	instead of
30분	half an hour	사로잡히게 되다	become obsessed with
짜증나다	feel annoyed	기술 관련한	technology-related

Day 05 Student Life 학교(학생) 생활

PART 1

1) What is your course or what course did you finish?
2) Why did you choose that subject?
3) What do you find most interesting about your course?
4) What was your favourite subject?
5) What do you dislike about your study?
6) What job would you like when you have completed all your studies?
7) What are the advantages of studying abroad?

PART 2

Describe a good study method you use.

You should say:

    what the method is

    where you learned it

    whether you think many other people use it

and explain why this method is effective for you.

PART 3

1) Should all students pay for their university education?
2) What advantages do universities bring to society?
3) How are education priorities today different from those in the past?
4) What changes do you think will happen in the classroom in the near future?

보이는 Speaking QR 코드

PART 1

1) What is your course or what course did you finish? 당신의 전공은 뭐예요? 혹은 어떤 전공을 마쳤나요?

Brainstorming	Direct Answer	영문학을 공부하고 있음
	Additional Information	다른 시대의 다양한 문학을 다룸

✏️ 다음 불법포인트를 참고해서 영어 문장을 완성해 보자. (주어와 시제, 품사와 단복수 등을 고려할 것!)

> ❶ 나는 영문학을 공부하고 있습니다.
> I am studying _____ .
> ※ 영문학 : English Literature
>
> ❷ 이 전공은 셰익스피어와 버지니아 울프 같은 작가들을 포함해서 다른 시대의 다양한 문학을 다룹니다.
> This _____ _____ a diverse range of _____ from different periods, including anthors such as Shakespeare and Virginia Woolf.
> ※ 전공 : course(전공이라고 하면 우리는 보통 major을 떠올리지만, 영국에서는 course라는 단어를 훨씬 더 많이 쓴다.)
> 다루다 : cover / 문학 : literature

Q. What is your course or what course did you finish?
A. I am studying English literature. This course covers a diverse range of literature from different periods, including authors such as Shakespeare and Virginia Woolf.

2) Why did you choose that subject? 당신은 왜 그 과목을 선택했어요?

Brainstorming	Direct Answer	독서에 대한 사랑과 서양 문화에 대한 관심
	Additional Information	영문과 교수가 되고 싶음

✏️ 다음 불법포인트를 참고해서 영어 문장을 완성해 보자. (주어와 시제, 품사와 단복수 등을 고려할 것!)

> ❶ 영문학은 독서에 대한 나의 사랑과 서양 문화에 대한 나의 관심을 결합해 줍니다.
> English literature _____ my love of reading and my interest in _____ .
> ※ 결합하다 : combine / 서양 문화 : Western culture
>
> ❷ 나는 장래에 이 과목의 교수가 되고 싶습니다.
> I would like to become a professor in the _____ in the future.
> ※ 과목 : subject

Q. Why did you choose that subject?
A. English literature combines my love of reading and my interest in Western culture. I would like to become a professor in the subject in the future.

3) **What do you find most interesting about your course?** 당신의 전공에서 가장 흥미로운 것은 뭐예요?

Brainstorming	Direct Answer	서양 역사와 생활 방식
	Additional Information	현대 소설도 배우지만, 고전들도 배움

✏️ 다음 불법포인트를 참고해서 영어 문장을 완성해 보자. (주어와 시제, 품사와 단복수 등을 고려할 것!)

❶ 이 전공의 가장 흥미로운 면은 서양의 역사와 생활 방식에 대해 배우는 것입니다.
The most interesting aspect of the course is learning about Western history and _____ .
※ 생활 방식 : lifestyle

❷ 우리가 공부하는 소설들 중 일부는 현대적이지만 몇몇은 오래된 고전들입니다.
Some of the novels we study are _____ but some are old _____ .
※ 현대적 : modern / 고전 : classic

Q. What do you find most interesting about your course?
A. The most interesting aspect of the course is learning about Western history and lifestyle. Some of the novels we study are modern but some are old classics.

4) **What was your favourite subject?** 당신이 가장 좋아하는 과목은 무엇이었어요?

Brainstorming	Direct Answer	역사
	Additional Information	과거에 사람들이 어떻게 살았는지 궁금

✏️ 다음 불법포인트를 참고해서 영어 문장을 완성해 보자. (주어와 시제, 품사와 단복수 등을 고려할 것!)

❶ 역사는 학교에서 내가 가장 좋아하는 과목이었습니다.
History was my _____ subject at school.
※ 가장 좋아하는 : favourite

❷ 나는 책과 영화로부터 이 과목을 배웠습니다. 나는 과거에 사람들이 어떻게 살았는지에 대해 매우 호기심이 많습니다.
I learned the subject from books and movies. I am so _____ about how people lived in the past.
※ 호기심이 많은 : curious

Q. What was your favourite subject?
A. History was my favourite subject at school. I learned the subject from books and movies. I am so curious about how people lived in the past.

5) What do you dislike about your study? 당신이 학업에 대해서 싫어하는 것은 무엇이에요?

Brainstorming	Direction Answer	소설을 읽는 재미를 망침
	Additional Information	상세하게 공부하므로 줄거리가 지루해질 수 있음

✏️ 다음 불법포인트를 참고해서 영어 문장을 완성해 보자. (주어와 시제, 품사와 단복수 등을 고려할 것!)

❶ 영문학을 공부하는 것은 소설을 읽는 재미를 망칠 수 있습니다.
Studying English literature can _____ the joy of reading a novel.
※ 망치다 : ruin

❷ 줄거리가 지루해지도록 아주 상세하게 (소설)책을 공부해야 합니다.
The book needs to be studied in such great detail that the _____ becomes _____ .
※ 줄거리 : storyline / 지루한 : boring

Q. What do you dislike about your study?
A. Studying English literature can ruin the joy of reading a novel. The book needs to be studied in such great detail that the storyline becomes boring.

6) What job would you like when you have completed all your studies?
당신은 모든 학업을 마치면 어떤 일을 하고 싶어요?

Brainstorming	Direct Answer	대학 교수
	Additional Information	좀 더 성숙한 학생들을 가르치는 것을 더 좋아함

✏️ 다음 불법포인트를 참고해서 영어 문장을 완성해 보자. (주어와 시제, 품사와 단복수 등을 고려할 것!)

❶ 학업을 마친 후에 나는 대학에서 교수가 되고 싶습니다.
After my studies, I would like to become a _____ at a university.
※ 교수 : professor

❷ 나는 초등학교 선생님이 되기를 원한 적이 있지만 지금은 더 성숙한 학생들을 가르치는 것을 더 좋아합니다.
I _____ want to be _____ teacher but now, I would _____ to teach more _____ students.
※ (과거에) ~ 한 적이 있다 : used to / 초등학교 : a primary school / 더 좋아하다 : prefer / 성숙한 : mature

Q. What job would you like when you have completed all your studies?
A. After my studies, I would like to become a professor at a university. I used to want to be a primary school teacher but now, I would prefer to teach more mature students.

7) What are the advantages of studying abroad?
해외에서 공부하는 것의 장점은 뭐예요?

Brainstorming	Direct Answer	문화에 대한 새로운 관점, 언어 능력, 배우려는 의지
	Additional Information	취업에 있어서 매력적

✏️ 다음 **불법포인트**를 참고해서 영어 문장을 완성해 보자. (주어와 시제, 품사와 단복수 등을 고려할 것!)

❶ 해외 유학 프로그램을 마친 학생들은 문화에 대한 새로운 관점, 언어 능력 그리고 배우려는 의지를 가지고 돌아옵니다.
Students who have finished a programme studying abroad return with a new _____ on culture, language skills and a _____ to learn.
※ 관점 : perspective / (기꺼이 하려는) 의지 : willingness

❷ 취업 기회에 대해서 말하자면, 말할 필요도 없이 이 모든 것이 미래의 고용주들에게 매력적입니다.
_____ job opportunities, _____ , all of these are _____ to future employers.
※ ~에 대해서 말하자면 : when it comes to(=as for / in terms of) / 말할 필요도 없이 : needless to say
매력적인 : attractive

Q. What are the advantages of studying abroad?
A. Students who have finished a programme studying abroad return with a new perspective on culture, language skills and a willingness to learn. When it comes to job opportunities, needless to say, all of these are attractive to future employers.

PART 2

Describe a good study method you use.

You should say :
   what the method is
   where you learned it
   whether you think many other people use it
and explain why this method is effective for you.

당신이 이용하는 좋은 학습법을 묘사하세요.

당신은 반드시 말해야 합니다.
   그 방법이 무엇인지
   그것을 어디에서 배웠는지
   당신은 많은 다른 사람들이 이것을 사용한다고 생각하는지
그리고 이 방법이 왜 당신에게 효과적인지 설명하세요.

※ 가끔은 다소 황당하다고 느껴지는 질문도 받을 수 있다. 평소에 되도록 많은 예상 질문들을 숙지하고 자신 없는 문제부터 답변을 준비하는 것이 중요하다. 지금 떠오르지 않는 아이디어가 시험장에서 갑자기 떠오르는 기적은 없다.

주어지는 1분을 어떻게 활용할 것인가? (How to Use Your 1 Minute Preparation Time)

1. 질문 파악 학습법 묘사에 초점을 맞추는 문제이다.	내가 영어로 잘 설명할 수 있는 학습법을 떠올린다.
2. 묘사 대상 결정하기 영어로 가장 자신 있게 묘사할 수 있는 학습법을 떠올린다.	나만의 특별한 학습법이 없는 경우에는 주변 친구들의 사례를 떠올리고 내 학습법이라 가정하고 스토리를 만들자.
3. 하위 질문 확인 + 스토리 작성 하위 질문의 개수를 확인하고, 각각에 대한 답을 적는다.	sub-questions는 3개처럼 보이지만, 마지막 문장의 'and explain why this method is effective for you'를 포함해서 4개이다. 반드시 4개의 질문에 모두 답하되, 답의 길이는 똑같지 않아도 상관없다.
4. 주제 관련 아카데믹 표현 사용 평소 학습법과 관련해서 학습한 아카데믹 표현들을 떠올린다.	the most effective method, flash cards, mix up the cards, look at the questions, try to remember the answers, this technique, simple and easy, useful, studying at home, revision, repetitive, stick in my mind
5. 주의해야 할 문법 문제의 시제 및 인칭 대명사 등을 확인한다.	method의 동의어 way와 technique도 적절하게 사용하면 method가 계속 반복되는 것을 막을 수 있다. 또한 2번째 질문에 대한 답을 할 때는 과거 시제를 정확하게 사용하는 것에 주의할 것!

Brainstorming

Sub-question 1 what the method is	플래시 카드, 카드 한 면에는 질문을 쓰고 다른 면에는 답변을 씀
Sub-question 2 where you learned it	이 방법을 쓰던 오빠에게 배움
Sub-question 3 whether you think many other people use it	간단하고 쉬워서 많은 학생들이 이용하는 학습법
Sub-question 4 and explain why this method is effective for you	복습을 반복할 수 있기 때문

다음 **불법포인트**를 참고해서 영어 문장을 완성해 보자. (주어와 시제, 품사와 단복수 등을 고려할 것!)

❶ 지금 나는 내가 이용하는 좋은 학습법에 대해 이야기하고 싶습니다.
Now, I would like to talk about a good _____ I use.
※ 학습법 : study method

❷ 공부하는 것을 돕기 위해 내가 선택한 가장 효과적인 방법은 플래시 카드를 사용하는 것입니다. 이것을 사용하는 방식은 카드 한 면에는 질문을 쓰고 다른 면에는 답변을 씁니다. 그리고 나는 공부할 때, 이 카드를 섞고 질문만 보고 제가 공부한 답변을 기억하려고 노력합니다.
_____ which I've chosen to help me study is using flash cards. The way it works is a question is written on one side of the card and the answer on the other side. Then when I am studying, I _____ the cards and just look at the questions and try to remember the answers that I have _____ .
※ 가장 효과적인 방법 : the most effective method / 섞다 : mix up / 공부하다, 복습하다 : revise

❸ 나는 학교와 대학교에 걸쳐서 이 기술을 사용한 내 오빠/형(으)로부터 이렇게 공부하는 방법을 배웠습니다.
I learnt this method of studying from my _____ who used this technique throughout school and university.
※ 오빠, 형 : elder brother

❹ 나는 플래시 카드는 하기 간단하고 쉽기 때문에 많은 학생들에 의해서 이용되는 방법이라고 생각합니다. 플래시 카드는 또한 가지고 다닐 수 있기 때문에 유용해서 나는 집에서 공부할 때뿐만 아니라 버스 안에서 또는 쇼핑할 때도 그것들로 공부할 수 있습니다.
I think using flash cards is a method used by many students since it is _____ . Flash cards are also useful because they can be carried around, so I can study from them when I am _____ or shopping as well as when I am studying _____ .
※ 하기 간단하고 쉬운 : simple and easy to do / 버스 안에서 : on the bus / 집에서 : at home

❺ 이 방법은 나에게는 특히 효과적인데, 나는 복습을 꽤 반복적으로 하는 것이 필요하고 그 결과 이 정보가 뇌에 정말로 박히기 때문입니다. 이 플래시 카드를 가지고, 나는 이것들을 자세히 볼 수 있고 내가 필요하다고 생각하는 만큼 같은 것들을 자주 재사용할 수 있습니다.
This method is _____ effective for me since I _____ my _____ to be quite _____ so that the information really _____ . With flash cards, I can look at them and _____ the same ones as often as I feel is necessary.
※ 특히 : particularly / 필요하다 : require / 시험 공부, 복습 : revision / 반복적인 : repetitive / 뇌에 박히다 : stick in one's mind / 재사용하다 : reuse

Sample Answer

> Describe a good study method you use.
>
> You should say:
>   what the method is
>   where you learned it
>   whether you think many other people use it
> and explain why this method is effective for you.

Now, I would like to talk about a good study method I use.

The most effective method which I've chosen to help me study is using flash cards. The way it works is a question is written on one side of the card and the answer on the other side. Then when I am studying, I mix up the cards and just look at the questions and try to remember the answers that I have revised.

I learnt this method of studying from my elder brother who used this technique throughout school and university.

I think using flash cards is a method used by many students since it is simple and easy to do. Flash cards are also useful because they can be carried around, so I can study from them when I am on the bus or shopping as well as when I am studying at home.

This method is particularly effective for me since I require my revision to be quite repetitive so that the information really sticks in my mind. With flash cards, I can look at them and reuse the same ones as often as I feel is necessary.

That's all from me, thank you very much for your attention.

PART 3

1) Should all students pay for their university education?
모든 학생들은 자신의 대학 교육을 위해서 돈을 지불해야 하나요?

Brainstorming	Direct Answer	등록금을 지불해야 한다고 생각하지 않음
	Supporting Sentence 1	가난한 사람에게 불리함
	Supporting Sentence 2	학생의 형편이 아닌 성적에 기반을 두어야 함

✏️ 다음 불법포인트를 참고해서 영어 문장을 완성해 보자. (주어와 시제, 품사와 단복수 등을 고려할 것!)

❶ 나는 대학생들이 등록금을 지불해야 한다고 생각하지 않습니다.
I don't think that university students should have to pay their _____ .
※ 등록금 : tuition fees

❷ 이것은 사회에서 더 가난한 사람들이 불리한 입장에 있는 것을 의미하는 불공정한 제도입니다.
It is an unfair system that means poorer people in society are _____ .
※ 불리한 입장에 있는 : at a disadvantage

❸ 대학에 다니는 것은 학생이 대학에 다닐 형편이 되는지 아닌지 대신에, 얼마나 학생의 성적이 좋은지에 기반을 두어야 합니다.
Attending university should be based on how good a student's grades are _____ whether a student can _____ to go to university.
※ 대신에 : instead of / 형편이(여유가) 되다 : afford

Q. Should all students pay for their university education?

A. I don't think that university students should have to pay their tuition fees. It is an unfair system that means poorer people in society are at a disadvantage. Attending university should be based on how good a student's grades are instead of whether a student can afford to go to university.

2) What advantages do universities bring to society?
대학들은 어떤 장점들을 사회에 가져다 주나요?

Brainstorming	Direct Answer	교육을 더 받고 지식이 많은 사람들을 사회에 제공
	Supporting Sentence 1	한 사회의 문화와 경제 발전을 가능하게 함
	Supporting Sentence 2	사회를 개선하는 데 도움을 주는 기술을 학생들에게 제공함

✏️ 다음 문법포인트를 참고해서 영어 문장을 완성해 보자. (주어와 시제, 품사와 단복수 등을 고려할 것!)

❶ 대학들은 유익한데 대학들이 교육을 더 받고 지식이 많은 사람들을 사회에 제공하기 때문입니다.
Universities are beneficial because they provide society with more educated, _____ people.
※ 지식이 많은 : knowledgeable

❷ 이것은 한 사회의 문화와 경제 발전을 가능하게 합니다.
This _____ advances to happen in a society's culture and economy.
※ 가능하게 하다 : allow

❸ 대학들은 사회를 개선하는 데 도움을 주는 기술들을 학생들에게 제공합니다.
Universities provide students with skills that help to _____ society.
※ 개선하다 : improve

Q. What advantages do universities bring to society?
A. Universities are beneficial because they provide society with more educated, knowledgeable people. This allows advances to happen in a society's culture and economy. Universities provide students with skills that help to improve society.

3) How are education priorities today different from those in the past?
오늘날 교육의 우선순위는 과거와 어떻게 다른가요?

Brainstorming	Direct Answer	지금은 학구적인 분위기에 더 초점을 맞춤
	Supporting Sentence 1	과거에는 일상적인 작업에 집중
	Supporting Sentence 2	사회가 발전하면서 언어와 과학에 우선순위를 둠

✏️ 다음 불법포인트를 참고해서 영어 문장을 완성해 보자. (주어와 시제, 품사와 단복수 등을 고려할 것!)

❶ 교육의 우선순위는 그들이 이전에 그랬던 것보다 지금은 학구적인 분위기에 훨씬 더 초점을 맞춥니다.
_____ in education focus on _____ much more now than they did previously.
※ 우선순위 : priority / 학계, 학구적인 분위기 : academia

❷ 과거에 교육은 요리, 농사 그리고 건설처럼 일상적인 작업을 어떻게 해야 하는지를 배우는 데 기초했습니다.
In the past, education was based on learning how to do _____ such as cooking, farming and _____ .
※ 일상적인 작업 : everyday task / 건설 : construction

❸ 사회가 발전하면서 교육적 우선순위는 언어와 과학 같은 과목으로 향해 가고 있습니다.
Since society has progressed, the _____ priority has _____ subjects such as language and science.
※ 교육적인 : educational / ~로 향해 가다 : move towards

Q. How are education priorities today different from those in the past?
A. Priorities in education focus on academia much more now than they did previously. In the past, education was based on learning how to do everyday tasks such as cooking, farming and construction. Since society has progressed, the educational priority has moved towards subjects such as language and science.

4) What changes do you think will happen in the classroom in the near future?
당신은 가까운 미래에 교실에는 어떤 변화들이 일어날 것이라고 생각해요?

Brainstorming	Direct Answer	직접적인 경험을 하는 것
	Supporting Sentence 1	현재는 교과서로 공부
	Supporting Sentence 2	미래에는 발전된 컴퓨터 기술로 실제 경험에 더 중점을 둠

✏️ 다음 불법포인트를 참고해서 영어 문장을 완성해 보자. (주어와 시제, 품사와 단복수 등을 고려할 것!)

❶ 교실에서의 미래 변화는 직접적인 경험을 하는 것입니다.
A future change in the classroom will be _____ .
※ 직접적인 경험을 하다 : gain hands-on experience

❷ 현재, 학생들은 주로 교과서를 공부하고 선생님들이 과목을 설명하는 것을 듣습니다.
Now, students mainly study _____ and listen to teachers explain subjects.
※ 교과서 : textbook

❸ 하지만 미래에는 클라우드 컴퓨팅, 증강 현실 그리고 3차원 인쇄 같은 발전된 컴퓨터 기술 덕택에 실제 경험을 통해서 배우는 것에 더 많은 중점을 둘 것입니다.
But in the future, there will be a greater _____ on learning through _____ thanks to advanced computer skills such as _____ , _____ and _____ .

※ 강조 : emphasis / 실제 경험 : practical experience / 클라우드 컴퓨팅 : cloud computing(인터넷상의 서버를 통하여 데이터 저장, 네트워크, 콘텐츠 사용 등 IT 관련 서비스를 한번에 사용할 수 있는 컴퓨팅 환경) / 증강 현실 : augmented reality(실제 세계에 3차원 가상물체를 겹쳐 보여주는 기술) / 3차원 인쇄 : 3D printing(디지털화된 디자인 데이터를 활용해 인쇄를 하듯 물체를 만들어 내는 방식)

Q. What changes do you think will happen in the classroom in the near future?
A. A future change in the classroom will be gaining hands-on experience. Now, students mainly study textbooks and listen to teachers explain subjects. But in the future, there will be a greater emphasis on learning through practical experience thanks to advanced computer skills such as cloud computing, augmented reality and 3D printing.

Day 5 Student Life 불법포인트 정리

영문학	English Literature	하기 간단하고 쉬운	simple and easy to do
전공	course / major	버스 안에서	on the bus
다루다	cover	집에서	at home
문학	literature	특히	particularly
결합하다	combine	필요하다	require
서양 문화	Western culture	시험 공부, 복습	revision
과목	subject	반복적인	repetitive
생활 방식	lifestyle	뇌리에 박히다	stick in one's mind
현대적	modern	재사용하다	reuse
고전	classic	등록금	tuition fees
가장 좋아하는	favourite	불리한 입장에 있는	at a disadvantage
호기심이 많은	curious	대신에	instead of
망치다	ruin	형편이(여유가) 되다	afford
줄거리	storyline	지식이 많은	knowledgeable
지루한	boring	가능하게 하다	allow
교수	professor	개선하다	improve
(과거에) ~ 한 적 있다	used to	우선순위	priority
초등학교	a primary school	학계, 학구적인 분위기	academia
더 좋아하다	prefer	일상적인 작업	everyday task
성숙한	mature	건설	construction
관점	perspective	교육적인	educational
(기꺼이 하려는) 의지	willingness	~로 향해 가다	move towards
~에 대해서 말하자면	when it comes to / as for / in terms of	직접적인 경험을 하다	gain hands-on experience
말할 필요도 없이	needless to say	교과서	textbook
매력적인	attractive	강조	emphasis
학습법	study method	실제 경험	practical experience
가장 효과적인 방법	the most effective method	클라우드 컴퓨팅	cloud computing
섞다	mix up	증강 현실	augmented reality
공부하다, 복습하다	revise	3차원 인쇄	3D printing
오빠, 형	elder brother		

Day 06 ▶ Communication 의사소통

PART 1

1) How do you usually keep in touch with members of your family?
2) Do you prefer to speak to people by phone or by writing e-mails?
3) Do you ever write letters by hand? [Why/Why not?]
4) Is there anything you dislike about mobile phones?
5) What languages do you speak?
6) Do you think it's important to learn a foreign language?
7) What do you find most difficult about learning English?

PART 2

Describe a letter you received recently.

You should say :
    when you received it
    who sent it to you
    what it is about
and explain whether it is important to you.

PART 3

1) What is the difference between letters and e-mails?
2) What is the difference between the past and present as regards communication?
3) What was the role of letters 50 years ago and what about at present?
4) Will post offices disapper in the next 50 years?

보이는 Speaking QR 코드

PART 1

1) How do you usually keep in touch with members of your family? 당신은 보통 가족 구성원들과 어떻게 연락을 하나요?

Brainstorming	Direct Answer	부모님과 조부모님과는 전화로 연락함
	Additional Information	형제 자매와는 카톡으로 의사소통

✏️ 다음 불법포인트를 참고해서 영어 문장을 완성해 보자. (주어와 시제, 품사와 단복수 등을 고려할 것!)

❶ 보통 나는 부모님과 조부모님과는 전화로 연락합니다.
Usually I _____ my parents and grandparents _____ .
※ 연락을 (유지)하다 : keep in touch with / 전화로 : over the phone(by phone도 OK!)

❷ 하지만 형제 자매들과는 무료 문자와 전화의 특징을 가진 스마트폰 전용 무료 모바일 인스턴트 메시징 앱인 카카오톡으로 의사소통 합니다.
But with my _____ , we _____ via KakaoTalk, which is a free mobile instant messaging application for smartphones with free text and call features.
※ 형제 자매 : sibling / 의사소통 하다 : communicate

Q. How do you usually keep in touch with members of your family?
A. Usually I keep in touch with my parents and grandparents over the phone. But with my siblings, we communicate via KakaoTalk, which is a free mobile instant messaging application for smartphones with free text and call features.

2) Do you prefer to speak to people by phone or by writing e-mails?
당신은 사람들과 전화로 말하는 것을 더 좋아해요? 아니면 이메일 쓰는 것을 더 좋아해요?

Brainstorming	Direct Answer	전화
	Additional Information	더 즉각적, 답장을 기다리는 것을 좋아하지 않음

✏️ 다음 불법포인트를 참고해서 영어 문장을 완성해 보자. (주어와 시제, 품사와 단복수 등을 고려할 것!)

❶ 나는 전화로 사람들과 연락하는 것을 더 좋아합니다.
I prefer _____ people over the phone.   ※ 연락하다 : contact

❷ 이것이 더 즉각적이고 나는 초조하게 이메일 답장을 기다리는 것을 좋아하지 않습니다.
It is more _____ and I don't like waiting for e-mail replies with _____ .
※ 즉각적인 : immediate / 초조함, 성급함 : impatience

Q. Do you prefer to speak to people by phone or by writing e-mails?
A. I prefer contacting people over the phone. It is more immediate and I don't like waiting for e-mail replies with impatience.

3) Do you ever write letters by hand? [Why/Why not?]
당신은 손으로 편지를 쓴 적이 있어요? [왜?/왜 아닌지?]

Brainstorming	Direct Answer	가끔 씀
	Additional Information	휴가 중에 친구들과 가족에게 엽서를 보낼것임

✏️ 다음 **불법포인트**를 참고해서 영어 문장을 완성해 보자. (주어와 시제, 품사와 단복수 등을 고려할 것!)

❶ 가끔 나는 여전히 손으로 편지를 씁니다.
Occasionally I still write _____ .   ※ 손으로 : by hand

❷ 요즘은 이메일을 쓰는 것이 더 쉽지만, 만약 내가 휴가 중이면 나는 나의 친구들과 가족에게 엽서를 보낼 것입니다.
It is easier to write e-mails nowadays but if I am _____ , I will send _____ to my friends and family.
※ 휴가 중 : on holiday / 엽서 : postcard

Q. Do you ever write letters by hand? [Why/Why not?]
A. Occasionally I still write by hand. It is easier to write e-mails nowadays but if I am on holiday, I will send postcards to my friends and family.

4) Is there anything you dislike about mobile phones? 당신은 휴대 전화에 대해서 싫어하는 점이 있나요?

Brainstorming	Direct Answer	얼굴을 직접 보며 사람들을 만나는 것이 덜 중요하게 됨
	Additional Information	그렇게 되지 않기를 바람

✏️ 다음 **불법포인트**를 참고해서 영어 문장을 완성해 보자. (주어와 시제, 품사와 단복수 등을 고려할 것!)

❶ 사회가 휴대 전화와 기술에 중독되어 있어서, 얼굴을 직접 보며 사람들을 만나는 것이 덜 중요하게 되었습니다.
Society has _____ to mobile phones and technology so seeing people _____ has become less important.
※ 중독되다 : become addicted / 얼굴을 직접 보고 : face to face

❷ 나는 실제로는 그렇지 않기를 바랍니다.
I wish that _____ .
※ 실제로는 그렇지 않다 : be not the case

Q. Is there anything you dislike about mobile phones?
A. Society has become addicted to mobile phones and technology so seeing people face to face has become less important. I wish that wasn't the case.

5) What languages do you speak? 당신은 어떤 언어들을 할 수 있나요?

Brainstorming	Direction Answer	한국어, 영어, 중국어
	Additional Information	5년 안에 5개 언어 구사하기를 희망함

✏️ 다음 불법포인트를 참고해서 영어 문장을 완성해 보자. (주어와 시제, 품사와 단복수 등을 고려할 것!)

❶ 나의 모국어는 한국어이지만, 나는 또한 영어를 말하고 최근에는 중국어를 공부하기 시작했습니다.
My _____ is Korean but I also speak English and have recently started studying Chinese.
※ 모국어 : mother tongue(=native language)

❷ 나는 지금부터 5년 안에 적어도 5개 언어를 구사할 수 있기를 희망합니다.
I wish to be able to speak _____ five languages in five years from now.
※ 적어도 : at least

Q. What languages do you speak?
A. My mother tongue is Korean but I also speak English and have recently started studying Chinese. I wish to be able to speak at least five languages in five years from now.

6) Do you think it's important to learn a foreign language?
당신은 외국어를 배우는 것이 중요하다고 생각해요?

Brainstorming	Direct Answer	중요함
	Additional Information	더 많은 사람들과 의사소통 가능, 여행할 때 필요함

✏️ 다음 불법포인트를 참고해서 영어 문장을 완성해 보자. (주어와 시제, 품사와 단복수 등을 고려할 것!)

❶ 네, 나는 적어도 제2언어를 배우는 것이 중요하다고 생각합니다.
Yes, I think it is important to learn at least a _____ .
※ 제2언어(모국어 다음의 언어, 제2외국어가 아니다.) : second language

❷ 이것은 모국어만을 구사하는 사람들보다 더 많은 사람들과 의사소통을 하는 것을 가능하게 하는데, 여행할 때 필요합니다.
It _____ me to communicate with more people than those who only speak my native language, which is _____ when travelling.
※ 가능하게 하다 : allow / 필요한 : necessary

Q. Do you think it's important to learn a foreign language?
A. Yes, I think it is important to learn at least a second language. It allows me to communicate with more people than those who only speak my native language, which is necessary when travelling.

7) What do you find most difficult about learning English?
당신이 영어를 배우는 데 가장 어려운 것은 무엇인가요?

Brainstorming	Direct Answer	발음을 정확하게 하는 것
	Additional Information	가끔 더듬거림

✏️ 다음 **불법포인트**를 참고해서 영어 문장을 완성해 보자. (주어와 시제, 품사와 단복수 등을 고려할 것!)

❶ 영어를 배우는 데 가장 어려운 점은 발음을 정확하게 하는 것입니다.
The most difficult aspect of learning English is getting the _____ right.
※ 발음 : pronunciation

❷ 때때로 나는 단어를 어떻게 말하는지 잊어버려서 약간 더듬거립니다.
Sometimes I _____ how to say a word so I _____ a little bit.
※ 잊어버리다 : forget / 말을 더듬다 : stutter

Q. What do you find most difficult about learning English?
A. The most difficult aspect of learning English is getting the pronunciation right. Sometimes I forget how to say a word so I stutter a little bit.

PART 2

Describe a letter you received recently.

You should say:
    when you received it
    who sent it to you
    what it is about
and explain whether it is important to you.

최근에 당신이 받은 편지에 대해 묘사하세요.

당신은 반드시 말해야 합니다.
    당신은 언제 이 편지를 받았는지
    누가 당신에게 이 편지를 보냈는지
    이 편지는 무엇에 관한 것인지
그리고 이 편지가 당신에게 중요한지 아닌지 설명하세요.

※ 여기에서 말하는 letter는 이메일이 아닌, 손으로 직접 쓴 우편으로 혹은 인편으로 받은 편지를 말한다.

주어지는 1분을 어떻게 활용할 것인가? (How to Use Your 1 Minute Preparation Time)

1. 질문 파악 편지내용 묘사에 초점을 맞추는 문제이다.	내가 영어로 잘 설명할 수 있는 편지를 떠올린다.
2. 묘사 대상 결정하기 영어로 가장 자신 있게 묘사할 수 있는 편지 내용을 떠올린다.	최근에 받은 편지가 없는 경우에는 감동적이거나 재미있는 내용의 편지를 받았다고 가정하고 스토리를 만들자.
3. 하위 질문 확인 + 스토리 작성 하위 질문의 개수를 확인하고, 각각에 대한 답을 적는다.	sub-questions는 3개처럼 보이지만, 마지막 문장의 'and explain whether it is important to you'를 포함해서 4개이다. 반드시 4개의 질문에 모두 답하되, 답의 길이는 똑같지 않아도 상관없다.
4. 주제 관련 아카데믹 표현 사용 평소 편지와 관련해서 학습한 아카데믹한 표현들을 떠올린다.	a letter I received lately, the last letter, my best friend, as a Christmas present, a thank you letter, rarely get to see each other, formal, the latest news in our lives, joyfully look forward to, handwritten, special
5. 주의해야 할 문법 문제의 시제 및 인칭 대명사 등을 확인한다.	첫 번째와 두 번째 질문은 과거 시제, 세 번째와 네 번째 질문은 현재 시제에 초점을 맞춰 대답하는 것에 주의하자!

Brainstorming

Sub-question 1 when you received it	크리스마스 직후
Sub-question 2 who sent it to you	초등학교 친구인 절친 진희, 지금은 서로 다른 나라에 살고 있어 거의 보지 못함, 생일 선물과 크리스마스 선물은 서로 주고 받음, 선물 받으면 서로 감사 편지를 씀
Sub-question 3 what it is about	서로의 삶에 대한 새로운 정보를 업데이트 함 이 편지에 새 남자 친구에 대해 이야기 함
Sub-question 4 and explain whether it is important to you	손으로 쓴 편지이기에 더 특별함 분홍색 튼튼한 상자에 이 편지들을 보관함

✏️ 다음 불법포인트를 참고해서 영어 문장을 완성해 보자. (주어와 시제, 품사와 단복수 등을 고려할 것!)

❶ 지금 나는 최근에 내가 받은 편지에 대해서 이야기하고 싶습니다.
Now, I would like to talk about a letter I received _____ .
※ 최근에 : lately

❷ 내가 받았던 최근 편지는 크리스마스 직후 진희라는 가장 친한 친구로부터 받은 것입니다.
The last letter that I received was _____ Christmas, from my best friend, Jinhee.
※ 직후 : just after

❸ 나는 크리스마스 선물로 그녀에게 모자를 보냈고 그녀는 그것을 받은 후 감사 편지를 나에게 보냈습니다. 초등학교 시절 이후로 나의 가장 친한 친구와 나는 친구로 지내 왔지만 우리는 대학생활을 시작한 이후 다른 나라에서 살고 있습니다. 우리는 멀리 떨어져 살아서 거의 서로 만날 수 없지만, 우리는 항상 생일 선물과 크리스마스 선물을 서로 보내는 것을 기억합니다. 우리는 선물을 받으면 보통 서로에게 감사의 편지를 보냅니다.
I sent her a hat as a Christmas present and she sent me a _____ after she received it. My best friend and I have been friends since we were at _____ but we have lived in different countries since we started university. As we _____ , we rarely _____ but we always remember to send each other birthday and Christmas presents. Once we have received our gifts, we usually send each other a thank you letter.
※ 감사 편지 : thank you letter / 초등학교 : primary school(primary school은 영국식, elementary school은 미국식 영어) / 멀리 떨어져 살다 : live so far apart / 서로 만나다 : get to see each other

❹ 감사 편지는 보통 매우 격식을 차린 것으로 간주되지만 우리의 메시지는 단지 우리의 삶에서 가장 최신 소식이 무엇인지에 대해 서로에게 업데이트하는 기회입니다. 이 편지에 그녀는 잘생기고 점잖은 새 남자친구, 토미에 대해 이야기 했습니다.
Thank you letters are usually considered to be very _____ but our messages are really just an opportunity to update each other on what _____ in our lives is. In this letter, she talked about her new boyfriend, Tommy, who is so handsome and gentle.
※ 격식을 차린 : formal / 가장 최신 소식 : the latest news

❺ 나는 이 편지들이 손으로 쓰여졌다는 사실이 이 편지들을 더욱 특별하게 만든다고 생각합니다. 그래서 나는 분홍색 튼튼한 상자 안에 모든 편지들을 보관합니다.
I think the fact that they are _____ makes our letters more special. So I keep all of them in a pink-coloured _____ box.
※ 손으로 쓰여진 : handwritten / 튼튼한 : sturdy

Sample Answer

Describe a letter you received recently.

You should say:
    when you received it
    who sent it to you
    what it is about
and explain whether it is important to you.

Now, I would like to talk about a letter I received lately.

The last letter that I received was just after Christmas, from my best friend, Jinhee.

I sent her a hat as a Christmas present and she sent me a thank you letter after she received it. My best friend and I have been friends since we were at primary school but we have lived in different countries since we started university. As we live so far apart, we rarely get to see each other but we always remember to send each other birthday and Christmas presents. Once we have received our gifts, we usually send each other a thank you letter.

Thank you letters are usually considered to be very formal but our messages are really just an opportunity to update each other on what the latest news in our lives is. In this letter, she talked about her new boyfriend, Tommy, who is so handsome and gentle.

I think the fact that they are handwritten makes our letters more special. So I keep all of them in a pink-coloured sturdy box.

That's all from me, thank you very much for your attention.

PART 3

1) What is the difference between letters and e-mails?
편지와 이메일의 차이점은 무엇인가요?

Brainstorming	Direct Answer	주된 차이점은 속도
	Supporting Sentence 1	이메일은 즉각적, 편지는 시간이 오래 걸릴 수 있음
	Supporting Sentence 2	손으로 쓴 편지가 더 개인적이고 매력적임

✏️ 다음 불법포인트를 참고해서 영어 문장을 완성해 보자. (주어와 시제, 품사와 단복수 등을 고려할 것!)

❶ 편지와 이메일의 주된 차이점은 수취인이 그것을 받는 속도입니다.
The main difference between letters and e-mails is the speed at which the _____ gets them.
※ 수취인 : recipient

❷ 이메일은 즉시 받을 수 있지만 편지는 이것이 어디로 보내지는가에 따라 시간이 오래 걸릴 수 있습니다.
An e-mail can be received _____ but a letter can _____ , depending on where it is being sent to.
※ 즉시 : instantly / 시간이 오래 걸리다 : take a long time

❸ 하지만 손으로 쓴 편지는 이메일보다 훨씬 더 개인적인 느낌이고 더 많은 매력을 지니고 있습니다.
However, a handwritten letter feels much more _____ than an e-mail and has more _____ .
※ 개인적인 : personal / 매력 : charm

Q. What is the difference between letters and e-mails?
A. The main difference between letters and e-mails is the speed at which the recipient gets them. An e-mail can be received instantly but a letter can take a long time, depending on where it is being sent to. However, a handwritten letter feels much more personal than an e-mail and has more charm.

2) What is the difference between the past and present as regards communication?
의사소통과 관련해서 과거와 현재의 차이점은 무엇인가요?

Brainstorming	Direct Answer	과거에는 시간이 오래 걸리고 노력을 필요로 한다는 것이 받아들여짐
	Supporting Sentence 1	현재는 보내기 쉽고 빨리 받아야 함
	Supporting Sentence 2	현대인의 성급함을 반영함

✏️ 다음 불법포인트를 참고해서 영어 문장을 완성해 보자. (주어와 시제, 품사와 단복수 등을 고려할 것!)

❶ 과거에는 의사소통이 발신과 수신 모두 시간이 오래 걸리고 보다 많은 노력을 필요로 한다는 것이 받아들여졌습니다.
In the past, it was accepted that _____ took a long time and more _____ to both send and receive.
※ 의사소통 : communication / 노력 : effort

❷ 의사소통에 대한 현재의 기대는 이것이 스마트폰으로 이메일이나 인스턴트 메시지 같은 것들을 통해서 보내기 쉬워야 하고 빨리 받아야 한다는 것입니다.
The present _____ of communication is that it should be easy to send and quickly received, such as via e-mail or an instant messaging service on a smart phone.
※ 기대 : expectation

❸ 이것은 현대인들의 성급함을 반영합니다.
It reflects modern people's _____ .
※ 성급함 : impatience

Q. What is the difference between the past and present as regards communication?
A. In the past, it was accepted that communication took a long time and more effort to both send and receive. The present expectation of communication is that it should be easy to send and quickly received, such as via e-mail or an instant messaging service on a smart phone. It reflects modern people's impatience.

3) What was the role of letters 50 years ago and what about at present?
50년 전과 현재에 편지의 역할이 무엇인가요?

Brainstorming	Direct Answer	신뢰받는 양식
	Supporting Sentence 1	중요한 정보의 인쇄된 자료
	Supporting Sentence 2	요즘은 구식이고 종이 낭비로 간주됨

✏️ 다음 **불법포인트**를 참고해서 영어 문장을 완성해 보자. (주어와 시제, 품사와 단복수 등을 고려할 것!)

❶ 50년 전 편지는 의사소통의 신뢰받는 양식이었습니다.
50 years ago, a letter was a _____ form of communication.
※ 신뢰받는 : trusted

❷ 사람들은 중요한 정보의 인쇄된 자료를 가지고 있기 원했고 인터넷 없이 편지를 보내는 것은 이것을 얻는 유일한 방법이었습니다.
People wanted to have a _____ of important information and without the Internet, sending a letter was the only way to achieve this.
※ 인쇄된 자료(하드카피) : hard copy(soft copy는 컴퓨터 상에 있는 자료, 이것을 종이로 출력한 자료가 hard copy이다.)

❸ 요즘에는 편지는 구식처럼 보이고 종이 낭비로 간주됩니다.
Nowadays, letters seem _____ and are considered _____ .
※ 구식인 : old fashioned / 종이 낭비 : a waste of paper

Q. What was the role of letters 50 years ago and what about at present?
A. 50 years ago, a letter was a trusted form of communication. People wanted to have a hard copy of important information and without the Internet, sending a letter was the only way to achieve this. Nowadays, letters seem old fashioned and are considered a waste of paper.

4) **Will post offices disapper in the next 50 years?**
50년 후에 우체국이 사라질까요?

Brainstorming	Direct Answer	사라지지 않음
	Supporting Sentence 1	더 많은 사람들이 해외 여행을 하고 해외에 살기 때문임
	Supporting Sentence 2	50년 내에 훨씬 더 많은 사람들이 해외로 돌아다닐 것이기에 물건을 우송할 필요성이 여전히 있음

✏️ 다음 불법포인트를 참고해서 영어 문장을 완성해 보자. (주어와 시제, 품사와 단복수 등을 고려할 것!)

❶ 아니요, 나는 그것들이 사라질 것이라고 생각하지 않습니다.
No, I don't think they will _____ .
※ 사라지다 : disappear

❷ 점점 더 많은 사람들이 해외 여행을 하고 해외에 살고 있기 때문에 여전히 소포와 같은 것들을 보낼 필요가 있을 것입니다.
There will still be a need to send things such as _____ since more and more people are travelling and living _____ .
※ 소포 : parcel / 해외에 : abroad

❸ 50년 내에 나는 훨씬 더 많은 사람들이 세계를 돌아다니는 것을 선택할 것이기에 물건을 우송할 필요성이 여전히 있을 것이라고 생각합니다.
In 50 years time, I think even more people will choose to _____ so there will still be a need to _____ goods.
※ 세계를 돌아다니다 : move around the world / 우송하다 : post

Q. Will post offices disappear in the next 50 years?
A. No, I don't think they will disappear. There will still be a need to send things such as parcels since more and more people are travelling and living abroad. In 50 years time, I think even more people will choose to move around the world so there will still be a need to post goods.

Day 6 Communication 불법포인트 정리

연락을 (유지)하다	keep in touch with	멀리 떨어져 살다	live so far apart
전화로	over the phone / by phone	서로 만나다	get to see each other
형제 자매	sibling	격식을 차린	formal
의사소통 하다	communicate	가장 최신 소식	the latest news
연락하다	contact	손으로 쓰여진	handwritten
즉각적인	immediate	튼튼한	sturdy
초조함, 성급함	impatience	수취인	recipient
손으로	by hand	즉시	instantly
휴가 중	on holiday	시간이 오래 걸리다	take a long time
엽서	postcard	개인적인	personal
중독되다	become addicted	매력	charm
얼굴을 직접 보고	face to face	의사소통	communication
실제로는 그렇지 않다	be not the case	노력	effort
모국어	mother tongue / native language	기대	expectation
적어도	at least	성급함	impatience
제2언어(모국어 다음의 언어)	second language	신뢰받는	trusted
가능하게 하다	allow	인쇄된 자료	hard copy
필요한	necessary	컴퓨터 상에 있는 자료	soft copy
발음	pronunciation	구식인	old fashioned
잊어버리다	forget	종이 낭비	a waste of paper
말을 더듬다	stutter	사라지다	disappear
최근에	lately	소포	parcel
직후	just after	해외에	abroad
감사 편지	thank you letter	세계를 돌아다니다	move around the world
초등학교(영국식) 초등학교(미국식)	primary school / elementary school	우송하다	post

Day 07 — Travelling & Transport
여행과 교통

PART 1

1) Do you like travelling?
2) Where was the last place you visited on holiday?
3) What kind of tourist destinations do you usually prefer?
4) Has a foreign visitor ever stayed at your home?
5) What is the best way to save money while travelling?
6) Do you like to travel alone or with your friends?
7) Do young people and older people benefit differently from travelling?

PART 2

Describe a transport system for commuters in your city or country.

You should say :
　　what kinds of transport are available
　　which kind of transport is the most popular
　　what the good points and bad points of the transport system are
and say how you think it should be changed in the future.

PART 3

1) How easy is it to travel around your country?
2) Which method of travel do you consider safest?
3) What are the pros and cons of low-cost air travel?
4) Have the types of transport people use changed much over the last few decades?

보이는 Speaking QR 코드

PART 1

1) Do you like travelling? 당신은 여행을 좋아해요?

Brainstorming	Direct Answer	덥고 햇살이 내리쬐는 나라로 여행가는 것을 좋아함
	Additional Information	특히 겨울, 계절적 정서 장애 때문임

✏️ 다음 불법포인트를 참고해서 영어 문장을 완성해 보자. (주어와 시제, 품사와 단복수 등을 고려할 것!)

❶ 네, 나는 덥고 햇살이 내리쬐는 나라로 여행가는 것을 좋아합니다.
Yes, I _____ travelling to hot and sunny countries.   ※ ~을 좋아하다 : be keen on

❷ 특히 겨울 시즌 동안 나는 이러한 국가로 여행을 떠나는데, 나는 계절성 정서 장애를 겪고 있고 하루에 적어도 한 번 해를 보지 못하면 정말로 우울하기 때문입니다.
Especially during the winter season, I travel to these countries because I suffer from _____ and it's really _____ not seeing the sun at least once a day.
※ 계절성 정서 장애 : seasonal affective disorder(겨울철 햇빛 부족으로 인한 우울증적 증상) / 우울한 : depressing

Q. Do you like travelling?

A. Yes, I am keen on travelling to hot and sunny countries. Especially during the winter season, I travel to these countries because I suffer from seasonal affective disorder and it's really depressing not seeing the sun at least once a day.

2) Where was the last place you visited on holiday? 당신이 최근 휴가 중에 방문한 장소는 어디였어요?

Brainstorming	Direct Answer	베트남
	Additional Information	친구 동진이와 1주일을 보냄, 호치민에서 쌀국수를 먹음

✏️ 다음 불법포인트를 참고해서 영어 문장을 완성해 보자. (주어와 시제, 품사와 단복수 등을 고려할 것!)

❶ 내가 최근 휴가간 장소는 베트남이었습니다.
The last place I _____ was to Vietnam.   ※ 휴가를 가다 : go on holiday

❷ 나는 동진이라는 나의 가장 친한 친구와 1주일을 보냈고, 우리는 호치민에서 베트남 국수인 포를 여러 번 먹었습니다.
I spent a week with my best friend, Dongjin, and we ate pho, the Vietnamese noodle soup, _____ in Ho Chi Minh City.   ※ 여러 번 : several times

Q. Where was the last place you visited on holiday?

A. The last place I went on holiday was to Vietnam. I spent a week with my best friend, Dongjin, and we ate pho, the Vietnamese noodle soup, several times in Ho Chi Minh City.

3) **What kind of tourist destinations do you usually prefer?**
당신은 보통 어떤 종류의 관광지를 더 좋아해요?

Brainstorming	Direct Answer	도심 관광지
	Additional Information	미술관, 상점들, 밤 문화를 즐김

✏️ 다음 **불법포인트**를 참고해서 영어 문장을 완성해 보자. (주어와 시제, 품사와 단복수 등을 고려할 것!)

❶ 나는 도심 관광지를 방문하는 것을 더 좋아합니다.
I prefer visiting _____ .
※ 도심 관광지 : city destination

❷ 미술관과 상점들 그리고 밤 문화를 통해 다른 나라의 문화를 보는 것을 즐깁니다.
I enjoy seeing other countries' culture through galleries, shops and _____ .
※ 밤 문화 : nightlife(밤 문화란 야간에 할 수 있는 유흥을 말한다.)

Q. What kind of tourist destinations do you usually prefer?
A. I prefer visiting city destinations. I enjoy seeing other countries' culture through galleries, shops and nightlife.

4) **Has a foreign visitor ever stayed at your home?** 외국인 방문객이 당신 집에 머문 적이 있나요?

Brainstorming	Direct Answer	한 번
	Additional Information	영국인 친구 줄리, 지난 여름 서울을 방문했을 때 우리 집에 머무름

✏️ 다음 **불법포인트**를 참고해서 영어 문장을 완성해 보자. (주어와 시제, 품사와 단복수 등을 고려할 것!)

❶ 네, 한 번이요.
Yes, _____ .
※ 한 번 : once(= one time)

❷ 나는 줄리라는 영국인 친구가 있는데, 그녀가 휴가로 지난 여름 서울을 방문했을 때 우리 집에서 나와 함께 머물렀습니다.
I had an English friend, Juli, and when she visited Seoul last summer on holiday, she _____ me in my family home.
※ (남)의 집에서 머물다 : stay with

Q. Has a foreign visitor ever stayed at your home?
A. Yes, once. I had an English friend, Juli, and when she visited Seoul last summer on holiday, she stayed with me in my family home.

5) What is the best way to save money while travelling?
여행하는 동안 돈을 아끼는 가장 좋은 방법은 무엇인가요?

Brainstorming	Direction Answer	비수기에 방문함
	Additional Information	비행기 표가 더 싸고 호텔도 더 경제적임

✏️ 다음 불법포인트를 참고해서 영어 문장을 완성해 보자. (주어와 시제, 품사와 단복수 등을 고려할 것!)

❶ 여행을 하는 동안 돈을 아끼는 최고의 방법은 비수기 동안에 어떤 나라를 방문하는 것입니다.
The best way to _____ while travelling is to visit a country _____ .
※ 돈을 아끼다 : save money / 비수기 동안에 : during the low season

❷ 그렇게 하면, 비행기 표를 구매하기에 더 싸고 호텔은 머물기에 더 경제적입니다.
_____ , _____ are cheaper to buy and hotels are more _____ to stay at.
※ 그렇게 하면 : that way / 비행기표 : flight ticket / 경제적인 : economical

Q. What is the best way to save money while travelling?
A. The best way to save money while travelling is to visit a country during the low season. That way, flight tickets are cheaper to buy and hotels are more economical to stay at.

6) Do you like to travel alone or with your friends?
당신은 혼자 여행하는 것을 좋아해요? 아니면 친구와 함께 여행하는 것을 좋아해요?

Brainstorming	Direct Answer	친구와 여행하는 것
	Additional Information	친구와 새로운 장소를 경험하고 길을 잃는 것은 더 재미있음

✏️ 다음 불법포인트를 참고해서 영어 문장을 완성해 보자. (주어와 시제, 품사와 단복수 등을 고려할 것!)

❶ 나는 친구와 여행하는 것을 더 좋아합니다.
I prefer to _____ .
※ 친구와 여행하다 : travel with friends

❷ 새로운 장소를 경험하고 거기에서 친구와 함께 길을 잃는 것은 더 재미있습니다.
It is more fun to _____ new places and _____ in them with friends.
※ 경험하다 : experience / 길을 잃다 : get lost

Q. Do you like to travel alone or with your friends?
A. I prefer to travel with friends. It is more fun to experience new places and get lost in them with friends.

7) Do young people and older people benefit differently from travelling?
젊은 사람과 나이든 사람들은 여행으로부터 다르게 이익을 얻나요?

Brainstorming	Direct Answer	개인에 따라 다름
	Additional Information	쉬는 것이라면 나이에 상관없이 같음

✏️ 다음 **문법포인트**를 참고해서 영어 문장을 완성해 보자. (주어와 시제, 품사와 단복수 등을 고려할 것!)

❶ 이것은 개인에 따라 다릅니다.
It depends on the _____ .
※ 개인 : individual

❷ 만약 여행의 목적이 태양 아래 해변에서 눕는 것이고 쉬는 것이라면 사람들의 나이와는 상관없이 이익은 같을 수 있습니다.
If _____ is to _____ in the sun and relax, the benefits could be the same, _____ people's age.
※ 여행의 목적 : the purpose of travelling / 해변에서 눕다 : lie on a beach / ~와는 상관없이 : regardless of

Q. Do young people and older people benefit differently from travelling?
A. It depends on the individual. If the purpose of travelling is to lie on a beach in the sun and relax, the benefits could be the same, regardless of people's age.

PART 2

Describe a transport system for commuters in your city or country.

You should say:
    what kinds of transport are available
    which kind of transport is the most popular
    what the good points and bad points of the transport system are
and say how you think it should be changed in the future.

당신의 도시나 나라에 있는 통근자들 위한 교통 시스템에 대해 묘사하세요.

당신은 반드시 말해야 합니다.
    어떤 종류의 교통수단이 이용가능한지
    어떤 교통수단이 가장 인기가 있는지
    교통 시스템의 좋은 점과 나쁜 점은 무엇인지
그리고 당신은 미래에 어떻게 교통 시스템이 바뀌어야 한다고 생각하는지 이야기하세요.

※ 가장 인기 있는 교통수단에 대해서 말할 땐, 자가용을 제외한 버스나 지하철과 같은 대중교통수단 중 하나를 선택한다.

주어지는 1분을 어떻게 활용할 것인가? (How to Use Your 1 Minute Preparation Time)

1. 질문 파악 교통수단 묘사에 초점을 맞추는 문제이다.	내가 영어로 잘 설명할 수 있는 교통수단을 떠올린다.
2. 묘사 대상 결정하기 영어로 가장 자신 있게 묘사할 수 있는 교통 수단을 떠올린다.	교통수단은 자주 나오는 문제이므로, 반드시 대중교통수단 중의 하나를 선택해서 수시로 연습해야 한다.
3. 하위 질문 확인 + 스토리 작성 하위 질문의 개수를 확인하고, 각각에 대한 답을 적는다.	sub-questions는 3개처럼 보이지만, 마지막 문장의 'and say how you think it should be changed in the future'를 포함해서 4개이다. 반드시 4개의 질문에 모두 답하되, 답의 길이는 똑같지 않아도 상관없다.
4. 주제 관련 아카데믹 표현 사용 평소 교통 수단과 관련해서 학습한 아카데믹한 표현들을 떠올린다.	a transport system, commuters, a variety of options, transportation, buses, subways, taxis, people who commute to work, this mode of transport, reliable and punctual, the network, stations, subway users, get stuck in traffic, late for work, double the price, compared with, lines, a burden for everyday passenger, vehicles, moving to the city, during peak hours, wait for a while, catch the next one
5. 주의해야 할 문법 문제의 시제 및 인칭 대명사 등을 확인한다.	commuters라는 단어만 여러 번 반복하지 말고 people who commute to work, subway users, everyday passengers 같은 의미상 동의어들을 사용해서 다양하게 표현해 보자.

Brainstorming

Sub-question 1 what kinds of transport are available	버스, 지하철, 택시
Sub-question 2 which kind of transport is the most popular	지하철
Sub-question 3 what the good points and bad points of the transport system is	좋은 점 : 믿을 만함, 시간 엄수, 넓은 교통망, 교통 체증 없음 나쁜 점 : 우리 동네 지하철 노선은 가격이 두 배, 매일 이용하는 승객에게는 부담
Sub-question 4 and say how you think it should be changed in the future	더 많은 통근자들을 수용하기 위해 더 커질 것임

✏️ **다음 불법포인트를 참고해서 영어 문장을 완성해 보자. (주어와 시제, 품사와 단복수 등을 고려할 것!)**

❶ 지금 나는 내 도시에 있는 통근자들을 위한 교통 시스템에 대해 이야기하고 싶습니다.
Now, I would like to talk about a transport system for _____ in my city.
※ 통근자 : commuter

❷ 내 도시, 분당에는 이용 가능한 교통수단의 다양한 선택권이 있습니다. 예를 들면, 버스, 지하철 그리고 택시들이 있습니다.
There are _____ transportation options available to commuters in my city, Bundang. For example, there are buses, subways and taxis.
※ 다양한 : a variety of

❸ 내가 알고 있는 한 지하철이 출퇴근하는 사람들에게 가장 인기가 있다고 여겨집니다.
_____, the subway is considered the most popular among people who _____ to work.
※ 내가 알고 있는 한 : as far as I am aware / 출퇴근하다 : commute

❹ 이 교통수단은 믿을 만하고 시간을 잘 엄수하고 교통망이 매우 넓은데 이것은 도시 전역에 많은 지하철역이 있다는 것을 의미하고, 대부분의 사람들을 위한 매우 편리한 선택입니다. 또한 지하철 이용자들은 통근자가 직장에 지각을 초래할지도 모르는 교통 체증에 갇히는것을 걱정하지 않습니다. 지하철을 이용하는 부정적인 면은, 분당에서 강남으로 향하는 노선은 다른 노선들에 비해 가격이 두 배이므로 매일 이용하는 승객에게는 부담이 될 수 있습니다.
This mode of transport is reliable and _____ and the network is so large, which means there are a lot of stations _____, making it a very convenient option for _____ people. Also subway users do not worry about _____, which may result in commuters being late for work. _____ the negative side of using the subway, the line heading to Gangnam is double the price _____ other lines so it could be a _____ for _____.
※ 시간을 엄수하는 : punctual / 도시 전역에 : all over the city / 대부분의 : the vast majority of / 교통 체증에 갇히다 : get stuck in traffic / ~에 관하여 : in terms of(=as far / when it comes to) / ~과 비교해서 : compared with 부담 : burden / 매일 이용하는 승객 : everyday passenger

❺ 미래에는 대중 교통에 사용되는 차량들은 더 많은 통근자를 수용하기 위해 더 커지게 될 것입니다. 지금 더욱 더 많은 사람들이 도시로 이주하고 있고 인구는 급속히 늘고 있습니다. 이것은 통근자가 가장 많은 시간에 버스나 지하철에 탈 공간이 충분치 않고 사람들은 다음 차량을 타기 위해 한참 동안 기다려야 하는 것을 의미합니다.
In the future, _____ used for _____ are going to become bigger so as to _____ more commuters. Right now, more and more people are moving to the city and the population is booming. This means that during peak hours, there is not enough room on buses or subways and people are having to _____ in order to catch the next one.
※ 차량 : vehicle / 대중교통 : public transport / 수용하다 : accommodate / 한참 동안 기다리다 : wait for a while

Sample Answer

> Describe a transport system for commuters in your city or country.
>
> You should say:
>
> what kinds of transport are available
>
> which kind of transport is the most popular
>
> what the good points and bad points of the transport system are
>
> and say how you think it should be changed in the future.

Now, I would like to talk about a transport system for commuters in my city.

There are a variety of transportation options available to commuters in my city, Bundang. For example, there are buses, subways and taxis.

As far as I am aware, the subway is considered the most popular among people who commute to work.

This mode of transport is reliable and punctual and the network is so large, which means there are a lot of stations all over the city, making it a very convenient option for the vast majority of people. Also subway users do not worry about getting stuck in traffic, which may result in commuters being late for work. In terms of the negative side of using the subway, the line heading to Gangnam is double the price compared with other lines so it could be a burden for everyday passengers.

In the future, vehicles used for public transport are going to become bigger so as to accommodate more commuters. Right now, more and more people are moving to the city and the population is booming. This means that during peak hours, there is not enough room on buses or subways and people are having to wait for a while in order to catch the next one.

That's all from me, thank you very much for your attention.

PART 3

1) How easy is it to travel around your country?
당신의 나라를 여기저기 여행하는 것은 얼마나 쉬워요?

Brainstorming		
	Direct Answer	매우 쉬움
	Supporting Sentence 1	비용이 모두 다른 다양한 선택들이 있음
	Supporting Sentence 2	KTX는 빨라서 인기가 있음
	Supporting Sentence 3	더 느린 기차나 버스 같은 더 값싼 선택들도 있음

✏️ 다음 **불법포인트**를 참고해서 영어 문장을 완성해 보자. (주어와 시제, 품사와 단복수 등을 고려할 것!)

❶ 우리 나라를 여기저기 여행하는 것은 매우 쉽습니다.
It is very easy to _____ my country.
※ 여기저기 여행하다 : travel around

❷ 비용이 모두 다른 다양한 다른 선택들이 있습니다.
There are a variety of different options which all _____ in cost.
※ 다르다 : vary

❸ KTX는 돌아다니기 위한 인기 있는 교통 수단인데 이것은 매우 빠르기 때문입니다.
The KTX is a popular method of transport to _____ because it is very fast.
※ 돌아다니다 : get around

❹ 더 느린 기차나 버스와 같은 더 값싼 선택들도 있습니다.
There are also _____ options such as _____ trains or buses.
※ 더 싼 : cheaper / 더 느린 : slower

Q. How easy is it to travel around your country?
A. It is very easy to travel around my country. There are a variety of different options which all vary in cost. The KTX is a popular method of transport to get around because it is very fast. There are also cheaper options such as slower trains or buses.

2) Which method of travel do you consider safest?
당신은 어떤 이동 방법이 가장 안전하다고 생각해요?

Brainstorming	Direct Answer	택시
	Supporting Sentence 1	믿을 만함, 하루 종일 운행
	Supporting Sentence 2	늦은 밤에 여성들에게 중요함

✏️ 다음 **불법포인트**를 참고해서 영어 문장을 완성해 보자. (주어와 시제, 품사와 단복수 등을 고려할 것!)

❶ 내 생각에는 택시가 가장 안전한 교통수단입니다.
As far as I am concerned, taxis are _____ .
※ 가장 안전한 교통수단 : the safest method of transport

❷ 택시들은 매우 믿을 만하고 하루 종일 운행하는 차들이 많이 있어서 사람들은 안전하지 못한 지역에서 버스나 지하철을 기다리면서 혼자 남겨질 필요가 없습니다.
They are very reliable and there are so many of them operating _____, so people do not have to _____ waiting for a bus or subway in an unsafe area.
※ 하루 종일 : at all hours / 혼자 남다 : be left alone

❸ 택시들은 특별히 늦은 밤에 여성들에게 중요합니다.
Taxis are particularly important for women _____ .
※ 늦은 밤에, 밤늦게 : late at night

Q. Which method of travel do you consider safest?
A. As far as I am concerned, taxis are the safest method of transport. They are very reliable and there are so many of them operating at all hours, so people do not have to be left alone waiting for a bus or subway in an unsafe area. Taxis are particularly important for women late at night.

3) What are the pros and cons of low-cost air travel?
저가항공 여행의 장·단점은 무엇이에요?

Brainstorming	Direct Answer	저가 항공의 성장은 양날의 칼
	Supporting Sentence 1	장점 - 수입과 사회적 지위에 상관없이 해외 여행과 새로운 문화 경험 가능
	Supporting Sentence 2	단점 - 더 많은 수요에 따른 더 많은 온실 가스 배출

✏️ 다음 불법포인트를 참고해서 영어 문장을 완성해 보자. (주어와 시제, 품사와 단복수 등을 고려할 것!)

❶ 저가 항공의 성장은 양날의 칼입니다.
The growth of low-cost air travel is _____ .
※ 양날의 칼 : a double-edged sword

❷ 장점은 사람들이 수입과 사회적 지위에 상관없이 해외 여행을 하고 새로운 문화를 경험하는 것을 더 쉽게 해 주는 것입니다.
The advantages are that it makes it easier for people to travel abroad and experience new cultures, regardless of their _____ and _____ .
※ 수입 : income / 사회적 지위 : social status

❸ 그러나 더 많은 사람들이 여행하고 싶어하면서 항공편에 대한 더 큰 수요가 있고, 그 결과 환경은 증가된 온실 가스 배출에 의해 부정적인 영향을 받고 있습니다.
However, with more people wanting to travel, it means that there is greater _____ for flights, so the environment is being adversely affected by increased _____ _____ .
※ 수요 : demand / 온실 가스 배출 : greenhouse gas emissions

Q. What are the pros and cons of low-cost air travel?
A. The growth of low-cost air travel is a double-edged sword. The advantages are that it makes it easier for people to travel abroad and experience new cultures, regardless of their income and social status. However, with more people wanting to travel, it means that there is greater demand for flights, so the environment is being adversely affected by increased greenhouse gas emissions.

4) Have the types of transport people use changed much over the last few decades?
지난 몇 십 년 동안 사람들이 이용하는 교통수단의 형태가 많이 바뀌었나요?

Brainstorming	Direct Answer	바뀌지 않음
	Supporting Sentence 1	수송량은 엄청나게 증가
	Supporting Sentence 2	더 많은 사람들이 도시로 이주했고 자가용 뿐만 아니라 대중교통에 대한 수요도 증가

✏️ 다음 불법포인트를 참고해서 영어 문장을 완성해 보자. (주어와 시제, 품사와 단복수 등을 고려할 것!)

❶ 나는 교통수단의 형태가 많이 바뀌었다고 생각하지 않는데, 우리는 여전히 지하철과 버스 그리고 택시를 이용하기 때문입니다.
_____ that the types of transport have changed much because we still use subways, buses and taxis.
※ 나는 ~라고 생각하지 않는다 : I don't think(부정문으로도 문장을 시작해 보자!)

❷ 하지만 나는 수송량은 엄청나게 늘어났다고 생각합니다.
However, I do think that _____ has increased hugely.
※ 수송량 : the volume of traffic

❸ 지난 수십 년 간 더 많은 사람들이 도시로 이주했기 때문에 개인용 차량 소유뿐 만 아니라 더 많은 대중교통에 대한 수요 증가도 있습니다.
Since more people have moved to cities _____ , there is a need for more public transport as well as _____ .
※ 지난 수십 년 간 : in the last few decades / 개인용 차량 소유 : private vehicle ownership

Q. Have the types of transport people use changed much over the last few decades?

A. I don't think that the types of transport have changed much because we still use subways, buses and taxis. However, I do think that the volume of traffic has increased hugely. Since more people have moved to cities in the last few decades, there is a need for more public transport as well as private vehicle ownership.

 **Day 7 Travelling & Transport 불법포인트 정리**

~을 좋아하다	be keen on	교통 체증에 갇히다	get stuck in traffic
계절성 정서 장애(겨울철 햇빛 부족으로 인한 우울증적 증상)	seasonal affective disorder	~에 관하여	in terms of / as far / when it comes to
우울한	depressing	~과 비교해서	compared with
휴가를 가다	go on holiday	부담	burden
여러 번	several times	매일 이용하는 승객	everyday passenger
도심 관광지	city destination	차량	vehicle
밤 문화	nightlife	대중 교통	public transport
한 번	once / one time	수용하다	accommodate
(남)의 집에서 머물다	stay with	한참 동안 기다리다	wait for a while
돈을 아끼다	save money	여기저기 여행하다	travel around
비수기 동안에	during the low season	다르다	vary
그렇게 하면	that way	돌아다니다	get around
비행기표	flight ticket	더 싼	cheaper
경제적인	economical	더 느린	slower
친구와 여행하다	travel with friends	가장 안전한 교통수단	the safest method of transport
경험하다	experience	하루 종일	at all hours
길을 잃다	get lost	혼자 남다	be left alone
개인	individual	늦은 밤에, 밤늦게	late at night
여행의 목적	the purpose of travelling	양날의 칼	a double-edged sword
해변에서 눕다	lie on a beach	수입	income
~와는 상관없이	regardless of	사회적 지위	social status
통근자	commuter	수요	demand
다양한	a variety of	온실 가스 배출	greenhouse gas emissions
내가 알고 있는 한	as far as I am aware	나는 ~라고 생각하지 않는다	I don't think
출퇴근하다	commute	수송량	the volume of traffic
시간을 엄수하는	punctual	지난 수십 년 간	in the last few decades
도시 전역에	all over the city	개인용 차량 소유	private vehicle ownership
대부분의	the vast majority of		

Day 08 ▶ Past & History 과거와 역사

PART 1

1) Do you like to learn about history?
2) Do you think history is important?
3) Do you like to watch programmes on TV about history?
4) Do you think you can really learn history from films and TV programmes?
5) Do you think the Internet is a good place to learn about history?
6) Can you name a person from history who you would like to learn more about?
7) Why would you like to learn more about him/her?

PART 2

Describe an important historical event.

You should say :
    what this event is
    when it happened and what happened
    who the most important people involved were
and say why you think it was important.

PART 3

1) What do you think we can learn by studying events of the past?
2) What important events do you think might take place in the future?
3) Are museums in your country popular with people of all ages? Why do you think that is?
   In your opinion, what could be done to make them more popular?
4) What do you think is the best way to make history interesting and accessible for children?

보이는 Speaking QR 코드

PART 1

1) Do you like to learn about history? 당신은 역사에 대해 배우는 것을 좋아해요?

Brainstorming	Direct Answer	좋아함
	Additional Information	고려왕조에 관심, 남녀 평등이 지금보다 더 나았기 때문임

✏️ 다음 불법포인트를 참고해서 영어 문장을 완성해 보자. (주어와 시제, 품사와 단복수 등을 고려할 것!)

❶ 네, 나는 과거에 무슨 일이 일어났는지를 배우는 것을 좋아합니다.
Yes, I enjoy leaning about _____ in the past.
※ 무슨 일이 일어나다 : what happen

❷ 나는 특히 918년부터 1392년 까지 고려왕조를 공부하는 것에 관심이 있는데, 이 시기에는 남녀 평등이 어떤 면에서는 지금보다 더 나았기 때문입니다.
I am particularly interested in studying the Koryo _____ from 918 to 1392 because in this period, _____ was better than it is now in some respects.
※ 왕조 : dynasty / 남녀 평등 : gender equality

Q. Do you like to learn about history?
A. Yes, I enjoy leaning about what happened in the past. I am particularly interested in studying the Koryo Dynasty from 918 to 1392 because in this period, gender equality was better than it is now in some respects.

2) Do you think history is important? 당신은 역사가 중요하다고 생각하나요?

Brainstorming	Direct Answer	중요함
	Additional Information	과거의 비극들로부터 배움

✏️ 다음 불법포인트를 참고해서 영어 문장을 완성해 보자. (주어와 시제, 품사와 단복수 등을 고려할 것!)

❶ 물론입니다. 역사상 발생한 사건들을 기억하는 것은 중요합니다.
Sure, it is important to remember events that _____ throughout history.
※ 발생하다 : take place

❷ 우리는 과거에 발생한 비극들로부터 배울 수 있습니다.
We can learn from the _____ that happened in the past.
※ 비극 : tragedy

Q. Do you think history is important?
A. Sure, it is important to remember events that took place throughout history. We can learn from the tragedies that happened in the past.

3) **Do you like to watch programmes on TV about history?**
당신은 TV에서 방영하는 역사 프로그램들을 시청하는 것을 좋아해요?

Brainstorming	Direct Answer	TV로 사극을 보는 것을 좋아함
	Additional Information	최근보다는 고대 역사에 관심이 있음

✏️ 다음 불법포인트를 참고해서 영어 문장을 완성해 보자. (주어와 시제, 품사와 단복수 등을 고려할 것!)

❶ 네, 나는 TV에서 방영하는 사극을 보는 것을 좋아합니다.
Yes, I love to watch _____ on TV.
※ 사극 : historical drama

❷ 나는 더 최근 역사보다는 특히 고대에 관한 프로그램 또는 다큐멘터리에 관심이 있습니다.
I am particularly interested in programmes or documentaries about _____ rather than more recent history.
※ 고대 : ancient times

Q. Do you like to watch programmes on TV about history?
A. Yes, I love to watch historical dramas on TV. I am particularly interested in programmes or documentaries about ancient times rather than more recent history.

4) **Do you think you can really learn history from films and TV programmes?**
당신은 영화나 TV 프로그램으로 역사를 정말로 배울 수 있다고 생각해요?

Brainstorming	Direct Answer	물론, 교과서보다 더 재미있게 배움
	Additional Information	그러나 이 내용들에는 약간의 허구적 이야기가 있음

✏️ 다음 불법포인트를 참고해서 영어 문장을 완성해 보자. (주어와 시제, 품사와 단복수 등을 고려할 것!)

❶ 물론, 영화와 TV 프로그램은 교과서로 공부하는 것보다 역사를 배우는 것을 더 재미있게 만듭니다.
Absolutely, films and TV programmes make learning about history more _____ than studying it from a _____ .
※ 재미있는 : entertaining / 교과서 : textbook

❷ 그러나 우리는 이 내용들에 약간의 허구적 측면들이 있다는 것을 명심해야 합니다.
But we need to bear in mind that there might be some _____ to their accounts.   ※ 허구적 측면들 : fictional aspects

Q. Do you think you can really learn history from films and TV programmes?
A. Absolutely, films and TV programmes make learning about history more entertaining than studying it from a textbook. But we need to bear in mind that there might be some fictional aspects to their accounts.

5) Do you think the Internet is a good place to learn about history?
당신은 인터넷이 역사에 대해서 배우는 데 좋은 장소라고 생각해요?

Brainstorming	Direction Answer	역사를 배우는 괜찮은 장소가 될 수 있음
	Additional Information	하지만 모든 정보가 사실에 기반을 두거나 정확한 것은 아님

✏️ 다음 **불법포인트**를 참고해서 영어 문장을 완성해 보자. (주어와 시제, 품사와 단복수 등을 고려할 것!)

> ❶ 인터넷은 단지 마우스 클릭 몇 번으로 역사를 배우는 괜찮은 장소가 될 수 있습니다.
> The Internet can be a decent place to learn about history _____ .
> ※ 단지 마우스 클릭 몇 번으로 : with just a few clicks of a mouse
>
> ❷ 하지만 인터넷에서의 문제는 우리가 찾은 모든 정보가 사실에 기반을 두거나 정확한 것은 아니라는 점입니다.
> But the problem with the Internet is that not all the information we find is _____ and correct.
> ※ 사실에 기반을 둔 : factual

Q. Do you think the Internet is a good place to learn about history?
A. The Internet can be a decent place to learn about history with just a few clicks of a mouse. But the problem with the Internet is that not all the information we find is factual and correct.

6) Can you name a person from history who you would like to learn more about?
당신이 더 배우고 싶은 역사 속 인물의 이름을 말할 수 있어요?

Brainstorming	Direct Answer	앨런 튜링
	Additional Information	영국의 선구적인 컴퓨터 과학자, 수학자, 논리학자, 암호 해독 전문가, 이론 생물학자

✏️ 다음 **불법포인트**를 참고해서 영어 문장을 완성해 보자. (주어와 시제, 품사와 단복수 등을 고려할 것!)

> ❶ '이미테이션 게임'을 본 이후, 나는 앨런 튜링의 삶과 업적에 관심을 갖게 되었습니다.
> Ever since watching 'The Imitation Game', I have become interested in Alan Turing's
> _____ .   ※ 삶과 업적 : life and work
>
> ❷ 그는 영국의 선구적인 컴퓨터 과학자이자 수학자, 논리학자, 암호 해독 전문가 그리고 이론 생물학자입니다.
> He was a British _____ computer scientist, _____ , _____ , cryptanalyst and theoretical biologist.
> ※ 선구적인 : pioneering / 수학자 : mathematician / 논리학자 : logician

Q. Can you name a person from history who you would like to learn more about?
A. Ever since watching 'The Imitation Game', I have become interested in Alan Turing's life and work. He was a British pioneering computer scientist, mathematician, logician, cryptanalyst and theoretical biologist.

7) Why would you like to learn more about him/her?
당신은 왜 그/그녀에 대해 더 배우고 싶어요?

Brainstorming	Direct Answer	튜링의 업적은 한동안 가려져 있었음
	Additional Information	영국 정부에 의한 고의적인 음모가 있었는지 알고 싶음

✏️ 다음 **불법포인트**를 참고해서 영어 문장을 완성해 보자. (주어와 시제, 품사와 단복수 등을 고려할 것!)

❶ 비록 튜링은 인공 지능의 아버지이고 세계 2차 대전의 기간을 단축시켰지만, 그의 업적은 한동안 가려져 있었습니다.
Although Turing is the father of _____ and he even shortened the duration of _____ , his work was hidden for a while.
※ 인공 지능 : artificial intelligence(AI) / 세계 2차 대전 : the Second World War(대문자로 쓰는 것에 주의!)

❷ 나는 영국 정부에 의한 고의적인 음모가 있었는지에 대해 알고 싶습니다.
I would like to know whether there was a _____ by the British government.
※ 고의적인 음모 : deliberate conspiracy

Q. Why would you like to learn more about him/her?
A. Although Turing is the father of artificial intelligence and he even shortened the duration of the Second World War, his work was hidden for a while. I would like to know whether there was a deliberate conspiracy by the British government.

PART 2

Describe an important historical event.

You should say:
  what this event is
  when it happened and what happened
  who the most important people involved were
and say why you think it was important.

중요한 역사적인 사건을 묘사하세요.

당신은 반드시 말해야 합니다.
  이 사건이 무엇인지
  이것은 언제 발생했고 무슨 일이 일어났는지
  관련된 가장 중요한 사람들은 누구였는지
그리고 당신은 왜 이 사건이 중요하다고 생각하는지 이야기하세요.

※ 역사에 자신이 없다면, 그럴 듯하게 지어내는 센스가 필요하다. 영화나 책에서 본 내용을 바탕으로 있음직하게 꾸며내는 것도 능력이다. 시험관에게는 내가 말한 내용이 사실인지 아닌지는 전혀 중요하지 않다.

주어지는 1분을 어떻게 활용할 것인가? (How to Use Your 1 Minute Preparation Time)

1. 질문 파악 역사적 사건 묘사에 초점을 맞추는 문제이다.	내가 영어로 잘 설명할 수 있는 역사적 사건을 떠올린다.
2. 묘사 대상 결정하기 영어로 가장 자신 있게 묘사할 수 있는 역사적 사건을 떠올린다.	세계사보다는 국사에 초점을 맞춘다. 영국인 시험관 앞에서 어설프게 산업혁명에 대해서 이야기하기보다는, 우리나라의 역사적 사건을 이야기해야 더 흥미롭게 들린다. 또한 말하는 도중 정확한 연도나 장소 등이 기억이 안 나더라도 적당히 지어서 말할 수 있는 이점이 있다. 한국사에 정통한 시험관을 만날 확률은 극히 드물다.
3. 하위 질문 확인 + 스토리 작성 하위 질문의 개수를 확인하고, 각각에 대한 답을 적는다.	sub-questions는 3개처럼 보이지만, 마지막 문장의 'and say why you think it was important'를 포함해서 4개이다. 반드시 4개의 질문에 모두 답하되, 답의 길이는 똑같이 않아도 상관없다.
4. 주제 관련 아카데믹 표현 사용 평소 역사와 관련해서 학습한 아카데믹한 표현들을 떠올린다.	a memorable moment in history, as a symbol of, democracy, take place, break out, the army and civilians, overthrown, the previous dictator, by force, result in, live in isolation, the foundations for Korea, a democratic country, a memorial, democracy, freedom
5. 주의해야 할 문법 문제의 시제 및 인칭 대명사 등을 확인한다.	역사적 사건, 즉 과거에 발생한 일에 대해 묘사하는 문제이기 때문에 과거 시제 사용에 주의하자!

Brainstorming

Sub-question 1 what this event is	광주 민주화 운동, 민주주의를 위한 대한민국 투쟁의 상징
Sub-question 2 when it happened and what happened	1980년 전라도 광주에서 발생, 군대와 전두환 대통령 통치에 반대하여 싸우는 민간인들
Sub-question 3 who the most important people involved were	군부대에 의해 수천 명의 시민들이 살해, 부상, 실종됨
Sub-question 4 and say why you think it was important	대한민국 민주주의의 토대

✎ 다음 불법포인트를 참고해서 영어 문장을 완성해 보자. (주어와 시제, 품사와 단복수 등을 고려할 것!)

❶ 지금 나는 역사상 기억에 남는 순간에 대해 이야기하고 싶습니다.
Now, I would like to talk about a _____ in history.
※ 기억에 남는 순간 : memorable moment

❷ 내가 선택한 사건은 광주 민주화 운동입니다. 비록 이 사건은 불과 몇 십 년 전에 발생했지만 민주주의를 위한 대한민국 투쟁의 상징으로 언급됩니다.
The event which I've chosen is the 'Gwangju Uprising'. Although it only happened _____ , it is referred to as a symbol of South Korea's _____ for _____ .
※ 몇 십 년 전 : a few decades ago / 투쟁 : struggle / 민주주의 : democracy

❸ 이 민주화 운동은 1980년에 일어났고 전라남도의 중심지인 광주에서 발생했습니다. 이것은 대통령이 된 전두환 장군에 의해 수행된 군사 쿠테타에 대한 대응이었습니다. 전 대통령은 이전 지도자를 무력으로 타도했고 그래서 시민들은 그에게 사임하기를 요구했습니다.
The _____ took place in 1980 and _____ in Gwangju, which was then the capital of South Jeolla Province. It was a response to a military coup d'état carried out by General Chun Doo-hwan, who went on to become president. Chun had _____ the previous leader _____ , so citizens were calling for him to _____ .
※ 민주화 운동, 봉기 : uprising / 발생하다 : break out / (지도자나 정부를) 타도하다 : overthrow / 무력으로 : by force
  사임하다 : resign

❹ 이러한 힘든 시기 동안 수천 명의 시민들이 군대에 의해 살해되거나 부상을 입었고 다른 사람들은 단순히 행방불명이 되었습니다. 수년 후 전 대통령은 대국민 사과를 발표했고 백담사라고 불리는 강원도에 있는 사찰에서 은둔 생활을 했습니다.
_____ civilians were killed or injured by the _____ during those difficult times, while others simply _____ . Years later, President Chun issued a public apology and went to _____ at a temple in Gangwon Province called Baekdamsa.
※ 수천 명의 : thousands of / 군대 : armed forces / 행방불명이 되다 : go missing
  은둔 생활을 하다 : live in isolation

❺ 광주 민주화 운동은 대한민국이 민주주의 국가가 되는 토대가 되었습니다. 자유를 위해 죽은 이 모든 사람들을 위한 기념비가 지금 광주에 있습니다.
The Gwangju Uprising laid the _____ for South Korea to become a _____ country. There is now a _____ in Gwangju for all those who died _____ .
※ 토대, 근간 : foundations / 민주주의의 : democratic / 기념비 : memorial / 자유를 위해 : for the sake of freedom

Sample Answer

> Describe an important historical event.
>
> You should say:
>   what this event is
>   when it happened and what happened
>   who the most important people involved were
> and say why you think it was important.

Now, I would like to talk about a memorable moment in history.

The event which I've chosen is the 'Gwangju Uprising'. Although it only happened a few decades ago, it is referred to as a symbol of South Korea's struggle for democracy.

The uprising took place in 1980 and broke out in Gwangju, which was then the capital of South Jeolla Province. It was a response to a military coup d'état carried out by General Chun Doo-hwan, who went on to become president. Chun had overthrown the previous leader by force, so citizens were calling for him to resign.

Thousands of civilians were killed or injured by the armed forces during those difficult times, while others simply went missing. Years later, President Chun issued a public apology and went to live in isolation at a temple in Gangwon Province called Baekdamsa.

The Gwangju Uprising laid the foundations for South Korea to become a democratic country. There is now a memorial in Gwangju for all those who died for the sake of freedom.

That's all from me, thank you very much for your attention.

PART 3

1) What do you think we can learn by studying events of the past?
당신은 과거의 사건들을 공부함으로써 우리가 무엇을 배울 수 있다고 생각해요?

Brainstorming	Direct Answer	시행착오로부터 배울 수 있음
	Supporting Sentence 1	과거를 공부하지 않으면 과거의 실수가 반복
	Supporting Sentence 2	현재 또는 다가오는 끔찍한 사건으로부터 우리를 구하고 삶을 번영하게 함

✏️ 다음 불법포인트를 참고해서 영어 문장을 완성해 보자. (주어와 시제, 품사와 단복수 등을 고려할 것!)

❶ 우리는 과거 사회의 지도자들에 의해 만들어진 시행착오로부터 배울 수 있습니다.
We can learn from the _____ made by leaders of communities in the past.
※ 시행착오 : trials and errors

❷ 만약 우리가 역사를 공부하지 않고 역사가 기억되도록 하지 않으면, 우리는 오래된 실수들을 반복하게 될 것입니다.
If we do not study history and make sure that it is remembered, then we _____ repeat old _____ .
※ ~하기 마련이다, ~할 운명이다 : be doomed to / 실수 : mistake

❸ 역사에 대한 정확한 이해는 더이상의 끔찍한 사건들로부터 우리를 구하는 것 뿐만 아니라 현재와 미래에 인류가 번영하는 것을 가능하게 합니다.
An _____ understanding of history not only helps to save us from further _____ but also allows humanity to _____ in the present and future.
※ 정확한 : accurate / 끔찍한 사건 : tragic event / 번영(번창)하다 : prosper

Q. What do you think we can learn by studying events of the past?
A. We can learn from the trials and errors made by leaders of communities in the past. If we do not study history and make sure that it is remembered, then we are doomed to repeat old mistakes. An accurate understanding of history not only helps to save us from further tragic events but also allows humanity to prosper in the present and future.

2) What important events do you think might take place in the future?
당신은 미래에 어떤 중요한 사건이 일어날 것이라고 생각해요?

Brainstorming	Direct Answer	의약 분야에 더 많은 발전
	Supporting Sentence 1	현재 과학자들은 치명적 질병에 대해 연구를 많이 함
	Supporting Sentence 2	수백만의 생명을 구하는 것은 시간 문제임

✏️ 다음 불법포인트를 참고해서 영어 문장을 완성해 보자. (주어와 시제, 품사와 단복수 등을 고려할 것!)

❶ 비록 미래에 어떤 중요한 사건이 일어날지 예측하기는 어렵지만, 내가 추측한다면 의약 분야에서 더 많은 발전이 있을 것이라고 생각합니다.
Although it is difficult to predict what important events might take place in the future, if I were to guess, I think there will be more advances in _____ .
※ 의약 분야 : the field of medicine

❷ 과학자들은 현재 아직은 치유가 가능하지 않지만 많은 사람들에게 발생하는 백혈병과 같은 많은 다른 치명적인 질병에 대해 많은 연구를 하고 있습니다.
Scientists are currently doing a lot of research into so many different _____ like _____ that affect many people but are not yet _____ .
※ 치명적 질병 : fatal disease / 백혈병 : leukemia / 치유 가능한 : curable

❸ 수백만의 생명을 구할 중요한 치유법이 발견되는 것은 시간 문제일 뿐입니다.
_____ important _____ are found that will save millions of lives.
※ ~하는 것은 시간 문제일 뿐이다 : it is only a matter of time before / 치유법 : cure

Q. What important events do you think might take place in the future?
A. Although it is difficult to predict what important events might take place in the future, if I were to guess, I think there will be more advances in the field of medicine. Scientists are currently doing a lot of research into so many different fatal diseases like leukemia that affect many people but are not yet curable. It is only a matter of time before important cures are found that will save millions of lives.

3) **Are museums in your country popular with people of all ages? Why do you think that is? In your opinion, what could be done to make them more popular?**

당신의 나라의 박물관은 모든 나이 대에 인기가 있나요? 당신은 왜 그렇다고 생각해요?
당신의 의견으로는 무엇이 박물관을 더 인기 있게 만들 수 있을 것 같아요?

Brainstorming	Direct Answer	십대들에게 인기가 없음
	Supporting Sentence 1	학교 현장학습으로 박물관을 감
	Supporting Sentence 2	스스로의 선택이 아닌, 그들은 박물관을 지루하다고 생각함
	Supporting Sentence 3	쌍방향 박물관, 직접 체험할 수 있게 된다면 더 인기가 있을 것임

✏️ 다음 불법포인트를 참고해서 영어 문장을 완성해 보자. (주어와 시제, 품사와 단복수 등을 고려할 것!)

❶ 박물관은 한국의 십대들에게 그다지 인기가 없습니다.
Museums are not very popular with _____ in Korea.
※ 십대 : teenager

❷ 그들은 학교 현장학습을 떠나면 박물관으로 가는 경향이 있습니다.
They tend to go to museums if it is on a _____ .
※ 학교 현장학습 : school field trip

❸ 나는 청소년들이 스스로의 선택으로 박물관에 가는 것을 선택할 것이라고 생각하지 않는데, 왜냐하면 그들은 박물관이 지루하다고 생각하기 때문입니다.
I don't think that they would choose to go there _____ because they think it is boring.
※ 스스로의 선택으로 : out of choice

❹ 만약 박물관이 더 쌍방향으로 만들어지고, 학습하는 데 좀 더 직접 손으로 만지며 다가가도록 아이들을 격려한다면 박물관은 더 인기가 있을 것입니다.
If museums were made more _____ and encouraged children to take a more _____ approach to learning, museums would be more popular.
※ 쌍방향의 : interactive / 직접 손으로 만지는 : hands-on

Q. Are museums in your country popular with people of all ages? Why do you think that is? In your opinion, what could be done to make them more popular?

A. Museums are not very popular with teenagers in Korea. They tend to go to museums if it is on a school field trip. I don't think that they would choose to go there out of choice because they think it is boring. If museums were made more interactive and encouraged children to take a more hands-on approach to learning, museums would be more popular.

4) What do you think is the best way to make history interesting and accessible for children?
당신은 아이들에게 역사를 흥미 있고 접근하기 쉽게 만드는 최고의 방법이 무엇이라고 생각해요?

Brainstorming	Direct Answer	아이들이 참여할 수 있도록 재미있게 만드는 것임
	Supporting Sentence 1	아이들은 직접적인 경험을 좋아함. 역사적 인물처럼 옷을 입은 배우들과 역사 테마 공원 여행
	Supporting Sentence 2	이순신 장군, 선덕여왕이 인기 있음

✏️ 다음 불법포인트를 참고해서 영어 문장을 완성해 보자. (주어와 시제, 품사와 단복수 등을 고려할 것!)

❶ 아마도 아이들이 역사에 좀 더 접근하기 쉽게하는 최고의 방법은 아이들이 참여할 수 있도록 재미있게 만드는 것입니다.
Perhaps the best way to ensure that history is more _____ to children is to make it fun so that they can _____ with it.
※ 접근하기 쉬운 : accessible / 참여하다 : engage

❷ 아이들은 직접적인 경험을 얻는 것을 좋아하기 때문에 아이들이 말을 건넬 수 있는 유명한 인물처럼 옷을 입은 배우들과 역사 테마 공원으로의 여행을 준비하는 것은 과거에 생명을 불어넣을 것입니다.
As kids love to get _____ , organising trips to historical theme parks with actors dressed as _____ who the children could talk to would _____ the past _____ .
※ 직접 경험 : first-hand experience / 유명한 인물 : famous figure / ~을 소생시키다, ~에 생명을 불어넣다 : bring ~ to life

❸ 이순신 장군과 선덕여왕이 인기가 있을 것입니다.
_____ Yi Sun-sin and the Great Queen Seondeok would be popular.
※ 장군 : general

Q. What do you think is the best way to make history interesting and accessible for children?
A. Perhaps the best way to ensure that history is more accessible to children is to make it fun so that they can engage with it. As kids love to get first-hand experience, organising trips to historical theme parks with actors dressed as famous figures who the children could talk to would bring the past to life. General Yi Sun-sin and the Great Queen Seondeok would be popular.

 **Day 8 Past & History 불법포인트 정리**

무슨 일이 일어나다	what happen	행방 불명이 되다	go missing
왕조	dynasty	은둔 생활을 하다	live in isolation
남녀 평등	gender equality	토대, 근간	foundations
발생하다	take place	민주주의의	democratic
비극	tragedy	기념비	memorial
사극	historical drama	자유를 위해	for the sake of freedom
고대	ancient times	시행착오	trials and errors
재미있는	entertaining	~하기 마련이다 ~할 운명이다	be doomed to
교과서	textbook	실수	mistake
허구적 측면들	fictional aspects	정확한	accurate
단지 마우스 클릭 몇 번으로	with just a few clicks of a mouse	끔찍한 사건	tragic event
사실에 기반을 둔	factual	번영(번창)하다	prosper
삶과 업적	life and work	의약 분야	the field of medicine
선구적인	pioneering	치명적 질병	fatal disease
수학자	mathematician	백혈병	leukemia
논리학자	logician	치유 가능한	curable
인공 지능	artificial intelligence(AI)	~하는 것은 시간 문제일 뿐이다	it is only a matter of time before
세계 2차 대전	the Second World War	치유법	cure
고의적인 음모	deliberate conspiracy	십대	teenager
기억에 남는 순간	memorable moment	학교 현장학습	school field trip
몇 십년 전	a few decades ago	스스로의 선택으로	out of choice
투쟁	struggle	쌍방향의	interactive
민주주의	democracy	직접 손으로 만지는	hands-on
민주화 운동, 봉기	uprising	접근하기 쉬운	accessible
발생하다	break out	참여하다	engage
(지도자나 정부를) 타도 하다	overthrow	직접 경험	first-hand experience
무력으로	by force	유명한 인물	famous figure
사임하다	resign	~을 소생시키다 ~에 생명을 불어넣다	bring ~ to life
수 천명의	thousands of	장군	general
군대	armed forces		

Day 09 Natural Environment & Wildlife
자연환경과 야생동식물

PART 1

1) Do you have a pet?
2) Is having a pet popular in your country?
3) Why do you think people like having pets?
4) Do you have your own garden?
5) What kind of plants or flowers do you like?
6) Is gardening a popular pastime where you live?
7) What are the advantages of having your own garden?

PART 2

Describe a lake, a river or a sea you have visited.

You should say:

    where the lake, river or sea is

    how often you have visited it

    what activities you do there

and explain why you like this particular place.

PART 3

1) What could be the consequences of deforestation?
2) Do you think your government is doing enough to save endangered species? Why do you think that?
3) What can be done to stop global warming, do you think?
4) Do you believe that people your age in your country live environmentally friendly lifestyles?

보이는 Speaking QR 코드

PART 1

1) Do you have a pet? 당신은 애완동물을 키우나요?

Brainstorming	Direct Answer	지금은 키우지 않음
	Additional Information	어릴 적에는 미미라는 개를 키웠음

✏️ 다음 불법포인트를 참고해서 영어 문장을 완성해 보자. (주어와 시제, 품사와 단복수 등을 고려할 것!)

❶ 아니요, 나는 현재 어떤 애완동물도 키우지 않습니다.
No, I don't have any pets _____ .
※ 현재, 지금 : at the moment

❷ 하지만 우리 가족은 내가 아이였을 때 함께 자란 미미라는 개를 키우곤 했습니다.
However, my family used to have a dog, Mimi, which I _____ with as a child.
※ 자라다 : grow up

Q. Do you have a pet?
A. No, I don't have any pets at the moment. However, my family used to have a dog, Mimi, which I grew up with as a child.

2) Is having a pet popular in your country? 당신의 나라에서는 애완동물을 키우는 것이 인기 있나요?

Brainstorming	Direct Answer	점점 더 인기 있음
	Additional Information	애완동물은 가족이기에 돈 쓰는 것을 주저하지 않음

✏️ 다음 불법포인트를 참고해서 영어 문장을 완성해 보자. (주어와 시제, 품사와 단복수 등을 고려할 것!)

❶ 네, 반려동물로써 애완동물을 키우는 것은 점점 더 인기가 있습니다.
Yes, it is becoming increasingly popular to have a pet as a _____ .
※ 반려동물 : companion animal

❷ 많은 사람들에게 애완동물은 가족이기에 그들은 애완동물에게 돈을 쓰는 것을 주저하지 않습니다.
For many people, pets are family so they don't _____ to spend money on them.
※ 주저하다 : hesitate

Q. Is having a pet popular in your country?
A. Yes, it is becoming increasingly popular to have a pet as a companion animal. For many people, pets are family so they don't hesitate to spend money on them.

3) Why do you think people like having pets?
당신은 왜 사람들이 애완동물 키우는 것을 좋아한다고 생각해요?

Brainstorming	Direct Answer	동료애 제공함
	Additional Information	혼자 사는 사람들에게 위로가 됨

✏️ 다음 **불법포인트**를 참고해서 영어 문장을 완성해 보자. (주어와 시제, 품사와 단복수 등을 고려할 것!)

❶ 애완동물을 키우는 것은 동료애를 제공합니다.
Having a pet offers _____ .
※ 동료애 : companionship

❷ 이것은 특히 혼자 사는 사람들에게 위로가 됩니다.
That might be especially _____ for people who live alone.
※ 위로가 되는 : comforting

Q. Why do you think people like having pets?
A. Having a pet offers companionship. That might be especially comforting for people who live alone.

4) Do you have your own garden? 당신은 당신 소유의 정원을 가지고 있나요?

Brainstorming	Direct Answer	아파트에 살아서 정원을 가지고 있지 않음
	Additional Information	부모님은 시골 주택에 살고 있고 커다란 정원을 가지고 있음

✏️ 다음 **불법포인트**를 참고해서 영어 문장을 완성해 보자. (주어와 시제, 품사와 단복수 등을 고려할 것!)

❶ 나는 아파트에서 살아서 정원을 가지고 있지 않습니다.
I live in a flat so I don't have a _____ .
※ 정원 : garden

❷ 그러나 나의 부모님은 시골의 주택에서 살고 있고 (집) 뒤에 커다란 정원을 가지고 있습니다.
But my parents live in a house in the countryside and they have a huge garden _____ .
※ 뒤에 : at the back

Q. Do you have your own garden?
A. I live in a flat so I don't have a garden. But my parents live in a house in the countryside and they have a huge garden at the back.

5) What kind of plants or flowers do you like? 당신은 어떤 종류의 식물이나 꽃을 좋아해요?

Brainstorming	Direction Answer	수국
	Additional Information	꽃말은 '감사'

✎ 다음 **불법포인트**를 참고해서 영어 문장을 완성해 보자. (주어와 시제, 품사와 단복수 등을 고려할 것!)

❶ 나는 식물에 그다지 관심이 있지는 않지만 내가 가장 좋아하는 꽃은 수국입니다.
I'm not that interested in plants but my favourite flower is the _____ .
※ 수국 : hydrangea

❷ 이 꽃의 꽃말은 '감사'입니다.
It means ' _____ ' in _____ .
※ 감사 : gratitude / 꽃말 : the language of flowers

Q. What kind of plants or flowers do you like?
A. I'm not that interested in plants but my favourite flower is the hydrangea. It means 'gratitude' in the language of flowers.

6) Is gardening a popular pastime where you live?
정원 가꾸기는 당신이 사는 곳에서 대중적인 취미인가요?

Brainstorming	Direct Answer	도심에 살고 있기에 인기 있는 취미는 아님
	Additional Information	서울 사람들은 정원 가꾸기를 할 기회가 많이 없음

✎ 다음 **불법포인트**를 참고해서 영어 문장을 완성해 보자. (주어와 시제, 품사와 단복수 등을 고려할 것!)

❶ 나는 도심에서 살고 있기 때문에 정원 가꾸기는 거주자들 사이에서 특별히 인기 있는 취미는 아닙니다.
Since I live in _____ , gardening isn't a particularly popular _____ amongst residents.
※ 도심 : the center of a city / 취미 : pastime

❷ 서울에 사는 대부분의 사람들에게는 정원 가꾸기를 할 기회가 많이 없습니다.
There is not much of an opportunity to do any _____ for most people in Seoul.
※ 원예, 정원 가꾸기 : gardening

Q. Is gardening a popular pastime where you live?
A. Since I live in the center of a city, gardening isn't a particularly popular pastime amongst residents. There is not much of an opportunity to do any gardening for most people in Seoul.

7) What are the advantages of having your own garden?
당신 소유의 정원을 갖는 것의 장점은 무엇인가요?

Brainstorming	Direct Answer	편히 쉬고 긴장을 풀 수 있는 장소를 갖는 것임
	Additional Information	조용한 곳에 있고 잘 관리되면 정말 고요할 것임

✏️ 다음 불법포인트를 참고해서 영어 문장을 완성해 보자. (주어와 시제, 품사와 단복수 등을 고려할 것!)

❶ 주된 장점은 편히 쉬고 긴장을 풀 수 있는 장소를 갖는다는 것입니다.
The main advantage is having a place to relax and _____ .
※ 긴장을 풀다 : unwind

❷ 만약 정원이 조용한 곳에 있고 잘 관리된다면, 정말 고요할 것입니다.
If the garden is in a quiet place and is well looked after, it can be very _____ .
※ 고요한 : serene

Q. What are the advantages of having your own garden?
A. The main advantage is having a place to relax and unwind. If the garden is in a quiet place and is well looked after, it can be very serene.

PART 2

Describe a lake, a river or a sea you have visited.

You should say:
- where the lake, river or sea is
- how often you have visited it
- what activities you do there

and explain why you like this particular place.

당신이 방문했던 호수, 강 또는 바다에 대해 묘사하세요.

당신은 반드시 말해야 합니다.
- 어디에 그 호수, 강 또는 바다가 있는지
- 얼마나 자주 당신은 그 곳을 방문하는지
- 그곳에서 당신은 어떤 활동을 하는지

그리고 당신은 왜 이 특정 장소를 좋아하는지 설명하세요.

※ 평소에 답안을 준비하지 않았다면 실제 시험에서 고득점을 받기 힘든 문제다. 시험이 얼마 남지 않은 학생이라면, 책의 순서와 상관없이 아이디어가 부족한 주제부터 공부하자!

주어지는 1분을 어떻게 활용할 것인가? (How to Use Your 1 Minute Preparation Time)

1. 질문 파악 호수, 강 또는 바다에 대한 묘사에 초점을 맞추는 문제이다.	내가 영어로 잘 설명할 수 있는 호수, 강 또는 바다를 떠올린다.
2. 묘사 대상 결정하기 영어로 가장 자신 있게 묘사할 수 있는 호수, 강 또는 바다를 떠올린다.	아무리 영어를 잘해도, 원어민이라 하더라도 아이디어가 없으면 상당히 낮은 점수를 받을 수 밖에 없다. '설마 이런 문제가 나오겠어?'라는 안이한 생각보다는 독특한 문제, 생소한 문제부터 답을 준비하자!
3. 하위 질문 확인 + 스토리 작성 하위 질문의 개수를 확인하고, 각각에 대한 답을 적는다.	sub-questions는 3개처럼 보이지만, 마지막 문장의 'and explain why you like this particular place'를 포함해서 4개이다. 반드시 4개의 질문에 모두 답하되, 답의 길이는 똑같지 않아도 상관없다.
4. 주제 관련 아카데믹 표현 사용 평소 호수, 강 또는 바다와 관련해서 학습한 아카데믹한 표현들을 떠올린다.	the River Thames, go on holiday, the main river, run through the whole city, along the river, a number of tourist attractions, hop-on hop-off, cruises, tourists, all the key sights, beautiful
5. 주의해야 할 문법 문제의 시제 및 인칭 대명사 등을 확인한다.	지금도 주기적으로 방문하면 현재 시제, 과거에는 방문했지만 요즘은 방문하지 않으면 과거 시제에 맞춰서 동사를 적절하게 사용하자.

Brainstorming

Sub-question 1 where the lake, river or sea is	템즈 강, 런던, 영국
Sub-question 2 how often you have visited it	런던은 한 번 갔지만 머무는 2주 동안 매일 봄
Sub-question 3 what activities you do there	유람선을 타고 템즈 강 주변의 모든 관광지를 방문
Sub-question 4 and explain why you like this particular place	아름다움, 거주자뿐만 아니라 관광객에게도 재미있는 활동 제공, 불꽃놀이 밤을 잊을 수 없음

✏️ 다음 불법포인트를 참고해서 영어 문장을 완성해 보자. (주어와 시제, 품사와 단복수 등을 고려할 것)

❶ 지금 나는 작년에 방문했던 강에 대해 이야기하고 싶습니다.
Now, I would like to talk about a river I visited _____ .
※ 작년 : last year

❷ 내가 선택한 강은 런던에 있는 템즈입니다. 지난 여름 나는 가족과 함께 영국으로 휴가를 갔습니다. 그곳에 있는 동안 우리는 자주 템즈 강을 구경했는데, 그 강은 도시 전체를 관통하여 흐르는 중요한 수로입니다.
The river I've chosen is the Thames in London. Last summer, I _____ to England with my family. While we were there we regularly saw the River Thames, which is the main _____ that runs through the capital.
※ 휴가 가다 : go on holiday / 수로 : waterway

❸ 나는 오직 한 번 런던을 갔었지만 우리는 그곳에서 2주를 보냈고 매일 이 강을 봤습니다. 우리 호텔이 있던 곳에서 이 도시의 반대편에 갈 때는 강을 건너야 했지만, 강 옆에는 또한 할것이 많이 있었습니다.
I have only been to London once but we spent two weeks there and saw the river every day. We had to _____ it to get to the other side of the city from where our hotel was, but there were also a number of things to do by the river itself.
※ 건너다 : cross

❹ 런던의 많은 관광지들인 런던 아이, 국회의사당, 빅 벤 그리고 테이트 모던과 같은 세계적으로 유명한 미술관들이 강을 따라 위치해 있습니다. 템즈 강을 따라 늘어선 관광 명소들 때문에 강을 따라 운행하는 자유롭게 타고 내리는 유람선이 있고 유람선에서 관광객들은 모든 주요 명소들을 볼 수 있습니다. 이 유람선 옵션 덕택에 우리는 모든 관광지를 방문할 수 있었습니다.
Many of London's _____ are located along the River Thames, such as the London Eye, _____ , Big Ben and world famous art galleries like the Tate Modern. Due to the number of tourist attractions that line the Thames, there is a _____ cruise ship that goes along the river, from which tourists can see all the key _____ . Thanks to that cruise option, we could visit all the attractions.
※ 관광지 : attraction / 국회의사당 : the Houses of Parliament / 자유롭게 타고 내리는 : hop-on hop-off
　명소 : sights

❺ 나는 이 장소를 특히 좋아하는데, 이 곳은 정말 아름답고 거주자들뿐만 아니라 관광객에게도 다양한 재미있는 활동들을 제공하기 때문입니다. 나는 템즈 강의 참으로 아름다웠던 불꽃놀이 밤을 결코 잊을 수 없을 것이고 곧 다시 그 곳을 방문하고 싶습니다.
I particularly like this place because it is very beautiful and offers such a variety of interesting activities for tourists as well as _____ . I will never forget the _____ fireworks night on the River Thames and I would love to visit there again soon.
※ 거주자 : resident / 참으로 아름다운 : magnificent

Sample Answer

> Describe a lake, a river or a sea you have visited.
>
> You should say:
>   where the lake, river or sea is
>   how often you have visited it
>   what activities you do there
> and explain why you like this particular place.

Now, I would like to talk about a river I visited last year.

The river I've chosen is the Thames in London. Last summer, I went on holiday to England with my family. While we were there we regularly saw the River Thames, which is the main waterway that runs through the capital.

I have only been to London once but we spent two weeks there and saw the river every day. We had to cross it to get to the other side of the city from where our hotel was, but there were also a number of things to do by the river itself.

Many of London's attractions are located along the River Thames, such as the London Eye, the Houses of Parliament, Big Ben and world famous art galleries like the Tate Modern. Due to the number of tourist attractions that line the Thames, there is a hop-on hop-off cruise ship that goes along the river, from which tourists can see all the key sights. Thanks to that cruise option, we could visit all the attractions.

I particularly like this place because it is very beautiful and offers such a variety of interesting activities for tourists as well as residents. I will never forget the magnificent fireworks night on the River Thames and I would love to visit there again soon.

That's all from me, thank you very much for your attention.

PART 3

1) What could be the consequences of deforestation?
산림 벌채의 결과는 무엇인가요?

Brainstorming	Direct Answer	특정 동물의 멸종을 초래함
	Supporting Sentence 1	온실가스 배출 증가
	Supporting Sentence 2	인간의 생존을 위협함

✏️ 다음 불법포인트를 참고해서 영어 문장을 완성해 보자. (주어와 시제, 품사와 단복수 등을 고려할 것!)

❶ 산림 벌채는 특정 동물의 멸종을 초래할 수 있는데, 이것은 서식지와 식량 공급의 감소를 초래하기 때문입니다.
_____ could lead to the _____ of certain animals since it results in the loss of _____ and food sources.
※ 산림 벌채 : deforestation / 멸종 : extinction / 서식지 : habitat

❷ 산림 벌채의 또 다른 결과는 그 지역의 온실가스 증가인데 나무들이 베일 때 배출됩니다.
Another _____ of deforestation is the increase in _____ , which are _____ when trees are _____ .
※ 결과 : consequence / 온실가스 : greenhouse gases / 배출하다 : release / 베어 넘기다 : chop down

❸ 이 모든 결과들은 모든 인류의 생존을 위협하는 것이 될 수도 있습니다.
All these outcomes could even be a _____ to the _____ of all human beings.
※ 위험 : threat / 생존 : survival

Q. What could be the consequences of deforestation?
A. Deforestation could lead to the extinction of certain animals since it results in the loss of habitat and food sources. Another consequence of deforestation is the increase in greenhouse gases, which are released when trees are chopped down. All these outcomes could even be a threat to the survival of all human beings.

2) **Do you think your government is doing enough to save endangered species? Why do you think that?**

당신의 정부는 멸종 위기에 처한 종을 구하는 것을 충분히 한다고 생각해요? 왜 그렇게 생각해요?

Brainstorming	Direct Answer	최선을 다하지 않음
	Supporting Sentence 1	자선 단체와 열정적인 개인들만이 의식을 제기함
	Supporting Sentence 2	정부가 긴급 조치를 취할 때임

✏️ 다음 **불법포인트**를 참고해서 영어 문장을 완성해 보자. (주어와 시제, 품사와 단복수 등을 고려할 것!)

❶ 아니요, 나는 정부가 최우선으로 멸종 위기에 처한 종들을 구하는 것에 대해 고려한다고 생각하지 않기 때문에 나는 그들이 최선을 다한다고 생각하지 않습니다.
No, I don't think that the government considers saving _____
as a _____ , and therefore I don't think that they _____ .
※ 멸종 위기에 처한 종들 : endangered species / 우선사항 : priority / 최선을 다하다 : do one's best

❷ 멸종 위기에 처한 동물들을 보호할 필요성에 제기된 모든 의식은 자선 단체와 열정적인 개인들에 의해 이루어진 것입니다.
All the _____ that is raised about the need to protect endangered animals is done
by _____ and _____ individuals.
※ 의식 : awareness / 자선 단체 : charity / 열정적인 : passionate

❸ 정부가 이런 종들을 돌보는 데 긴급 조치를 취할 때입니다.
_____ for the government to take _____ to look after such species.
※ ~할 때다 : it is time / 긴급 조치 : urgent action

Q. Do you think your government is doing enough to save endangered species? Why do you think that?

A. No, I don't think that the government considers saving endangered species as a priority, and therefore I don't think that they do their best. All the awareness that is raised about the need to protect endangered animals is done by charities and passionate individuals. It is time for the government to take urgent action to look after such species.

3) What can be done to stop global warming, do you think?
당신은 지구 온난화를 멈추기 위해서 무엇을 할 수 있다고 생각해요?

Brainstorming	Direct Answer	가정 내 탄소 발자국 감소
	Supporting Sentence 1	정부의 법률 시행
	Supporting Sentence 2	나무 심기

✏️ 다음 불법포인트를 참고해서 영어 문장을 완성해 보자. (주어와 시제, 품사와 단복수 등을 고려할 것!)

---

❶ 모든 사람들이 가정에서 사용하는 에너지의 양같은 그들의 탄소 발자국을 감소시키기 위한 책임을 진다면 지구 온난화는 줄어들 수 있습니다.

_____ could be reduced if everyone _____ decreasing their _____, such as the amount of energy that they use in their own homes.

※ 지구 온난화 : global warming / 책임지다 : take responsibility for / 탄소 발자국(가정에서 쓰는 에너지의 양) : carbon footprint

❷ 하지만 지구 온난화의 문제를 막기 위해서 정부가 주요 온실가스 배출자들에 의해 생성된 이산화탄소의 양과 관련한 법률을 시행하는 것은 중요합니다.

However, to stop the problem of global warming, it is important for governments to _____ regarding the amount of _____ produced by major greenhouse gas emitters.

※ 법률을 시행하다 : impose laws / 이산화탄소 : carbon dioxide(CO_2)

❸ 또한, 나무를 심는 것은 좋은 생각일 수 있는데 광합성을 하는 동안 나무는 이산화탄소를 흡수하고 산소를 배출하기 때문입니다.

In addition, planting trees would be a good idea because during _____, they _____ carbon dioxide and _____ oxygen.

※ 광합성 : photosynthesis / 흡수하다 : absorb / 배출하다 : give off

Q. What can be done to stop global warming, do you think?

A. Global warming could be reduced if everyone took responsibility for decreasing their carbon footprint, such as the amount of energy that they use in their own homes. However, to stop the problem of global warming, it is important for governments to impose laws regarding the amount of carbon dioxide produced by major greenhouse gas emitters. In addition, planting trees would be a good idea because during photosynthesis, they absorb carbon dioxide and give off oxygen.

4) Do you believe that people your age in your country live environmentally friendly lifestyles?
당신의 나라에서 당신 또래 사람들은 환경 친화적인 생활 방식으로 산다고 생각해요?

Brainstorming	Direct Answer	개인에게 달림
	Supporting Sentence 1	지구의 미래에 있어 그들의 역할의 중요성을 인식함
	Supporting Sentence 2	환경 친화적이 되는 것을 신경 쓰지 않는 사람들도 있음

✏️ 다음 불법포인트를 참고해서 영어 문장을 완성해 보자. (주어와 시제, 품사와 단복수 등을 고려할 것!)

❶ 그것은 매우 개인에 달려있습니다.
It very much _____ the individual.
※ ~에 달려있다 : depend on

❷ 내 세대의 많은 사람들은 지구의 미래에 있어 그들의 역할의 중요성을 인식하기에 환경 친화적이 되기 위해서 의식적으로 노력합니다.
Many people of my _____ recognise the importance of their role in the future of the planet and therefore _____ to be _____ .
※ 세대 : generation / 의식적으로 노력하다 : make a conscious effort / 환경 친화적인 : green(=environmentally friendly / eco-friendly)

❸ 하지만 일상생활에서 환경 친화적이 되는 것을 신경 쓰지 않는 사람도 많은데, 그들은 그들의 기여도가 너무 작고 중요하지 않을 것이라고 생각하기 때문입니다.
However, there are also many people who don't care to be eco-friendly in their _____ , because they believe that their _____ would be so small and insignificant.
※ 일상 생활 : day to day life / 기여도 : contribution

Q. Do you believe that people your age in your country live environmentally friendly lifestyles?
A. It very much depends on the individual. Many people of my generation recognise the importance of their role in the future of the planet and therefore make a conscious effort to be green. However, there are also many people who don't care to be eco-friendly in their day to day lives, because they believe that their contribution would be so small and insignificant.

Day 9 Natural Environment & Wildlife 불법포인트 정리

현재, 지금	at the moment	결과	consequence
자라다	grow up	온실가스	greenhouse gases
반려동물	companion animal	배출하다	release
주저하다	hesitate	베어 넘기다	chop down
동료애	companionship	위험	threat
위로가 되는	comforting	생존	survival
정원	garden	멸종 위기에 처한 종들	endangered species
뒤에	at the back	우선사항	priority
수국	hydrangea	최선을 다하다	do one's best
감사	gratitude	의식	awareness
꽃말	the language of flowers	자선 단체	charity
도심	the center of a city	열정적인	passionate
취미	pastime	~할 때다	it is time
원예, 정원 가꾸기	gardening	긴급 조치	urgent action
긴장을 풀다	unwind	지구 온난화	global warming
고요한	serene	책임지다	take responsibility for
작년	last year	탄소 발자국(가정에서 쓰는 에너지의 양)	carbon footprint
휴가를 가다	go on holiday	법률을 시행하다	impose laws
수로	waterway	이산화 탄소	carbon dioxide(CO_2)
건너다	cross	광합성	photosynthesis
관광지	attraction	흡수하다	absorb
국회의사당	the Houses of Parliament	배출하다	give off
자유롭게 타고 내리는	hop-on hop-off	~에 달려있다	depend on
명소	sights	세대	generation
거주자	resident	의식적으로 노력하다	make a conscious effort
참으로 아름다운	magnificent	환경 친화적인	green / environmentally friendly / eco-friendly
산림 벌채	deforestation	일상 생활	day to day life
멸종	extinction	기여도	contribution
서식지	habitat		

Day 10 — Neighbours & Politeness
이웃과 예의범절

PART 1

1) How well do you know your next-door neighbours?
2) How often do you see them?
3) What problems do people sometimes have with their neighbours?
4) Would you say you are a polite person?
5) Who taught you to be polite?
6) Do you think people should be polite?
7) In your country, have there been any changes in politeness in the past few decades?

PART 2

Describe a situation in which you were very polite.

You should say :
    when it was
    where the situation took place
    how you showed that you were polite
and explain why you needed to be so polite.

PART 3

1) How important is it to be polite in your culture?
2) In your country's culture, how do you show that you are being polite?
3) Are we less polite with members of our families than with people we don't know?
4) What are some behaviours that are considered impolite in your culture?

보이는 Speaking QR 코드

PART 1

1) How well do you know your next-door neighbours? 당신은 옆집에 사는 이웃을 얼마나 잘 알아요?

Brainstorming	Direct Answer	잘 모름
	Additional Information	지나치면 인사하지만 어울리지는 않음

✏️ 다음 불법포인트를 참고해서 영어 문장을 완성해 보자. (주어와 시제, 품사와 단복수 등을 고려할 것!)

❶ 나는 나의 이웃을 잘 알지 못합니다.
I don't know my _____ very well.
※ 이웃 : neighbour

❷ 우리는 지나치면 서로 인사를 건네지만 우리는 결코 함께 어울린 적이 없습니다.
We say hello to each other if we pass but we have never _____ together.
※ 어울리다, 교제하다 : socialise

Q. How well do you know your next-door neighbours?
A. I don't know my neighbours very well. We say hello to each other if we pass but we have never socialised together.

2) How often do you see them? 당신은 얼마나 자주 그들을 만나요?

Brainstorming	Direct Answer	주중 대부분의 아침
	Additional Information	우리는 거의 동시에 출근하기 때문임

✏️ 다음 불법포인트를 참고해서 영어 문장을 완성해 보자. (주어와 시제, 품사와 단복수 등을 고려할 것!)

❶ 나는 주중 대부분의 아침에 그들을 봅니다.
I see them most mornings _____ .
※ 주중에 : during the week

❷ 이것은 우리가 보통 거의 동시에 출근을 하기 때문입니다.
This is because we usually _____ at around the same time.
※ 출근하다 : leave for work

Q. How often do you see them?
A. I see them most mornings during the week. This is because we usually leave for work at around the same time.

3) **What problems do people sometimes have with their neighbours?**
사람들은 때때로 그들의 이웃 사람들과 어떤 문제가 있어요?

Brainstorming	Direct Answer	소음 문제
	Additional Information	파티를 하거나 애완동물을 기르는 이웃이 불만을 줄 수 있음

✏️ 다음 불법포인트를 참고해서 영어 문장을 완성해 보자. (주어와 시제, 품사와 단복수 등을 고려할 것!)

❶ 사람들이 이웃들과 갖는 전형적인 문제는 소음 문제입니다.
A typical problem people have with their neighbours is _____ .
※ 소음 문제 : the issue of noise

❷ 파티를 하거나 시끄러운 애완동물을 기르는 이웃 사람이 불만을 줄 수 있습니다.
A neighbour who has parties or noisy pets can be _____ .
※ 불만스럽게 만들다, 좌절감을 주다 : frustrate

Q. **What problems do people sometimes have with their neighbours?**
A. A typical problem people have with their neighbours is the issue of noise. A neighbour who has parties or noisy pets can be frustrating.

4) **Would you say you are a polite person?** 당신은 당신이 예의바른 사람이라고 말할 수 있어요?

Brainstorming	Direct Answer	내 자신이 예의바르다고 생각함
	Additional Information	모르는 사람들과 있을 때 더 정중하려고 함

✏️ 다음 불법포인트를 참고해서 영어 문장을 완성해 보자. (주어와 시제, 품사와 단복수 등을 고려할 것!)

❶ 네, 나는 내 자신이 예의가 바르다고 생각합니다.
Yes, I would _____ myself to be polite.
※ 생각하다, 여기다 : consider

❷ 특히 내가 모르는 사람들과 함께 있을 때, 나는 그들에게 좀 더 정중하려고 합니다.
Especially when I am with people who I don't know, I try to be more _____ to them.
※ 정중한 : courteous(=polite)

Q. **Would you say you are a polite person?**
A. Yes, I would consider myself to be polite. Especially when I am with people who I don't know, I try to be more courteous to them.

5) Who taught you to be polite? 누가 당신을 예의 바르게 가르쳤어요?

Brainstorming	Direction Answer	부모님
	Additional Information	엄격했음

✏️ 다음 불법포인트를 참고해서 영어 문장을 완성해 보자. (주어와 시제, 품사와 단복수 등을 고려할 것!)

❶ 나의 부모님은 내가 선생님들과 낯선 사람들에게 예의 바르고 존경하는 법을 알도록 키웠습니다.
My parents _____ me _____ making sure that I knew how to be polite and respectful to teachers and _____ .
※ 기르다, 키우다 : bring up / 낯선 사람 : stranger

❷ 그들은 나에게 매우 엄격했습니다.
They were very _____ with me.
※ 엄격한 : strict

Q. Who taught you to be polite?
A. My parents brought me up making sure that I knew how to be polite and respectful to teachers and strangers. They were very strict with me.

6) Do you think people should be polite? 당신은 사람들이 정중해야 한다고 생각해요?

Brainstorming	Direct Answer	물론, 엄마가 항상 말함
	Additional Information	킹스맨의 '매너가 사람을 만든다'라는 표현을 좋아함

✏️ 다음 불법포인트를 참고해서 영어 문장을 완성해 보자. (주어와 시제, 품사와 단복수 등을 고려할 것!)

❶ 물론입니다! 나의 어머니는 예절은 돈이 한 푼도 들지 않는다고 항상 나에게 말했습니다.
Of course! My mother always told me that manners don't _____ anything.
※ 비용이 들다 : cost

❷ 나는 또한 '킹스맨' 영화의 '매너가 사람을 만든다'라는 표현을 좋아합니다.
I also like the _____ , 'Manners maketh man', from the movie 'Kingsman'.
※ 표현 : expression

Q. Do you think people should be polite?
A. Of course! My mother always told me that manners don't cost anything. I also like the expression, 'Manners maketh man', from the movie 'Kingsman'.

7) In your country, have there been any changes in politeness in the past few decades?
당신의 나라에서는 과거 몇 십 년간 예의 범절에 있어 어떤 변화가 있었나요?

Brainstorming	Direct Answer	특별한 변화 없음
	Additional Information	경의를 표하는 것은 언제나 우리 문화의 중요한 측면임

✏️ 다음 **불법포인트**를 참고해서 영어 문장을 완성해 보자. (주어와 시제, 품사와 단복수 등을 고려할 것!)

❶ 아니요. 나는 예의 범절에 있어서 어떤 특별한 변화가 있었다고 생각하지 않습니다.
No, I don't think that there have been any particular changes in _____ .
※ 예의 범절 : politeness

❷ 경의를 표하는 것은 언제나 우리나라에서 문화의 중요한 측면이었습니다.
_____ has always been an important aspect of the culture in my country.
※ 경의를 표하다 : show respect

Q. **In your country, have there been any changes in politeness in the past few decades?**
A. No, I don't think that there have been any particular changes in politeness. Showing respect has always been an important aspect of the culture in my country.

PART 2

Describe a situation in which you were very polite.

You should say:
- when it was
- where the situation took place
- how you showed that you were polite

and explain why you needed to be so polite.

당신이 아주 공손했던 상황에 대해 묘사하세요.

당신은 반드시 말해야 합니다.
- 그 상황이 언제였는지
- 그 상황이 어디에서 일어났는지
- 당신이 공손하다는 것을 어떻게 보여줬는지

그리고 당신이 왜 그렇게 공손할 필요가 있었는지 설명하세요.

※ 공손했던 상황이라는 주제가 막연하게 느껴질 수 있다. 스피킹 기출 문제 중의 하나인, 'Describe something you do to help others.', (남을 돕기 위해서 한 것을 묘사하세요.)와 비슷한 문제로, 남을 도왔던 상황, 내가 남에게 친절하게 행동했던 상황을 떠올린다. 이런 경험이 특별히 없다면 영화나 책에서의 에피소드를 내 경험인양 인용해보자.

주어지는 1분을 어떻게 활용할 것인가? (How to Use Your 1 Minute Preparation Time)

1. 질문 파악 공손하게 행동했던 상황 묘사에 초점을 맞추는 문제이다.	내가 영어로 잘 설명할 수 있는 공손하게 행동했던 상황을 떠올린다.
2. 묘사 대상 결정하기 영어로 가장 자신 있게 묘사할 수 있는 공손하게 행동했던 상황을 떠올린다.	공손하게 행동했던 상황이 떠오르지 않는다면, 남을 도왔던 경험을 이야기한다.
3. 하위 질문 확인 + 스토리 작성 하위 질문의 개수를 확인하고, 각각에 대한 답을 적는다.	sub-questions는 3개처럼 보이지만, 마지막 문장의 'and explain why you needed to be so polite'를 포함해서 4개이다. 반드시 4개의 질문에 모두 답하되, 답의 길이는 똑같지 않아도 상관없다.
4. 주제 관련 아카데믹 표현 사용 공손하게 행동했던 상황과 관련해서 학습한 아카데믹한 표현들을 떠올린다.	very polite, help my grandmother, elderly, appreciate my help, running backwards and forwards from the kitchen, well mannered, a certain form of polite language, clear the table, washing up
5. 주의해야 할 문법 문제의 시제 및 인칭 대명사 등을 확인한다.	과거에 있었던 상황을 묘사하는 문제이다. 적절한 시제 사용에 주의하자!

Brainstorming

Sub-question 1 when it was	3주 전
Sub-question 2 where the situation took place	외할머니 댁, 어수
Sub-question 3 how you showed that you were polite	할머니 친구분 중 한 분의 생신, 할머니가 생신 점심을 준비하는 것을 도움, 부엌에서 왔다 갔다 뛰어다님
Sub-question 4 and explain why you needed to be so polite	어른들에게 공손한 말투 사용, 할머니가 요청한 모든 것을 함, 식탁을 치우고 설거지 함

✏️ 다음 **불법포인트**를 참고해서 영어 문장을 완성해 보자. (주어와 시제, 품사와 단복수 등을 고려할 것!)

❶ 지금 나는 내가 특히 공손했던 경우에 대해 이야기하고 싶습니다.
Now, I would like to talk about an occasion when I was _____ polite.
※ 특히 : particularly

❷ 내가 선택한 상황은 3주전 외할머니 댁을 최근 방문한 동안이었습니다.
The situation that I've chosen was during a visit to my _____ house about three weeks ago.
※ 외할머니 : maternal grandmother

❸ 나는 보통 두 달에 한 번씩 할머니를 방문합니다. 할머니는 우리나라의 다른 끝, 여수에 삽니다. 그래서 나에게는 여행하기에 꽤 긴 여정입니다. 할머니는 가까이에 사는 많은 친구들이 있고 할머니들은 규칙적으로 만나서 함께 골프를 치거나 카드 놀이를 하거나 온천에 갑니다.
I usually visit my grandmother at least _____ . She lives at the other end of the country, in Yeosu, so it is quite a long journey for me to make. My grandmother has many friends who live near her and they regularly _____ to play golf or cards or _____ together.
※ 두 달에 한 번 : once every couple of months / 만나다 : meet up / 온천에 가다 : go to the spa

❹ 나의 최근 방문 동안에, 할머니 친구분 중 한 분의 생신이어서 나는 할머니가 생신 점심을 준비하는 것을 도왔습니다. 모든 여성이 나이가 든 분들이어서 부엌에서 왔다 갔다 뛰어다니는 나의 도움을 고마워했습니다. 그들은 나의 행동을 매우 공손하고 예의 바르다고 여겼습니다.
During my recent visit, it was one of her friend's birthdays so I helped my grandmother _____ a birthday lunch. Since all of the women are elderly, they _____ my help, running _____ from the kitchen. They considered my actions very polite and _____ .
※ 준비하다 : prepare / 고마워하다 : appreciate / 왔다 갔다, 앞뒤로 : backwards and forwards
  예절 바른 : well mannered

❺ 우리 문화에서는 어른들에게 말할 때 특정한 형태의 공손한 말투를 사용하는 것이 중요합니다. 물론 나는 정중한 말투를 사용했습니다. 나는 또한 할머니들이 모두 편안한지 확인했고 할머니가 요청한 모든 것을 했습니다. 점심이 끝날 쯤, 할머니들이 밖에 햇볕에 앉아서 친목을 나누는 동안 나는 식탁을 치우고 설거지를 했습니다.
In my culture, it is important to use a certain form of polite language when talking to our elders, which I did of course. I also made sure that they were all _____ and did everything my grandmother asked. At the end of the lunch, I _____ and did the _____ while they sat outside in the sun and enjoyed each other's company.
※ 편안한 : comfortable / 식탁을 치우다 : clear the table / 설거지 : washing up

Sample Answer

> Describe a situation in which you were very polite.
>
> You should say:
>   when it was
>   where the situation took place
>   how you showed that you were polite
> and explain why you needed to be so polite.

Now, I would like to talk about an occasion when I was particularly polite.

The situation that I've chosen was during a visit to my maternal grandmother's house about three weeks ago.

I usually visit my grandmother at least once every couple of months. She lives at the other end of the country, in Yeosu, so it is quite a long journey for me to make. My grandmother has many friends who live near her and they regularly meet up to play golf or cards or go to the spa together.

During my recent visit, it was one of her friend's birthdays so I helped my grandmother prepare a birthday lunch. Since all of the women are elderly, they appreciated my help, running backwards and forwards from the kitchen. They considered my actions very polite and well mannered.

In my culture, it is important to use a certain form of polite language when talking to our elders, which I did of course. I also made sure that they were all comfortable and did everything my grandmother asked. At the end of the lunch, I cleared the table and did the washing up while they sat outside in the sun and enjoyed each other's company.

That's all from me, thank you very much for your attention.

PART 3

1) How important is it to be polite in your culture? 당신의 문화에서 예의 바른 것은 얼마나 중요해요?

Brainstorming	Direct Answer	상당히 중요함
	Supporting Sentence 1	누구와 이야기하느냐에 따라 다른 언어 형태 사용함
	Supporting Sentence 2	손위 사람이나 선배에게는 격식 차린 언어, 또래에게는 격식 차리지 않은 언어를 사용함

✏️ 다음 **불법포인트**를 참고해서 영어 문장을 완성해 보자. (주어와 시제, 품사와 단복수 등을 고려할 것!)

❶ 우리 문화에서 예의 바른 행동은 상당히 중요하게 여겨집니다.
In my culture, _____ is considered extremely important.
※ 예의 바른 행동 : polite behaviour

❷ 한국에서 예의 바른 것은 경의를 표하는 방법이어서 우리는 누구와 이야기를 하느냐에 따라 다른 언어 형태를 사용합니다.
Being polite in Korea is a way of showing respect so we use different forms of language _____ who we are talking to.
※ ~에 따라 다르다 : depend on

❸ 예를 들면 우리는 손위 사람이나 선배에게 이야기할 때 격식 차린 언어를 사용하지만, 우리는 또래에게 말할 때는 격식을 차리지 않은 형태를 사용합니다.
For example, we use formal language when _____ elders or _____ but we use a more casual form when speaking with peers.
※ 말을 걸다, 이야기하다 : address / 선배, 상사 : superior

Q. How important is it to be polite in your culture?
A. In my culture, polite behaviour is considered extremely important. Being polite in Korea is a way of showing respect so we use different forms of language depending on who we are talking to. For example, we use formal language when addressing elders or superiors but we use a more casual form when speaking with peers.

2) In your country's culture, how do you show that you are being polite?
당신 나라의 문화에서 당신은 당신이 예의 바르다는 것을 어떻게 보여주나요?

Brainstorming		
	Direct Answer	많은 방법이 있음
	Supporting Sentence 1	상황에 의해 결정됨
	Supporting Sentence 2	동료들과 회식 때 술잔을 채워주는 것임
	Supporting Sentence 3	손위 사람이나 선배에게 격식 차린 언어를 사용하고 인사함

✏️ 다음 **불법포인트**를 참고해서 영어 문장을 완성해 보자. (주어와 시제, 품사와 단복수 등을 고려할 것!)

❶ 좋은 매너와 예의 바른 것을 보여주는 데는 많은 다른 방법들이 있습니다.
There are so many different ways to _____ good manners and being polite.
※ 보여주다 : demonstrate

❷ 그것은 정말 상황에 의해 결정됩니다.
It really depends on the _____ .
※ 상황 : situation

❸ 예를 들면, 저녁 회식에서 동료들과 식사를 할 때 참석자들은 누군가 술을 다 마셨는지 주시하고 그런 다음 술잔이 비었을 때 다시 채우는 것이 예의입니다.
For example, when dining with _____ at a staff dinner, it is polite for attendees to make sure that they _____ when someone has finished their drink and then _____ it when it's empty.
※ 직장 동료 : co-worker / 주시하다, 관찰하다 : observe / 다시 채우다 : refill

❹ 격식 차린 언어와 직장에서 손위 사람들이나 선배들에게 말을 걸 때 몸을 굽혀 인사하기와 같은 특정 몸짓을 사용하는 것은 또한 예의 범절을 보여주는 방법입니다.
Using formal language and certain _____ , such as bowing when addressing elders or superiors at work, are also ways to show politeness.
※ 몸짓 : gesture

Q. In your country's culture, how do you show that you are being polite?
A. There are so many different ways to demonstrate good manners and being polite. It really depends on the situation. For example, when dining with co-workers at a staff dinner, it is polite for attendees to make sure that they observe when someone has finished their drink and then refill it when it's empty. Using formal language and certain gestures, such as bowing when addressing elders or superiors at work, are also ways to show politeness.

3) Are we less polite with members of our families than with people we don't know?
우리는 모르는 사람들보다 가족 구성원들에게 덜 예의 바른가요?

Brainstorming	Direct Answer	덜 예의 바름
	Supporting Sentence 1	집에서는 격식을 차릴 필요가 덜 함
	Supporting Sentence 2	모르는 사람에게 필요한 격식들은 가족들과 있을 때는 필요하지 않음

✏️ 다음 불법포인트를 참고해서 영어 문장을 완성해 보자. (주어와 시제, 품사와 단복수 등을 고려할 것!)

❶ 일반적으로, 나는 우리가 낯선 사람들보다 가족 구성원들에게 덜 예의 바르다고 생각합니다.
In general, I suppose we are less polite with family members than with _____ .
※ 낯선 사람 : stranger

❷ 편안한 환경인 집에 있을 때는 격식을 차릴 필요가 덜 합니다.
There is less need to be formal when at home, in a _____ environment.
※ 편안한 : relaxed

❸ '해 주세요'와 '감사합니다'라고 말하는 것을 기억하는 것과 같이 작은 측면에서 여전히 예의 바르게 해야 하는 것은 중요하지만, 우리가 모르는 사람들을 공경하는 것에 포함되는 격식들은 가족들과 있을 때는 필요하지 않습니다.
It is still important to be polite in small ways, such as remembering to say "please" and "thank you" but the _____ involved in being respectful to people we don't know are not _____ when around family.
※ 격식 : formality / 필요한 : necessary

Q. Are we less polite with members of our families than with people we don't know?
A. In general, I suppose we are less polite with family members than with strangers. There is less need to be formal when at home, in a relaxed environment. It is still important to be polite in small ways, such as remembering to say "please" and "thank you" but the formalities involved in being respectful to people we don't know are not necessary when around family.

4) **What are some behaviours that are considered impolite in your culture?**
당신의 문화에서 무례하게 생각되는 몇 가지 행동들은 무엇인가요?

Brainstorming	Direct Answer	식사하는 것과 관련된 몇 가지 무례한 행동들이 있음
	Supporting Sentence 1	외식은 우리 문화의 큰 부분, 해야 할 것과 하지 말아야 할 것이 있음
	Supporting Sentence 2	식탁에서 코를 푸는 것
	Supporting Sentence 3	밥을 먹지 않고 남기는 것

✏️ 다음 **불법포인트**를 참고해서 영어 문장을 완성해 보자. (주어와 시제, 품사와 단복수 등을 고려할 것!)

❶ 한국 문화에서는, 식사하는 것과 관련된 몇 가지 무례한 행동들이 있습니다.
In Korean culture, there are several _____ actions related to dining.
※ 무례한 : impolite

❷ 외식은 우리 문화의 커다란 부분이어서 식사와 관련해서 해야 할 것과 하지 말아야 할 것들이 있습니다.
_____ is a huge part of our culture so there are dos and don'ts when it comes to eating.
※ 외식 : dining out

❸ 예를 들면, 식탁에서 코를 푸는 것은 무례한 것으로 여겨집니다.
For example, it is considered impolite to _____ at the table.
※ 코를 풀다 : blow one's nose

❹ 또한 밥을 먹지 않고 남기는 것은 무례한 것입니다.
It is also _____ to leave rice uneaten.
※ 무례함 : bad form

Q. What are some behaviours that are considered impolite in your culture?
A. In Korean culture, there are several impolite actions related to dining. Dining out is a huge part of our culture so there are dos and don'ts when it comes to eating. For example, it is considered impolite to blow your nose at the table. It is also bad form to leave rice uneaten.

Day 10 Neighbours & Politeness 불법포인트 정리

이웃	neighbor	예절 바른	well mannered
어울리다, 교제하다	socialise	편안한	comfortable
주중에	during the week	식탁을 치우다	clear the table
출근하다	leave for work	설거지	washing up
소음 문제	the issue of noise	예의 바른 행동	polite behaviour
불만스럽게 만들다 좌절감을 주다	frustrate	~에 따라 다르다	depend on
생각하다, 여기다	consider	말을 걸다, 이야기하다	address
정중한	courteous(=polite)	선배, 상사	superior
기르다, 키우다	bring up	보여주다	demonstrate
낯선 사람	stranger	상황	situation
엄격한	strict	직장 동료	co-worker
비용이 들다	cost	주시하다, 관찰하다	observe
표현	expression	다시 채우다	refill
예의범절	politeness	몸짓	gesture
경의를 표하다	show respect	낯선 사람	stranger
특히	particularly	편안한	relaxed
외할머니	maternal grandmother	격식	formality
두 달에 한 번	once every couple of months	필요한	necessary
만나다	meet up	무례한	impolite
온천에 가다	go to the spa	외식	dining out
준비하다	prepare	코를 풀다	blow one's nose
고마워하다	appreciate	무례함	bad form
왔다 갔다, 앞뒤로	backwards and forwards		

Day 11 — Building & Design
빌딩과 디자인

PART 1

1) Tell me about the kind of accommodation you live in?
2) How long have you lived there?
3) What do you like about living there?
4) What sort of accommodation would you most like to live in?
5) Do you prefer big or small houses?
6) Would you like to take part in designing your house?
7) Do people like to design their own houses in your country?

PART 2

Describe an interesting building.

You should say :
    where it is located
    what it looks like
    when it was built
and explain why you like this building.

PART 3

1) What role do old buildings and new buildings play in modern society?
2) What changes have taken place in architecture in the past two decades?
3) Do you think it is necessary to protect old buildings?
4) What do the houses in your country look like?

보이는 Speaking QR 코드

PART 1

1) Tell me about the kind of accommodation you live in? 당신이 사는 주거 형태에 대해 말하세요.

Brainstorming	Direct Answer	방 3개 아파트
	Additional Information	3층, 칸막이가 없는 거실과 부엌이 있음

✏️ 다음 불법포인트를 참고해서 영어 문장을 완성해 보자. (주어와 시제, 품사와 단복수 등을 고려할 것!)

❶ 나는 내 친구와 함께 침실이 3개 있는 아파트에서 삽니다.
I live in _____ with my friend.
※ 침실이 3개 있는 아파트 : a three bedroom flat(=a flat with three bedrooms)

❷ 3층에 있고 칸막이가 없는 거실과 부엌이 있습니다.
It is on the third floor and has an _____ living room and kitchen.
※ 칸막이가 없는, 오픈 플랜식의 : open-plan(다양한 용도를 위해 칸막이를 최소한으로 줄인)

Q. Tell me about the kind of accommodation you live in?
A. I live in a three bedroom flat with my friend. It is on the third floor and has an open-plan living room and kitchen.

2) How long have you lived there? 당신은 거기에서 얼마 동안 살았어요?

Brainstorming	Direct Answer	1년 반
	Additional Information	대학을 졸업하고 일하기 시작한 후에 이사옴

✏️ 다음 불법포인트를 참고해서 영어 문장을 완성해 보자. (주어와 시제, 품사와 단복수 등을 고려할 것!)

❶ 나는 지금까지 1년 반 동안 나의 멋진 아파트에서 살고 있습니다.
I have been living in my lovely apartment for a year and a half _____ .
※ 지금까지 : so far

❷ 나는 대학을 졸업하고 일하기 시작한 후에 이사 왔습니다.
I moved in after I _____ and started working.
※ 대학을 졸업하다 : graduate from university

Q. How long have you lived there?
A. I have been living in my lovely apartment for a year and a half so far. I moved in after I graduated from university and started working.

3) **What do you like about living there?** 당신은 그곳에 사는 것에 대해 무엇이 좋아요?

Brainstorming	Direct Answer	이 지역을 좋아함
	Additional Information	가까이에 많은 부티크 상점과 술집들이 있음

✏️ 다음 불법포인트를 참고해서 영어 문장을 완성해 보자. (주어와 시제, 품사와 단복수 등을 고려할 것!)

❶ 나는 이 아파트가 있는 분당 정자동 지역을 좋아합니다.
I love the area that the _____ is in, Jeongjadong in Bundang.
※ 아파트 : flat(=apartment)

❷ 이 곳은 가까이에 많은 부티크 상점들과 술집들이 있는 매우 유망한 지역입니다.
It is a very _____ part of town with a lot of _____ shops and bars nearby.
※ 유망한, 떠오르는 : up and coming / 부티크 : boutique(값비싼 옷이나 선물류를 파는 작은 가게)

Q. What do you like about living there?
A. I love the area that the flat is in, Jeongjadong in Bundang. It is a very up and coming part of town with a lot of boutique shops and bars nearby.

4) **What sort of accommodation would you most like to live in?**
당신이 가장 살고 싶은 주거 형태는 무엇인가요?

Brainstorming	Direct Answer	커다란 해안가 집
	Additional Information	바다 바로 옆, 이웃이 없는 모든 것이 내 것인 집

✏️ 다음 불법포인트를 참고해서 영어 문장을 완성해 보자. (주어와 시제, 품사와 단복수 등을 고려할 것!)

❶ 나는 언젠가 커다란 해안가 집에서 살고 싶습니다.
I would like to live in a large beach house _____ .
※ 언젠가 : some day

❷ 이 집이 바로 바다 옆에 있어서 이웃이 없다면 이상적으로 완벽할 것입니다.
Ideally, the house would be all mine with no neighbours, _____ by the ocean would be perfect.
※ 바로 : right

Q. What sort of accommodation would you most like to live in?
A. I would like to live in a large beach house some day. Ideally, the house would be all mine with no neighbours, right by the ocean would be perfect.

5) **Do you prefer big or small houses?** 당신은 큰 주택을 더 좋아해요? 아니면 작은 주택을 더 좋아해요?

Brainstorming	Direction Answer	큰 집, 아름답게 보임
	Additional Information	수영장이 있는 침실이 5개인 집에서 파티를 하고 싶음

✏️ 다음 불법포인트를 참고해서 영어 문장을 완성해 보자. (주어와 시제, 품사와 단복수 등을 고려할 것!)

❶ 나는 큰 집들을 더 좋아하는데, 이 집들은 정말 아름답게 보이기 때문입니다.
I prefer big houses because they look _____ .
※ 정말 아름다운 : just beautiful

❷ 수영장이 있는 침실이 5개 있는 집을 소유하고 금요일 밤마다 파티를 할 수 있었으면 좋겠습니다.
I wish I could own a five-bedroom house with a swimming pool and _____ there _____ .
※ 파티를 하다 : have a party / 금요일 밤마다 : every Friday night

Q. Do you prefer big or small houses?
A. I prefer big houses because they look just beautiful. I wish I could own a five-bedroom house with a swimming pool and have a party there every Friday night.

6) **Would you like to take part in designing your house?** 당신은 당신의 집을 설계하는 데 참여하고 싶어요?

Brainstorming	Direct Answer	집 설계에 관여하고 싶음
	Additional Information	편안하고 창의적인 장소가 되길 원함

✏️ 다음 불법포인트를 참고해서 영어 문장을 완성해 보자. (주어와 시제, 품사와 단복수 등을 고려할 것!)

❶ 네, 나는 나의 집을 설계하는 데 관여하고 싶습니다.
Yes, I would like to _____ designing my house.
※ 관여하다, 역할을 하다 : play a part in

❷ 나는 집에서 글을 쓰면서 많은 시간을 보내는 것을 좋아해서 나는 집이 편안하고 창의적이라고 느껴지는 아름다운 장소가 되길 원합니다.
I like to spend a lot of time at home writing, so I want it to be a beautiful place where I feel comfortable and _____ .
※ 창의적인 : creative

Q. Would you like to take part in designing your house?
A. Yes, I would like to play a part in designing my house. I like to spend a lot of time at home writing, so I want it to be a beautiful place where I feel comfortable and creative.

7) Do people like to design their own houses in your country?
당신의 나라에서는 사람들이 자신의 주택을 설계하는 것을 좋아해요?

Brainstorming	Direct Answer	집을 설계한 사람에 대해 들어본 적 없음
	Additional Information	특별히 관심 있다고 생각하지 않음

✏️ 다음 **불법포인트**를 참고해서 영어 문장을 완성해 보자. (주어와 시제, 품사와 단복수 등을 고려할 것!)

❶ 개인적으로, 나는 자신의 집을 설계한 적이 있는 사람에 대해 들어본 적이 없습니다.
Personally, I have not heard of anyone having ever _____ their own house.
※ 설계하다 : design

❷ 그래서 나는 우리나라 사람들은 특별히 그것에 관심을 가지고 있다고 생각하지 않습니다.
So I don't think people in my country particularly _____ it.
※ ~에 관심 갖다, 신경 쓰다 : care about

Q. Do people like to design their own houses in your country?
A. Personally, I have not heard of anyone having ever designed their own house. So I don't think people in my country particularly care about it.

PART 2

Describe an interesting building.

You should say:
    where it is located
    what it looks like
    when it was built
and explain why you like this building.

흥미로운 건물을 묘사하세요.

당신은 반드시 말해야 합니다.
    이 건물은 어디에 있는지
    이 건물은 어떻게 생겼는지
    이 건물은 언제 지어졌는지
그리고 당신이 왜 이 건물을 좋아하는지 설명하세요.

※ 건물 묘사에 대한 답은 '본인 출처'가 아닌, '전문가 출처'로 반드시 준비되어야 한다. 평소에 관심 있게 본 건물, 혹은 실제로 본적은 없지만 유명한 건물을 하나 정한 후, 그 건물의 웹사이트에 방문해서 영문으로 된 소개를 꼼꼼히 읽고 적절하게 내 답으로 인용한다. 이렇게 준비된 답은 더 아카데믹하게 들릴 뿐만 아니라 문법적 오류도 적다. 한국에 있는 건물 중에는 영어로 된 소개가 없는 경우도 종종 있으니, 영어권 나라에 있는 건물이나 세계적으로 유명한 역사적인 건물을 선택하는 것이 좋다.

주어지는 1분을 어떻게 활용할 것인가? (How to Use Your 1 Minute Preparation Time)

1. 질문 파악 건물 묘사에 초점을 맞추는 문제이다.	내가 영어로 잘 설명할 수 있는 건물을 떠올린다.
2. 묘사 대상 결정하기 영어로 가장 자신 있게 묘사할 수 있는 건물을 떠올린다.	건물에 대해서 생각해보지 않았다면, 상상력을 동원해서 허구의 건물을 만들어 자세하게 이야기 한다.
3. 하위 질문 확인 + 스토리 작성 하위 질문의 개수를 확인하고, 각각에 대한 답을 적는다.	sub-questions는 3개처럼 보이지만, 마지막 문장의 'and explain why you like this building' 를 포함해서 4개이다. 반드시 4개의 질문에 모두 답하되, 답의 길이는 똑같지 않아도 상관없다.
4. 주제 관련 아카데믹 표현 사용 건물과 관련해서 학습한 아카데믹한 표현들을 떠올린다.	the building, Sagrada Familia, located in, the famous building. a large Roman Catholic church, situated in, was designed by, a famous architect, Gaudi, a very distinctive style, impressively huge, a very gothic appearance, apparent, the towering spires, fascinating, construction, architecture, just amazing, the amount of detail and the vastness of this building, an astounding piece of architecture, a great tourist attraction
5. 주의해야 할 문법 문제의 시제 및 인칭 대명사 등을 확인한다.	building이라는 단어를 여러 번 반복하기 보다는 church, construction, architecture 등 동의어를 다양하게 활용하자. 또한 건물이 지어진 것은 과거이지만, 이 건물의 특징이나 멋스러움을 이야기 할 때는 현재 시제를 사용해야 한다.

Brainstorming

Sub-question 1 where it is located	스페인 바르셀로나에 있는 로마 가톨릭 교회, 사그라다 파밀리아
Sub-question 2 what it looks like	크고 완전한 고딕 풍의 외관, 우뚝 솟은 첨탑들
Sub-question 3 when it was built	1882년에 건축 시작, 스페인 내전으로 중단, 교회 건축의 중간 지점을 지난 건 2010년, 아직 미완성
Sub-question 4 and explain why you like this building	세부 양식(디테일)의 양과 광대함, 건물의 역사와 가우디와의 관계가 대단한 관광 명소로 만듦

다음 불법포인트를 참고해서 영어 문장을 완성해 보자. (주어와 시제, 품사와 단복수 등을 고려할 것!)

❶ 지금 나는 흥미로운 건물에 대해 이야기하고 싶습니다.
Now, I would like to talk about an _____ .
※ 흥미로운 건물 : interesting building

❷ 내가 선택한 구조물은 스페인에 있는 사그라다 파밀리아입니다. 작년에 나는 나의 가족과 함께 바르셀로나를 방문했습니다. 우리가 거기에 머무는 동안 나는 이 유명한 건물, 거대한 로마 카톨릭 교회를 보러 갔습니다.
The structure which I've chosen is Sagrada Familia located in Spain. Last year, I visited Barcelona with my family. While we were there, I went to see this famous building, a large _____
_____ .
※ 로마 가톨릭 교회 : Roman Catholic church

❸ 그 건물은 가우디라는 유명한 건축가에 의해서 설계되었습니다. 그가 도시에서 설계했던 것으로 인정을 받은 다른 건물들에서 볼 수 있듯이 가우디는 매우 독특한 스타일을 가지고 있는 것으로 알려졌습니다. 그 교회는 인상적으로 크고 완전한 고딕 풍의 외관을 가지고 있어서 우뚝 솟은 첨탑들을 통해 누가 봐도 알 수 있습니다.
The building _____ a famous _____ called Gaudi. Gaudi _____ have a very distinctive style as can be seen in other buildings that he _____ having designed in the city. The church is impressively huge and has a very gothic appearance, which is _____ through its _____ .
※ ~에 의해 설계되다 : be designed by / 건축가 : architect / ~에게 알려지다 : be known to
   인정받다 : be credited for / 누가 봐도 알 수 있는, 분명한 : apparent / 우뚝 솟은 첨탑 : towering spire

❹ 내가 매혹적이라고 생각했던 이 건물의 한 측면은 비록 이 건축이 1882년, 100년도 더 이전에 시작됐지만 이것이 아직 완성되지 않았다는 것입니다. 이것은 스페인 내전과 같은 사건들을 포함한 스페인의 파괴적인 역사 때문에 교회 건축이 중단되어야만 했다는 것을 의미합니다. 사실 이 건축의 중간 지점을 지난 건 2010년이었습니다.
One aspect of this building that I found _____ is that it has not yet been completed, even though its construction started over 100 years ago, in 1882. This is because Spain's disruptive history, including such events as _____ , meant that building work on the church had to be _____ . In fact, it was only in 2010 that the _____ point of its construction was passed.
※ 매혹적인, 대단히 흥미로운 : fascinating / 스페인 내전 : the Spanish Civil War / 중단하다, 잠시 멈추다 : pause
   중간의 : midway

❺ 건축적인 측면에서, 이 건물은 정말 놀랍습니다. 세부 양식(디테일)의 양과 광대함은 사그라다 파밀리아를 믿기 어려울 정도의 건축 작품으로 만들었고 이 건물의 역사와 가우디가 연결되어 이것을 대단한 관광 명소로 만들었습니다.
In terms of the _____ , this building is just amazing. The amount of detail and its _____ make the Sagrada Familia an _____ piece of architecture and its history and connection to Gaudi make it a great _____ .
※ 건축 : architecture / 광대함 : vastness / 믿기 어려운, 놀라운 : astounding / 관광 명소 : tourist attraction

Sample Answer

Describe an interesting building.

You should say:
- where it is located
- what it looks like
- when it was built
- and explain why you like this building.

Now, I would like to talk about an interesting building.

The structure which I've chosen is Sagrada Familia located in Spain. Last year, I visited Barcelona with my family. While we were there, I went to see this famous building, a large Roman Catholic church.

The building was designed by a famous architect called Gaudi. Gaudi was known to have a very distinctive style as can be seen in other buildings that he is credited for having designed in the city. The church is impressively huge and has a very gothic appearance, which is apparent through its towering spires.

One aspect of this building that I found fascinating is that it has not yet been completed, even though its construction started over 100 years ago, in 1882. This is because Spain's disruptive history, including such events as the Spanish Civil War, meant that building work on the church had to be paused. In fact, it was only in 2010 that the midway point of its construction was passed.

In terms of the architecture, this building is just amazing. The amount of detail and its vastness make the Sagrada Familia an astounding piece of architecture and its history and connection to Gaudi make it a great tourist attraction.

That's all from me, thank you very much for your attention.

PART 3

1) What role do old buildings and new buildings play in modern society?
현대 사회에서 오래된 건물들과 새로운 건물들은 어떤 역할을 해요?

Brainstorming	Direct Answer	오래된 건물들은 전통을 지키기 위해 유지됨
	Supporting Sentence 1	지역을 아름답게 만들고 관광명소가 될 수 있음
	Supporting Sentence 2	경제에 도움이 됨
	Supporting Sentence 3	새로운 건물들은 건강, 안전, 향상된 생활 수준을 위해 중요함

✏️ 다음 불법포인트를 참고해서 영어 문장을 완성해 보자. (주어와 시제, 품사와 단복수 등을 고려할 것!)

❶ 오래된 건물들은 전통을 지키는 것을 돕기 위해서 유지됩니다.
Old buildings are _____ in order to help keep tradition.
※ 유지하다 : maintain(= keep)

❷ 미학적으로 궁전들이나 전통가옥들과 같은 많은 오래된 건물들은 지역을 더 아름답게 보이게 만들고 또한 좋은 관광 명소가 될 수 있습니다.
_____, many old buildings such as _____ or traditional houses make an area look more beautiful and can also be good _____.
※ 미학적으로 : aesthetically / 궁전 : palace / 관광 명소 : tourist attraction

❸ 이것은 관광객들이 이러한 장소들을 방문할 것이기에 경제에 도움이 되는 데 현대 사회에서 중요합니다.
This helps with the _____ since tourists will pay to visit those places, which is important in _____.
※ 경제 : economy / 현대 사회 : modern society

❹ 새로운 건물들은 건강과 안전의 목적 그리고 향상된 생활 수준을 위해서 중요합니다.
New buildings are important for health and _____ and _____ _____.
※ 안전의 목적 : safety purpose / 향상된 생활 수준 : an improved standard of living

Q. What role do old buildings and new buildings play in modern society?
A. Old buildings are maintained in order to help keep tradition. Aesthetically, many old buildings such as palaces or traditional houses make an area look more beautiful and can also be good tourist attractions. This helps with the economy since tourists will pay to visit those places, which is important in modern society. New buildings are important for health and safety purposes and an improved standard of living.

2) What changes have taken place in architecture in the past two decades?
지난 20년 동안 건축에서 어떤 변화들이 일어났어요?

Brainstorming	Direct Answer	현대적이고 서구화됨
	Supporting Sentence 1	서울 같은 도시에서 뚜렷하게 나타남
	Supporting Sentence 2	전면이 유리로 된 고층 건물들이 많이 생김
	Supporting Sentence 3	과거에는 더 작게 설계됨

✏️ 다음 **불법포인트**를 참고해서 영어 문장을 완성해 보자. (주어와 시제, 품사와 단복수 등을 고려할 것!)

❶ 한국에서 건물들의 양식은 매우 현대적이고 한때 지배했던 전통적인 아시아 양식과 비교해서 더 서구화되었습니다.
In Korea, the style of buildings has become very modern and more _____ compared to the traditional Asian style that used to _____ .
※ 서구화된 : westernised / 지배하다 : dominate

❷ 이것은 서울 같은 도시들에서 특히 뚜렷하게 나타납니다.
It is particularly _____ in cities such as Seoul.
※ 뚜렷한 : noticeable

❸ 점점 더 많은 건물들은 전면이 유리로 된 고층 건물들입니다.
More and more buildings are _____ , with glass _____ .
※ 고층 건물 : high-rise skyscraper / (건물의) 전면 : facade

❹ 과거에 빌딩들은 단지 몇 층으로만 구성되어 훨씬 더 작게 설계되었습니다.
In the past, buildings were designed to be much smaller, _____ of just a few floors.
※ 구성되다 : comprise

Q. What changes have taken place in architecture in the past two decades?
A. In Korea, the style of buildings has become very modern and more westernised compared to the traditional Asian style that used to dominate. It is particularly noticeable in cities such as Seoul. More and more buildings are high-rise skyscrapers, with glass facades. In the past, buildings were designed to be much smaller, comprising of just a few floors.

3) Do you think it is necessary to protect old buildings?
당신은 오래된 건물들을 보호하는 것이 필요하다고 생각해요?

Brainstorming	Direct Answer	분명히 그러함
	Supporting Sentence 1	오래된 건물들은 과거와 연결되어 있고 이야기와 전통을 가짐
	Supporting Sentence 2	과거의 기억들을 살아있게 하는데 좋은 방법임

✏️ 다음 불법포인트를 참고해서 영어 문장을 완성해 보자. (주어와 시제, 품사와 단복수 등을 고려할 것!)

❶ 분명히 그렇습니다. 의미 있는 오래된 건물들을 보호하는 것이 대단히 중요합니다.
_____ yes, it is _____ to protect old buildings of _____ .
※ 분명히 : definitely / 대단히 중요한 : crucial / 의미, 중요성 : significance

❷ 오래된 건물들은 과거와 연결되어 있고 그 건물들과 관련된 이야기와 전통을 가지고 있습니다.
Old buildings are connections to the past and have stories and tradition _____ them.
※ ~와 관련된 : associated with

❸ 나는 상당히 감상적인 사람이어서 과거의 기억들을 살아있게 하는 것은 중요하고 오래된 건물들을 보호하고 유지하는 것은 그렇게 하는 데 좋은 방법입니다.
I am quite a _____ person so it is important to _____ the memories of the past _____ and protecting and maintaining old buildings is a good way to do that.
※ 감성적인 : sentimental / ~을 살아있게 하다 : keep ~ alive

Q. Do you think it is necessary to protect old buildings?

A. Definitely yes, it is crucial to protect old buildings of significance. Old buildings are connections to the past and have stories and tradition associated with them. I am quite a sentimental person so it is important to keep the memories of the past alive and protecting and maintaining old buildings is a good way to do that.

4) What do the houses in your country look like?
당신의 나라에 있는 집들은 어떻게 생겼어요?

Brainstorming	Direct Answer	침실이 3개 있는 아파트가 가장 일반적임
	Supporting Sentence 1	도시의 부자들은 고층 아파트 단지에서 삶
	Supporting Sentence 2	정원이 있는 주택은 시골에서 더 흔함

✏️ 다음 **불법포인트**를 참고해서 영어 문장을 완성해 보자. (주어와 시제, 품사와 단복수 등을 고려할 것!)

❶ 요즘 한국에는 몇 가지 다른 형태의 집들이 있지만 침실이 3개 있는 아파트가 가장 일반적입니다.
Nowadays, there are _____ of houses in Korea but three-bedroom flats are the most common.
※ 몇 가지 다른 형태들 : several different types

❷ 도시에서 기반을 둔 일부 부자들은 수영장, 헬스장 그리고 심지어 골프 연습장과 같은 편의 시설을 갖춘 고층아파트 단지에서 삽니다.
Some rich people based in cities live in high-rise apartment blocks with _____ such as a swimming pool, gym and even a _____ .
※ 편의 시설 : convenient facility / 골프 연습장 : driving range

❸ 정원이 있는 주택에서 사는 것은 시골에서 더 흔합니다.
Living in a house with a garden is more common _____ .
※ 시골에서 : in the countryside

Q. What do the houses in your country look like?
A. Nowadays, there are several different types of houses in Korea but three-bedroom flats are the most common. Some rich people based in cities live in high-rise apartment blocks with convenient facilities such as a swimming pool, gym and even a driving range. Living in a house with a garden is more common in the countryside.

Day 11 Building & Design 불법포인트 정리

침실이 3개 있는 아파트	a three bedroom flat / a flat with three bedrooms	건축	architecture
칸막이가 없는, 오픈 플랜식의	open-plan	광대함	vastness
지금까지	so far	믿기 어려운, 놀라운	astounding
대학을 졸업하다	graduate from university	관광 명소	tourist attraction
아파트	flat / apartment	유지하다	maintain / keep
유망한, 떠오르는	up and coming	미학적으로	aesthetically
부티크	boutique	궁전	palace
언젠가	some day	경제	economy
바로	right	현대 사회	modern society
정말 아름다운	just beautiful	안전의 목적	safety purpose
파티를 하다	have a party	향상된 생활 수준	an improved standard of living
금요일 밤마다	every Friday night	서구화된	westernised
관여하다, 역할을 하다	play a part in	지배하다	dominate
창의적인	creative	뚜렷한	noticeable
설계하다	design	고층 건물	high-rise skyscraper
~에 관심 갖다, 신경 쓰다	care about	(건물의) 전면	facade
흥미로운 건물	interesting building	구성되다	comprise
로마 가톨릭 교회	Roman Catholic church	분명히	definitely
~에 의해 설계되다	be designed by	대단히 중요한	crucial
건축가	architect	의미, 중요성	significance
~에게 알려지다	be known to	~와 관련된	associated with
인정받다	be credited for	감성적인	sentimental
누가 봐도 알 수 있는, 분명한	apparent	~을 살아있게 하다	keep ~ alive
우뚝 솟은 첨탑	towering spire	몇 가지 다른 형태들	several different types
매혹적인, 대단히 흥미로운	fascinating	편의 시설	convenient facility
스페인 내전	the Spanish Civil War	골프 연습장	driving range
중단하다, 잠시 멈추다	pause	시골에서	in the countryside
중간의	midway		

Day 12 · IT(Information Technology) 정보기술

PART 1

1) How often do you use the Internet?
2) What are your favourite websites?
3) Would you like to have your own website?
4) Do you think there should be restrictions on what is published on the Internet?
5) What do you use your computer for?
6) Do you think computers are necessary for modern day life?
7) Are there any problems with using computers too much?

PART 2

Describe an Internet business you would like to start.

You should say:
    what the business would be
    what it would involve
    how you would start it
and explain why you think the business would be successful.

PART 3

1) Which websites are popular among your generation?
2) Is using the Internet a social or solitary activity?
3) How has the Internet changed social behaviour?
4) Should companies check job applicants' online profiles?

보이는 Speaking QR 코드

PART 1

1) How often do you use the Internet? 당신은 인터넷을 얼마나 자주 사용해요?

Brainstorming	Direct Answer	매일
	Additional Information	인터넷은 나의 놀이터

✏️ 다음 불법포인트를 참고해서 영어 문장을 완성해 보자. (주어와 시제, 품사와 단복수 등을 고려할 것!)

❶ 나는 연구와 학문, 소셜 미디어 그리고 게임 하기와 같은 다양한 목적으로 매일 인터넷을 이용합니다.
I use the Internet every day for _____ , such as research and study, social media and playing games.
※ 다양한 목적들 : a variety of purposes

❷ 인터넷은 나의 놀이터입니다.
The Internet is my _____ .
※ 놀이터 : playground

Q. How often do you use the Internet?
A. I use the Internet every day for a variety of purposes, such as research and study, social media and playing games. The Internet is my playground.

2) What are your favourite websites? 당신이 가장 좋아하는 웹사이트는 무엇인가요?

Brainstorming	Direct Answer	유투브와 인스타그램
	Additional Information	규칙적으로 확인함

✏️ 다음 불법포인트를 참고해서 영어 문장을 완성해 보자. (주어와 시제, 품사와 단복수 등을 고려할 것!)

❶ 나는 유투브에서 많은 동영상을 보고 인스타그램에서 많은 디자이너들과 예술가들을 추종합니다.
I watch a lot of videos on Youtube and I _____ a lot of designers and artists on Instagram.
※ 추종하다, 따르다 : follow

❷ 그래서 나는 그 사이트들을 규칙적으로 확인합니다.
So, I check those sites out _____ .
※ 규칙적으로 : regularly

Q. What are your favourite websites?
A. I watch a lot of videos on Youtube and I follow a lot of designers and artists on Instagram. So, I check those sites out regularly.

3) **Would you like to have your own website?** 당신 자신의 웹사이트를 가지고 싶으세요?

Brainstorming	Direct Answer	기술에 능숙하지 않기 때문에 별로임
	Additional Information	유지를 계속할 수 없을 것 같음

✏️ 다음 불법포인트를 참고해서 영어 문장을 완성해 보자. (주어와 시제, 품사와 단복수 등을 고려할 것!)

❶ 아니요, 별로, 나는 기술에 매우 능숙하지 않기 때문입니다.
No, _____ because I am not very _____ with technology.
※ 별로, 그다지 : not really / 능숙한 : proficient

❷ 나는 내가 웹사이트를 소유하는 데 필요한 유지를 계속할 수 있다고 생각하지 않습니다.
I don't think I could _____ the _____ required to own a website.
※ 계속하다, 따라가다 : keep up with / 유지 : maintenance

Q. Would you like to have your own website?
A. No, not really because I am not very proficient with technology. I don't think I could keep up with the maintenance required to own a website.

4) **Do you think there should be restrictions on what is published on the Internet?**
당신은 인터넷에 게재되는 것에 대한 제한이 있어야 한다고 생각해요?

Brainstorming	Direct Answer	그렇게 생각하지 않음
	Additional Information	인터넷은 누구에게나 자유롭고 열려있어야 하며, 언론의 자유는 침해 당해서는 안됨

✏️ 다음 불법포인트를 참고해서 영어 문장을 완성해 보자. (주어와 시제, 품사와 단복수 등을 고려할 것!)

❶ 아니요, 나는 그렇게 생각하지 않습니다.
No, _____ .
※ 나는 그렇게 생각하지 않다 : I don't think so

❷ 인터넷은 누구에게나 자유롭고 열려있어야 하며, 어떤 사람의 언론의 자유도 침해 당해서는 안됩니다.
The Internet should be free and open to everyone and anyone's _____ should not be _____ .
※ 언론(표현)의 자유 : freedom of speech / 침해하다 : infringe

Q. Do you think there should be restrictions on what is published on the Internet?
A. No, I don't think so. The Internet should be free and open to everyone and anyone's freedom of speech should not be infringed.

5) What do you use your computer for? 당신은 컴퓨터를 왜 사용해요?

Brainstorming	Direction Answer	업무, 보고서 작성, 프레젠테이션 문서를 만들기 위해 사용함
	Additional Information	페이스북을 통해 친구나 가족에게 연락하기 위해 사용함

✏️ 다음 불법포인트를 참고해서 영어 문장을 완성해 보자. (주어와 시제, 품사와 단복수 등을 고려할 것!)

❶ 나는 업무, 보고서 작성 그리고 프레젠테이션 문서를 만드는 데 컴퓨터를 사용합니다.
I use the computer for work, writing reports and _____ presentations.
※ 만들다 : create

❷ 나는 또한 컴퓨터를 페이스북과 같은 소셜 미디어 사이트를 통해서 내 친구들과 가족에게 연락하기 위해 사용합니다.
I also use it for _____ with my friends and family through social media sites like Facebook.
※ 연락하다 : keep in touch

Q. What do you use your computer for?
A. I use the computer for work, writing reports and creating presentations. I also use it for keeping in touch with my friends and family through social media sites like Facebook.

6) Do you think computers are necessary for modern day life?
당신은 현대의 삶을 위해 컴퓨터가 필요하다고 생각해요?

Brainstorming	Direct Answer	연구와 의사소통을 위한 수단으로 필요함
	Additional Information	이런 종류의 기술 없이는 이러한 것들을 잃게 됨

✏️ 다음 불법포인트를 참고해서 영어 문장을 완성해 보자. (주어와 시제, 품사와 단복수 등을 고려할 것!)

❶ 네, 오늘날 사람들은 컴퓨터를 연구와 의사소통을 위한 수단으로써 의지하고 있습니다.
Yes, nowadays people _____ computers as tools for research and _____ .
※ 의지하다 : be dependent on / 의사소통 : communication

❷ 우리는 이런 종류의 기술이 없이는 (이러한 것들을) 잃게 될 것입니다.
We would be lost without this sort of _____ .
※ 기술 : technology

Q. Do you think computers are necessary for modern day life?
A. Yes, nowadays people are dependent on computers as tools for research and communication. We would be lost without this sort of technology.

7) Are there any problems with using computers too much?
컴퓨터를 너무 많이 사용하는 것에는 어떤 문제들이 있어요?

Brainstorming	Direct Answer	시력 손상
	Additional Information	근육 피로

✏️ 다음 불법포인트를 참고해서 영어 문장을 완성해 보자. (주어와 시제, 품사와 단복수 등을 고려할 것!)

❶ 장시간 동안 컴퓨터 화면을 쳐다보는 것에 의한 사람의 시력 손상과 같은 문제들은 컴퓨터를 너무 많이 사용하는 것에서 발생할 수 있습니다.

Problems can occur from using computers too much, such as _____ to a person's eyesight from looking at a computer screen for _____ .

※ 손상 : damage / 장시간 동안 : prolonged periods of time

❷ 또한 근육 피로도 자주 컴퓨터를 사용하는 사람들의 가장 흔한 통증 중의 하나입니다.

Also _____ is one of the most common _____ of _____ _____ .

※ 근육 피로 : muscle fatigue / (가벼운)통증 : complaint / 자주 컴퓨터를 사용하는 사람 : regular computer user

Q. Are there any problems with using computers too much?
A. Problems can occur from using computers too much, such as damage to a person's eyesight from looking at a computer screen for prolonged periods of time. Also muscle fatigue is one of the most common complaints of regular computer users.

PART 2

Describe an Internet business you would like to start.

You should say:
    what the business would be
    what it would involve
    how you would start it
and explain why you think the business would be successful.

당신이 시작하고 싶은 인터넷 사업을 묘사하세요.

당신은 반드시 말해야 합니다.
    어떤 사업인지
    어떤 것을 포함할 것인지
    어떻게 사업을 시작할 것인지
그리고 당신은 왜 그 사업이 성공할 것이라고 생각하는지 설명하세요.

※ 아직 사회 경험이 없는 어린 학생에게는 이런 질문이 다소 난감하게 느껴질지도 모른다. 너무 거창하게 생각하지 말고, 내가 영어로 잘 설명할 수 있는 아이템을 선정해서, 그것을 인터넷으로 판다고 가정해보자. 아주 자세하게 작성한 사업 계획서를 투자자 앞에서 프레젠테이션 한다는 기분으로 대답해보자.

주어지는 1분을 어떻게 활용할 것인가? (How to Use Your 1 Minute Preparation Time)

1. 질문 파악 인터넷 사업에 초점을 맞추는 문제이다.	내가 영어로 잘 설명할 수 있는 인터넷 사업을 떠올린다.
2. 묘사 대상 결정하기 영어로 가장 자신 있게 묘사할 수 있는 인터넷 사업 아이템을 떠올린다.	인터넷 사업에 대해서 생각해보지 않았다면, 내가 영어로 잘 설명할 수 있는 아이템을 선정해서, 그것을 인터넷으로 판다고 가정해보자.
3. 하위 질문 확인 + 스토리 작성 하위 질문의 개수를 확인하고, 각각에 대한 답을 적는다.	ssub-questions는 3개처럼 보이지만, 마지막 문장의 'and explain why you think the business would be successful'를 포함해서 4개이다. 반드시 4개의 질문에 모두 답하되, 답의 길이는 똑같지 않아도 상관없다.
4. 주제 관련 아카데믹 표현 사용 인터넷 사업과 관련해서 학습한 아카데믹한 표현들을 떠올린다.	an Internet business, start in the near future, an online magazine, a variety of sections, lifestyle, travel and events, so many different sections, international, encourage, freelance writers, contribute, advertise on my web magazine, generate revenue, successful, be full of, well written, informative and interesting, all over the world, guarantee, information, accurate and up-to-date
5. 주의해야 할 문법 문제의 시제 및 인칭 대명사 등을 확인한다.	미래에 할 사업에 대해 상상력을 동원해서 대답해야 하는 문제이다. 미래에 대한 강의 의지를 내포한 'will' 보다는 '~일(할) 것이다'는 의미의 'would'를 사용하자. 미래에 벌어질 상상하는 일의 결과에 대해 말할 때는 'would'가 더 자연스럽다. would = wIll + 상상/가정

Brainstorming

Sub-question 1 what the business would be	'열심히 일하고 열심히 놀아라'라는 온라인 잡지
Sub-question 2 what it would involve	음식, 패션, 생활방식, 여행 그리고 행사가 포함된 다양한 섹션을 가진 잡지
Sub-question 3 how you would start it	나와 프리랜서 작가들이 국제적인 기사를 씀. 수익 창출을 위해 회사들의 광고 유치
Sub-question 4 and explain why you think the business would be successful	다른 어떤 곳에서도 게재되지 않은 잘 작성되고, 유익하며, 재미있는 기사들로 가득. 전 세계에서 기사들을 기고할 프리랜서 작가들을 통해, 정확하고 최신의 정보라는 것을 보장

✎ **다음 불법포인트를 참고해서 영어 문장을 완성해 보자. (주어와 시제, 품사와 단복수 등을 고려할 것!)**

❶ 지금 나는 가까운 미래에 내가 시작하고 싶은 인터넷 사업에 대해 말할 것입니다.
Now, I'm going to talk about an Internet business I would like to start _____ .
※ 가까운 미래에 : in the near future

❷ 내가 선택한 사업은 '열심히 일하고 열심히 놀아라'라는 온라인 잡지입니다.
The business that I've chosen is an online _____ , called 'Work Hard Play Hard'.
※ 잡지 : magazine

❸ 나는 이미 음식 블로그를 쓰고 있지만 나는 패션, 생활방식, 여행 그리고 행사가 포함된 다양한 섹션을 가진 잡지로 확장하고 싶습니다.
I already write a food blog but I would like to _____ it into a magazine with a variety of sections, including fashion, _____ , travel and events.
※ 확장하다 : expand / 생활방식 : lifestyle

❹ 나는 내 스스로 많은 기사들을 쓰고 싶지만, 나는 정말 많은 다른 섹션을 가진 잡지를 원하고 이 잡지가 국제적이기를 원하기 때문에 나는 기사들을 기고하도록 프리랜서 작가들을 장려할 것입니다. 나는 또한 수익을 창출하기 위해서 내 온라인 잡지에 회사들이 광고하도록 일할 필요가 있을 것입니다.
I would like to write a lot of the _____ myself but since I want the magazine to have so many different sections and I would like it to be _____ , I would _____ freelance writers to _____ pieces. I would also need to work on getting companies to _____ on my web magazine in order for me to _____ .
※ 기사 : article / 국제적인 : international / 장려하다 : encourage / 기고하다, 기여하다 : contribute
  광고하다 : advertise / 수익을 창출하다 : generate revenue

❺ 나는 온라인 잡지가 성공할 것이라고 생각하는데, 다른 어떤 곳에서도 게재되지 않은 잘 작성되고, 유익하며, 재미있는 기사들로 가득할 것이기 때문입니다. 전 세계에서 기사들을 기고할 프리랜서 작가들을 통해 정확하고 최신의 정보라는 것을 보장할 것입니다.
I think it would be _____ because it would _____ well written, _____ and interesting pieces that have not been published anywhere else. By getting freelance writers from all over the world to contribute articles, it would _____ that information is accurate and _____ .
※ 성공적인 : successful / ~로 가득 차다 : be full of / 유익한 : informative / 보장하다 : guarantee
  최신의 : up-to-date

Sample Answer

Describe an Internet business you would like to start.

You should say:
- what the business would be
- what it would involve
- how you would start it

and explain why you think the business would be successful.

Now, I'm going to talk about an Internet business I would like to start in the near future.

The business that I've chosen is an online magazine, called 'Work Hard Play Hard'.

I already write a food blog but I would like to expand it into a magazine with a variety of sections, including fashion, lifestyle, travel and events.

I would like to write a lot of the articles myself but since I want the magazine to have so many different sections and I would like it to be international, I would encourage freelance writers to contribute pieces. I would also need to work on getting companies to advertise on my web magazine in order for me to generate revenue.

I think it would be successful because it would be full of well written, informative and interesting pieces that have not been published anywhere else. By getting freelance writers from all over the world to contribute articles, it would guarantee that information is accurate and up-to-date.

That's all from me, thank you very much for your attention.

PART 3

1) Which websites are popular among your generation? 당신 세대에는 어떤 웹사이트가 인기 있어요?

Brainstorming	Direct Answer	소셜 미디어 관련 웹사이트
	Supporting Sentence 1	페이스북, 트위터, 인스타그램으로 서로 연락이 가능함
	Supporting Sentence 2	사람들의 일을 홍보, 스스로 시사 문제와 친구들의 생활을 업데이트

✏️ 다음 불법포인트를 참고해서 영어 문장을 완성해 보자. (주어와 시제, 품사와 단복수 등을 고려할 것!)

❶ 소셜 미디어와 관련된 웹사이트가 내 세대에서 특히 인기가 있습니다.
Websites related to social media are particularly popular among my _____ .
※ 세대 : generation

❷ 페이스북, 트위터 그리고 인스타그램과 같은 사이트들은 사람들이 서로 연락하는 것을 가능하게 합니다.
Sites such as Facebook, Twitter and Instagram allow people to _____ .
※ 서로 연락하다 : connect with each other

❸ 이러한 웹사이트들은 또한 그들의 일을 홍보하고 그들에게 시사 문제들과 친구들의 생활에 대해 지속적으로 업데이트하게 합니다.
Those websites also _____ their work and keep them updated on _____ and their friends' lives.
※ 홍보하다 : promote / 시사 문제 : current event

Q. Which websites are popular among your generation?
A. Websites related to social media are particularly popular among my generation. Sites such as Facebook, Twitter and Instagram allow people to connect with each other. Those websites also promote their work and keep them updated on current events and their friends' lives.

2) Is using the Internet a social or solitary activity?

인터넷을 이용하는 것은 사회 활동이에요? 혼자 하는 활동이에요?

Brainstorming	Direct Answer	인터넷 서핑은 개인 활동
	Supporting Sentence 1	우리가 얼굴을 맞대고 이야기하는 양을 줄임
	Supporting Sentence 2	우리 모두를 더 은둔하게 만듦

✏️ 다음 **불법포인트**를 참고해서 영어 문장을 완성해 보자. (주어와 시제, 품사와 단복수 등을 고려할 것!)

❶ 비록 요즘 가장 인기 있는 웹사이트 중 일부가 소셜 미디어 사이트이기는 하지만, 나는 인터넷을 서핑 하는 것은 혼자 하는 활동이라고 생각합니다.
Although some of the most popular websites these days are social media sites, I think that surfing the net is a _____ .
※ 혼자 하는 활동 : solitary activity

❷ 소셜 미디어는 사람과 접촉하는 편리한 방법이지만, 이것은 근본적으로 우리가 사람들과 얼굴을 맞대고 이야기하는 시간의 양을 줄입니다.
While social media is a _____ of contacting people, it is ultimately reducing the amount of time we spend talking to people face to face.
※ 편리한 방법 : convenient method

❸ 더 심각하게 인터넷은 틀림없이 우리 모두를 약간 더 은둔하게 만듭니다.
More seriously, the Internet arguably makes us all a little more _____ .
※ 은둔한 : reclusive

Q. Is using the Internet a social or solitary activity?

A. Although some of the most popular websites these days are social media sites, I think that surfing the net is a solitary activity. While social media is a convenient method of contacting people, it is ultimately reducing the amount of time we spend talking to people face to face. More seriously, the Internet arguably makes us all a little more reclusive.

3) **How has the Internet changed social behaviour?** 인터넷은 사회적 행동을 어떻게 변화시켰어요?

Brainstorming	Direct Answer	더 낫게 변화 - 오랜 친구들과 다시 연결
	Supporting Sentence 1	사람들을 더 용감하게 만듦
	Supporting Sentence 2	얼굴을 맞대기 보다는 컴퓨터 화면 뒤에서 의견을 표현하는 게 더 쉬움
	Supporting Sentence 3	더 나쁘게 변화시키기도 함
	Supporting Sentence 4	사람들은 메시지에 의존함

✏️ 다음 불법포인트를 참고해서 영어 문장을 완성해 보자. (주어와 시제, 품사와 단복수 등을 고려할 것!)

❶ 어떤 면에서 사람들은 연락이 끊겼을지도 모를 오랜 친구들과 다시 연결되는 것이 더 쉬워졌기 때문에 인터넷은 사회적 행동을 더 낫게 변화시켰습니다.

In one sense, the Internet has changed _____ for the better since it is easier to reconnect with old friends that people may have _____ .

※ 사회적 행동 : social behaviour / 연락이 끊기다 : lose contact with

❷ 인터넷은 또한 사람들이 말하는 것에 있어 더 용감하게 했습니다.

The Internet has also made people _____ with what they say.   ※ 더 용감한 : braver

❸ 이것은 서로 얼굴을 맞대고 누군가에게 말하는 것과는 대조적으로 컴퓨터 화면 뒤에 있다는 안전 장치를 갖고 의견을 표현하기가 더 쉽기 때문입니다.

This is because it is easier to _____ with the safety of being behind a computer screen _____ saying it to someone, face to face.

※ 의견을 표현하다 : express an opinion / ~과는 대조적으로 : as opposed to

❹ 하지만 인터넷은 더 나쁘게 사회적 활동을 변화시켰습니다.

However, the Internet has changed social behaviour _____ .

※ 더 나쁘게 : for the worse

❺ 사람들은 메시지에 의존하는 경향이 있는데, 이것은 노력은 덜 요구하면서도 덜 개인적일 수 있기 때문입니다.

People tend to rely on messages to communicate since it requires less effort, but that can also feel less _____ .

※ 개인적인 : personal

Q. How has the Internet changed social behaviour?

A. In one sense, the Internet has changed social behaviour for the better since it is easier to reconnect with old friends that people may have lost contact with. The Internet has also made people braver with what they say. This is because it is easier to express an opinion with the safety of being behind a computer screen as opposed to saying it to someone, face to face. However, the Internet has changed social behaviour for the worse. People tend to rely on messages to communicate since it requires less effort, but that can also feel less personal.

4) Should companies check job applicants' online profiles?
회사들은 구직자들의 온라인 프로필을 확인해야 할까요?

Brainstorming	Direct Answer	사생활 침해이기에 확인하면 안됨
	Supporting Sentence 1	한 개인의 사생활이 업무를 반영하지 않음
	Supporting Sentence 2	하지만 회사들이 지원자들의 온라인 프로필을 확인할 것이기에 스스로 조심해야 함

✏️ 다음 불법포인트를 참고해서 영어 문장을 완성해 보자. (주어와 시제, 품사와 단복수 등을 고려할 것!)

❶ 나는 회사들이 구직자들의 온라인 프로필을 확인해야 한다고 생각하지 않는데, 이것은 누군가의 사생활 침해이기 때문입니다.
I don't think that companies should check job applicants' online profiles since that is an _____ of someone's _____ .
※ 침해 : invasion / 사생활 : private life

❷ 한 개인의 사생활은 그들이 근무 상황에서 고용인으로서 어떻게 업무를 수행할지를 반영하지 않을지도 모릅니다.
A person's private lifestyle may bear no _____ on how they would _____ as an employee in a work situation.
※ 반영 : reflection / (일을) 수행하다 : perform

❸ 하지만 회사들이 지원자의 온라인 프로필을 확인할 것이라고 점점 더 예상되기 때문에, 나는 그들이 인터넷 상에서 모든 사람들에게 어떻게 보여지는지에 대해 조심하는 것이 중요하다고 생각합니다.
However, since it is increasingly expected that companies will check _____ online profiles, I think it is important for people to be careful about how they are representing themselves _____ on the Internet.
※ 지원자 : applicant / 모든 사람들이 볼 수 있게, 누가 봐도 : for all to see

Q. Should companies check job applicants' online profiles?

A. I don't think that companies should check job applicants' online profiles since that is an invasion of someone's private life. A person's private lifestyle may bear no reflection on how they would perform as an employee in a work situation. However, since it is increasingly expected that companies will check applicants' online profiles, I think it is important for people to be careful about how they are representing themselves for all to see on the Internet.

Day 12 IT(Information Technology) 불법포인트 정리

다양한 목적들	a variety of purposes	기고하다, 기여하다	contribute
놀이터	playground	광고하다	advertise
추종하다, 따르다	follow	수익을 창출하다	generate revenue
규칙적으로	regularly	성공적인	successful
별로, 그다지	not really	~로 가득차다	be full of
능숙한	proficient	유익한	informative
계속하다, 따라가다	keep up with	보장하다	guarantee
유지	maintenance	최신의	up-to-date
나는 그렇게 생각하지 않다	I don't think so	세대	generation
언론(표현)의 자유	freedom of speech	서로 연락하다	connect with each other
침해하다	infringe	홍보하다	promote
만들다	create	시사 문제	current event
연락하다	keep in touch	혼자 하는 활동	solitary activity
의지하다	be dependent on	편리한 방법	convenient method
의사소통	communication	은둔한	reclusive
기술	technology	사회적 행동	social behaviour
손상	damage	연락이 끊기다	lose contact with
장시간 동안	prolonged periods of time	더 용감한	braver
근육 피로	muscle fatigue	의견을 표현하다	express an opinion
(가벼운) 통증	complaint	~과는 대조적으로	as opposed to
자주 컴퓨터를 사용하는 사람	regular computer user	더 나쁘게	for the worse
가까운 미래에	in the near future	개인적인	personal
잡지	magazine	침해	invasion
확장하다	expand	사생활	private life
생활방식	lifestyle	반영	reflection
기사	article	(일을) 수행하다	perform
국제적인	international	지원자	applicant
장려하다	encourage	모든 사람들이 볼 수 있게, 누가 봐도	for all to see

Day 13 Shopping & Party 쇼핑과 파티

PART 1

1) Do you like shopping?
2) Why doesn't everyone like shopping?
3) Why do you think that some people prefer to use the Internet for shopping?
4) Are there any kinds of products that are easier to buy online?
5) Why are some people late for parties intentionally?
6) Why do some people like to party while others hate it?
7) Do you think parties will become more popular in the future?

PART 2

Describe a traditional festival in your country.

You should say:
   what it is
   when it is celebrated
   how you celebrate it
and explain what you like and what you don't like about it.

PART 3

1) Is shopping a popular activity in your country?
2) How have shopping habits changed over recent years?
3) To what extent do you think advertising affects the way people shop?
4) Do you think shopping habits are likely to change in the future?

보이는 Speaking QR 코드

PART 1

1) Do you like shopping? 당신은 쇼핑을 좋아해요?

Brainstorming	Direct Answer	좋아함, 신발 쇼핑 중독
	Additional Information	발렌티노 락스터드 플랫 슈즈 시리즈를 모으고 있음

✏️ 다음 **불법포인트**를 참고해서 영어 문장을 완성해 보자. (주어와 시제, 품사와 단복수 등을 고려할 것!)

> ❶ 네, 나는 쇼핑을 좋아합니다. 나는 특히 신발에 있어서 약간 쇼핑 중독자입니다.
> Yes, I do. I am a bit of a _____ , particularly for shoes.
> ※ 쇼핑 중독자 : shopaholic
>
> ❷ 나는 요즘 발렌티노 락스터드 플랫 슈즈 시리즈를 모으고 있습니다.
> I am _____ a series of Valentino Rockstud _____ nowadays.
> ※ 모으다, 수집하다 : collect / 플랫 슈즈, 굽이 낮은 신발 : flat shoes

Q. Do you like shopping?
A. Yes, I do. I am a bit of a shopaholic, particularly for shoes. I am collecting a series of Valentino Rockstud flat shoes nowadays.

2) Why doesn't everyone like shopping? 왜 모든 사람들이 쇼핑을 좋아하지 않아요?

Brainstorming	Direct Answer	긴 활동이어서 싫증이 날 수 있음
	Additional Information	남자들 대부분이 쇼핑을 좋아하지 않음

✏️ 다음 **불법포인트**를 참고해서 영어 문장을 완성해 보자. (주어와 시제, 품사와 단복수 등을 고려할 것!)

> ❶ 쇼핑은 긴 활동이 될 수 있어서 몇몇 사람들은 쇼핑을 지루해합니다.
> Since shopping can be a long activity, some people _____ it.
> ※ ~에 지루해하다 : get bored with
>
> ❷ 영국에서 실시한 어떤 설문조사에 따르면, 80%의 남자들이 그들의 파트너와 쇼핑하는 것을 좋아하지 않았고 45%는 무슨 수를 써서라도 그렇게 하는 것을 피했습니다.
> According to a survey _____ in England, 80 percent of men didn't like shopping with their partners, and 45 percent avoided doing so _____ .
> ※ 실시하다 : conduct / 무슨 수를 써서라도 : at all costs

Q. Why doesn't everyone like shopping?
A. Since shopping can be a long activity, some people get bored with it. According to a survey conducted in England, 80 percent of men didn't like shopping with their partners, and 45 percent avoided doing so at all costs.

3) **Why do you think that some people prefer to use the Internet for shopping?**
당신은 왜 어떤 사람들이 쇼핑을 하기 위해 인터넷을 이용하는 것을 더 좋아한다고 생각해요?

Brainstorming	Direct Answer	찾는 것을 정확하게 검색할 수 있어서 편리함
	Additional Information	현관까지 곧바로 배송됨

✏️ 다음 불법포인트를 참고해서 영어 문장을 완성해 보자. (주어와 시제, 품사와 단복수 등을 고려할 것!)

❶ 어떤 사람들은 인터넷 쇼핑을 더 좋아하는데, 그들이 찾는 것을 정확하게 검색할 수 있다는 점에서 매우 편리하기 때문입니다.
Some people prefer Internet shopping because it is very convenient in that a person can search for exactly what they are _____ . ※ 찾다 : look for

❷ 또 다른 이유는 집에서 나갈 필요도 없이 고객의 현관까지 곧바로 제품이 배송된다는 점입니다.
Another reason is that products are _____ directly to the customer's _____ , without them ever having to leave the house.
※ 배송하다 : deliver / 현관 : front door

Q. Why do you think that some people prefer to use the Internet for shopping?
A. Some people prefer Internet shopping because it is very convenient in that a person can search for exactly what they are looking for. Another reason is that products are delivered directly to the customer's front door, without them ever having to leave the house.

4) **Are there any kinds of products that are easier to buy online?** 온라인에서 사는 게 더 쉬운 제품의 종류가 있어요?

Brainstorming	Direct Answer	가전 제품
	Additional Information	몇 번의 마우스 클릭으로 가격과 제품 사양을 비교할 수 있음

✏️ 다음 불법포인트를 참고해서 영어 문장을 완성해 보자. (주어와 시제, 품사와 단복수 등을 고려할 것!)

❶ 나는 다리미와 커피 메이커와 같은 작은 제품부터 냉장고와 식기 세척기 같은 더 큰 것들까지, 가전 제품들은 온라인으로 사는 것이 더 쉽다고 생각합니다.
I find it easier to buy _____ online, ranging from small products such as irons and coffee makers, to larger ones like refrigerators and dishwashers.
※ 가전 제품 : electrical home appliances

❷ 이 제품들은 예를 들면 옷처럼 입어볼 필요가 없고 온라인 쇼핑객들은 구매 버튼을 누르기 전에 가격과 제품 사양을 비교할 수 있기 때문입니다.
This is because these items don't need to be tried on like clothes, for example, and online shoppers can easily compare prices and _____ before hitting the purchase button.   ※ 제품 사양 : product description

Q. Are there any kinds of products that are easier to buy online?
A. I find it easier to buy electrical home appliances online, ranging from small products such as irons and coffee makers, to larger ones like refrigerators and dishwashers. This is because these items don't need to be tried on like clothes, for example, and online shoppers can easily compare prices and product descriptions before hitting the purchase button.

5) **Why are some people late for parties intentionally?** 왜 어떤 사람들은 의도적으로 파티에 늦어요?

Brainstorming	Direction Answer	파티가 한창 진행 중일 때 도착하기를 원함
	Additional Information	멋지게 등장하는 것을 좋아함

✏️ 다음 불법포인트를 참고해서 영어 문장을 완성해 보자. (주어와 시제, 품사와 단복수 등을 고려할 것!)

❶ 어떤 사람들은 일부러 늦게 도착하는데, 그들은 파티가 한창 진행 중 때 도착하기를 원하기 때문입니다.
Some people are _____ because they want to arrive at a party when it is _____ .
※ 일부러 늦게 도착하는 : fashionably late(제 시간에 올 수도 있지만 중요한 사람처럼 보이려고 일부러 약간 늦게 나타나는 것)
한창 진행 중인 : in full swing

❷ 그들은 멋지게 등장하는 것을 좋아할지도 모릅니다.
They may like to _____ .   ※ 멋지게 등장하다 : make a big entrance

Q. **Why are some people late for parties intentionally?**
A. Some people are fashionably late because they want to arrive at a party when it is in full swing. They may like to make a big entrance.

6) **Why do some people like to party while others hate it?**
왜 다른 사람들은 파티를 싫어하는 반면 어떤 사람들은 파티를 좋아해요?

Brainstorming	Direct Answer	사교적인 사람들은 새로운 사람들을 만나고 어울릴 기회를 얻어서 좋아함
	Additional Information	내성적인 사람들은 벽의 꽃이 되는 경향이 있어 싫어함

✏️ 다음 불법포인트를 참고해서 영어 문장을 완성해 보자. (주어와 시제, 품사와 단복수 등을 고려할 것!)

❶ 사교적인 사람들은 보통 파티를 좋아하는데 새로운 사람을 만나고 어울릴 기회를 그들에게 주기 때문입니다.
People who are _____ usually like parties since it gives them an opportunity to meet new people and _____ .
※ 사교적인, 외향적인 : outgoing / 어울리다 : mingle

❷ 하지만 좀 더 내성적인 사람들은 파티를 싫어할지도 모르는데 그들은 이러한 모임에서 벽의 꽃이 되는 경향이 있기 때문입니다.
However, others who are more _____ may hate parties because they tend to be _____ at such gatherings.
※ 내성적인 : introverted / 벽의 꽃 : wallflower(파티에서 파트너가 없어 춤을 추지 못해 벽에 붙어 서있는 인기 없는 사람)

Q. **Why do some people like to party while others hate it?**
A. People who are outgoing usually like parties since it gives them an opportunity to meet new people and mingle. However, others who are more introverted may hate parties because they tend to be wallflowers at such gatherings.

7) Do you think parties will become more popular in the future?
당신은 미래에 파티가 더 인기가 있을 것이라고 생각해요?

Brainstorming	Direct Answer	사람들이 더 많이 파티에 갈 것이라고 생각하지 않음
	Additional Information	온라인 커뮤니티의 성장으로 인터넷으로 교류하고 사귈 것임

✎ 다음 불법포인트를 참고해서 영어 문장을 완성해 보자. (주어와 시제, 품사와 단복수 등을 고려할 것!)

❶ 아니요. 나는 사람들이 자주 파티에 갈 것이라고 생각하지 않습니다.
No, I don't think that people will go to parties _____ .
※ 자주 : frequently

❷ 온라인 커뮤니티의 급속한 성장으로 사람들은 직접 (만나기) 보다는 인터넷으로 서로 교류하고 사귈 것입니다.
Due to a boom in online communities, individuals will interact and socialise with each other _____ rather than in person.
※ 인터넷으로 : via the Internet

Q. Do you think parties will become more popular in the future?
A. No, I don't think that people will go to parties frequently. Due to a boom in online communities, individuals will interact and socialise with each other via the Internet rather than in person.

PART 2

Describe a traditional festival in your country.

You should say:
    what it is
    when it is celebrated
    how you celebrate it
and explain what you like and what you don't like about it.

당신 나라의 전통적인 축제에 대해서 묘사하세요.

당신은 반드시 말해야 합니다.
    그것이 무엇인지
    언제 기념하는지
    당신은 어떻게 축하하는지
그리고 이 축제에 대해 당신이 좋아하는 것과 좋아하지 않는 것은 무엇인지 설명하세요.

※ 전통적인 축제에 대한 대답을 준비할 때 본인의 아이디어로 무작정 영작하기 보다는, 구글(www.google.co.uk)에서 Chuseok이나 Korean New Year라고 영어로 된 검색어를 넣어서 영문으로 된 내용들을 인용해보자. 문법적 오류를 줄일 수 있고, reading 실력 향상에도 도움이 된다.

주어지는 1분을 어떻게 활용할 것인가? (How to Use Your 1 Minute Preparation Time)

1. 질문 파악 전통적인 축제 묘사에 초점을 맞추는 문제이다.	내가 영어로 잘 설명할 수 있는 전통적인 축제를 떠올린다. 최근에 만들어진 머드 축제나 부산 국제 영화제 등은 '전통적인' 축제와는 거리가 있다.
2. 묘사 대상 결정하기 영어로 가장 자신 있게 묘사할 수 있는 전통적인 축제를 떠올린다.	traditional festival이라고 하면 어떤 것을 말해야 할지 고민일 수도 있다. 우리나라의 명절도 traditional festival이다. 답변을 미리 준비하지 못했다면, 설날이나 추석을 떠올리자.
3. 하위 질문 확인 + 스토리 작성 하위 질문의 개수를 확인하고, 각각에 대한 답을 적는다.	sub-questions는 3개처럼 보이지만, 마지막 문장의 'and explain what you like and what you don't like about it'를 포함해서 4개이다. 반드시 4개의 질문에 모두 답하되, 답의 길이는 똑같지 않아도 상관없다.
4. 주제 관련 아카데믹 표현 사용 전통적인 축제와 관련해서 학습한 아카데믹한 표현들을 떠올린다.	an important festival, Chuseok, a harvest festival, spend time with their families, pay respects to the spirits of their ancestors, a lot of traditional foods and games, very difficult to travel around, ancestral hometowns, be overrun with crowds, the holiday
5. 주의해야 할 문법 문제의 시제 및 인칭 대명사 등을 확인한다.	전통적인 축제를 묘사하는 문제로 현재 시제를 쓴다.

Brainstorming

Sub-question 1 what it is	추석, 추수 감사제
Sub-question 2 when it is celebrated	가을 중순, 음력 8월 15일, 3일간
Sub-question 3 how you celebrate it	가족들과 시간을 보내고 조상들의 영혼을 기리기 위해 고향으로 돌아감, 많은 전통 음식과 가족들과 하는 게임들이 있음
Sub-question 4 and explain what you like and what you don't like about it	흩어진 가족들이 모여 이야기 나누기에 좋은 시간, 하지만 대중 교통은 사람들로 넘쳐 남

✏️ **다음 불법포인트를 참고해서 영어 문장을 완성해 보자. (주어와 시제, 품사와 단복수 등을 고려할 것!)**

❶ 지금 나는 한국의 중요한 축제에 대해 이야기하고 싶습니다.
Now, I would like to talk about an important _____ in Korea.
※ 축제 : festival

❷ 나는 추수 감사제인 추석을 선택했습니다.
I've chosen Chuseok, which is a _____ .
※ 추수 감사제 : harvest festival

❸ 가을 중순에 특별히, 음력 8월 15일에 3일 동안에 기념합니다.
It is celebrated for three days in the middle of autumn, _____ on the 15th day of the eighth _____ month.
※ 구체적으로 말하면 : specifically / 음력의 : lunar

❹ 이 기간 동안 한국 사람들은 그들의 가족들과 시간을 보내고 산소 방문으로 조상들의 영혼을 기리기 위해 고향으로 돌아갑니다. 보통 많은 전통 음식과 친척들끼리 하는 게임들이 있습니다.
During this period, Korean people travel back to their hometowns in order to spend time with their families and _____ to the spirits of their _____ by visiting their _____ . Usually, there are a lot of traditional foods and games played amongst relatives.
※ 기리다, 경의를 표하다 : pay respects / 조상 : ancestor / 산소, 무덤 : grave

❺ 대가족들은 보통 전국적으로 많은 다른 장소나 전 세계에까지 흩어져 있기 때문에 추석은 한 장소에서 모든 사람들과 못다한 이야기를 나누기에 좋은 시간입니다. 하지만 한국의 모든 사람들이 같은 계획을 염두에 두기 때문에, 그 기간 동안 이동하는 것은 매우 어려울 수 있습니다. 대부분의 사람들은 오늘날 도시에서 살지만 조상의 고향은 보통 더 작거나 더 시골의 외딴 지역입니다. 그래서 모두가 같은 시간, 같은 장소에 도착하려고 할 때 대중교통은 사람들로 넘쳐 납니다. 이동적인 측면이 내가 기대하지 않은 유일한 부분입니다.
It is a great time to _____ everyone in one place because large families are usually _____ in many different locations around the country, or even across the world. However, since everyone in Korea _____ the same plan _____ , it can be very difficult to travel around during that time. Most people these days live in cities but _____ hometowns are usually in smaller, more remote areas of the country. So when everyone tries to get to the same places at the same time, public transport _____ . The travel aspect is the only part of the holiday that I don't _____ .
※ 못다한 이야기를 나누다, 따라잡다 : catch up with / 흩어지게 하다 : scatter / ~을 염두하다 : have ~ in mind
   조상의 : ancestral / 사람들로 가득 차다 : get overrun with crowds / 기대하다 : look forward to

Sample Answer

> Describe a traditional festival in your country.
>
> You should say:
> what it is
> when it is celebrated
> how you celebrate it
> and explain what you like and what you don't like about it.

Now, I would like to talk about an important festival in Korea.

I've chosen Chuseok, which is a harvest festival.

It is celebrated for three days in the middle of autumn, specifically on the 15th day of the eighth lunar month.

During this period, Korean people travel back to their hometowns in order to spend time with their families and pay respects to the spirits of their ancestors by visiting their graves. Usually, there are a lot of traditional foods and games played amongst relatives.

It is a great time to catch up with everyone in one place because large families are usually scattered in many different locations around the country, or even across the world. However, since everyone in Korea has the same plan in mind, it can be very difficult to travel around during that time. Most people these days live in cities but ancestral hometowns are usually in smaller, more remote areas of the country. So when everyone tries to get to the same places at the same time, public transport gets overrun with crowds. The travel aspect is the only part of the holiday that I don't look forward to.

That's all from me, thank you very much for your attention.

PART 3

1) Is shopping a popular activity in your country? 당신의 나라에서 쇼핑은 인기 있는 활동인가요?

Brainstorming		
	Direct Answer	현지인과 관광객 모두에게 매우 있기 있는 활동임
	Supporting Sentence 1	명동과 동대문 같은 쇼핑 명소들이 있음
	Supporting Sentence 2	몇몇 다른 국가들 보다는 더 저렴함
	Supporting Sentence 3	명품 브랜드 옷과 화장품은 중국보다 더 저렴해서 중국인 관광객이 많이 옴

✎ 다음 **불법포인트**를 참고해서 영어 문장을 완성해 보자. (주어와 시제, 품사와 단복수 등을 고려할 것!)

❶ 네, 쇼핑은 한국에서 현지인들과 관광객들 모두에게 매우 인기 있는 활동입니다.
Yes, shopping is a very popular activity in Korea, for both _____ and tourists.
※ 현지인들 : locals

❷ 사람들로 항상 붐비는 명동과 동대문 같이 쇼핑 명소로 알려진 몇몇 장소들이 있습니다.
There are several areas which are renowned as _____ like Myeongdong and Dongdaemoon, and they are always crowded with people.
※ 쇼핑 명소 : shopping destination

❸ 한국에서 쇼핑이 저렴하지는 않지만 몇몇 다른 국가들 보다는 더 저렴합니다.
While shopping is not cheap in Korea, it is _____ than in some other countries.
※ 더 저렴한, 더 싼 : more affordable

❹ 예를 들어, 많은 중국인 관광객들은 중국에서보다 여기에서 사는 것이 더 싸기 때문에 명품 브랜드 옷들과 화장품을 사기 위해서 한국에 옵니다.
For example, many Chinese _____ come to Korea to buy luxury brand clothes and cosmetics since they are cheaper to buy here than they are in China.
※ 관광객 : tourist

Q. Is shopping a popular activity in your country?
A. Yes, shopping is a very popular activity in Korea, for both locals and tourists. There are several areas which are renowned as shopping destinations like Myeongdong and Dongdaemun, and they are always crowded with people. While shopping is not cheap in Korea, it is more affordable than in some other countries. For example, many Chinese tourists come to Korea to buy luxury brand clothes and cosmetics since they are cheaper to buy here than they are in China.

2) How have shopping habits changed over recent years?
최근 몇 년 간 쇼핑 습관은 어떻게 변했어요?

Brainstorming		
	Direct Answer	더 많은 가처분 수입으로 더 많은 사치품들을 살 수 있음
	Supporting Sentence 1	패션으로 명확하게 증명됨
	Supporting Sentence 2	서울은 최고의 패션 도시 중의 하나가 됨
	Supporting Sentence 3	유행에 민감한 이미지를 따라 잡기 위해 쇼핑 습관을 바꿈

✏️ 다음 불법포인트를 참고해서 영어 문장을 완성해 보자. (주어와 시제, 품사와 단복수 등을 고려할 것!)

❶ 사람들은 더 많은 가처분 수입을 가지고 있고 이것은 사람들이 더 많은 불필요한 물건들과 사치품들을 살 수 있다는 것을 의미합니다.
People have more _____ now, which means that they are able to buy more unnecessary goods and luxury items.
※ 가처분 소득 : disposable income(개인소득 가운데 소비 또는 저축을 자유롭게 할 수 있는 소득)

❷ 이것은 패션을 통해서 가장 명확하게 증명됩니다.
This is most clearly _____ through fashion.
※ 증명하다 : demonstrate

❸ 서울은 런던, 뉴욕 그리고 파리와 같은 장소들과 함께 패션과 관련된 최고의 도시들 중의 하나가 되었습니다.
Seoul has become one of the top cities associated with fashion _____ places such as London, New York and Paris.
※ ~와 함께, 나란히 : alongside

❹ 그러므로 사람들이 이 나라가 보여주는 유행에 민감한 이미지를 따라 잡기 위해서 그들의 쇼핑 습관을 바꾼 것은 놀랍지 않습니다.
Therefore, it is no surprise that people have changed their shopping habits to _____ the _____ image the country portrays.
※ 따라잡다, 뒤지지 않다 : keep up with / 유행에 민감한 : fashion conscious

Q. How have shopping habits changed over recent years?
A. People have more disposable income now, which means that they are able to buy more unnecessary goods and luxury items. This is most clearly demonstrated through fashion. Seoul has become one of the top cities associated with fashion alongside places such as London, New York and Paris. Therefore, it is no surprise that people have changed their shopping habits to keep up with the fashion conscious image the country portrays.

3) To what extent do you think advertising affects the way people shop?
당신은 사람들이 쇼핑하는 방식에 광고가 어느 정도로 영향을 미친다고 생각해요?

Brainstorming	Direct Answer	엄청난 영향을 줌
	Supporting Sentence 1	사람들이 갈망하는 무언가로서 상품과 서비스를 묘사함
	Supporting Sentence 2	사람들의 감성을 자극함

✏️ 다음 불법포인트를 참고해서 영어 문장을 완성해 보자. (주어와 시제, 품사와 단복수 등을 고려할 것!)

❶ 비록 나는 대부분이 잠재의식이라고 생각하지만 광고는 사람들이 쇼핑하는 방식에 엄청난 영향을 줍니다.
Advertising _____ the way people shop, although I believe most of it to be _____ .
※ ~에 엄청난 영향을 주다 : have a huge effect on / 잠재의식적인 : subconscious

❷ 광고는 사람들이 성취하거나 소유하기를 갈망하는 무언가로서 상품과 서비스를 묘사합니다.
Advertising _____ goods or services as something for people to _____ to achieve or to own.
※ 묘사하다 : portray / 갈망하다 : aspire

❸ 이것은 그들의 감정을 자극하고, 만약 광고에서 치장한 모델을 본다면 같은 것을 취하기를 원하도록 그들을 납득시킵니다.
This _____ their minds and if they see a model in an advert _____ _____ , it _____ them to want to achieve the same.
※ (감정)을 자극하다 : play on / 치장하다 : make something look good / 납득시키다, 설득시키다 : convince

Q. To what extent do you think advertising affects the way people shop?
A. Advertising has a huge effect on the way people shop, although I believe most of it to be subconscious. Advertising portrays goods or services as something for people to aspire to achieve or to own. This plays on their minds and if they see a model in an advert make something look good, it convinces them to want to achieve the same.

4) Do you think shopping habits are likely to change in the future?
당신은 미래에 쇼핑 습관이 바뀔 것이라고 생각해요?

Brainstorming	Direct Answer	바뀔 것임
	Supporting Sentence 1	유행과 경제 변화에 따라 쇼핑 습관이 바뀌는 것은 불가피함
	Supporting Sentence 2	명품과 세계적인 브랜드의 급상승 예측함

✏️ 다음 **불법포인트**를 참고해서 영어 문장을 완성해 보자. (주어와 시제, 품사와 단복수 등을 고려할 것!)

❶ 네, 쇼핑 습관은 미래에 바뀔 것입니다.
Yes, _____ are likely to change in the future.
※ 쇼핑 습관 : shopping habit

❷ 유행과 경제의 변화에 따라 쇼핑 습관이 바뀌는 것은 불가피합니다.
It is _____ that they will shift depending on changes in style and the economy.
※ 불가피한 : inevitable

❸ 나는 개인의 증가된 풍요로움과 세계화 때문에 명품과 세계적인 브랜드에 있어 훨씬 더 큰 급상승이 있을 것이라고 예측합니다.
I predict that with individuals' increased personal _____ and _____ , there will be an even greater _____ in luxury goods and international brands.
※ 풍요로움 : affluence / 세계화 : globalisation / 급상승 : surge

Q. Do you think shopping habits are likely to change in the future?
A. Yes, shopping habits are likely to change in the future. It is inevitable that they will shift depending on changes in style and the economy. I predict that with individuals' increased personal affluence and globalisation, there will be an even greater surge in luxury goods and international brands.

Day 13 Shopping & Party 불법포인트 정리

쇼핑 중독자	shopaholic	못다한 이야기를 나누다 따라잡다	catch up with
모으다, 수집하다	collect	흩어지게 하다	scatter
플랫 슈즈 굽이 낮은 신발	flat shoes	~을 염두하다	have ~ in mind
~에 지루해하다	get bored with	조상의	ancestral
실시하다	conduct	사람들로 가득 차다	get overrun with crowds
무슨 수를 써서라도	at all costs	기대하다	look forward to
찾다	look for	현지인들	locals
배송하다	deliver	쇼핑 명소	shopping destination
현관	front door	더 저렴한, 더 싼	more affordable
가전 제품	electrical home appliances	관광객	tourist
제품 사양	product description	가처분 소득	disposable income
일부러 늦게 도착하는	fashionably late	증명하다	demonstrate
한창 진행 중인	in full swing	~와 함께, 나란히	alongside
멋지게 등장하다	make a big entrance	따라잡다, 뒤지지 않다	keep up with
사교적인, 외향적인	outgoing	유행에 민감한	fashion conscious
어울리다	mingle	~에 엄청난 영향을 주다	have a huge effect on
내성적인	introverted	잠재의식적인	subconscious
벽의 꽃	wallflower	묘사하다	portray
자주	frequently	갈망하다	aspire
인터넷으로	via the Internet	(감정)을 자극하다	play on
축제	festival	치장하다	make something look good
추수 감사제	harvest festival	납득시키다, 설득시키다	convince
구체적으로 말하면	specifically	쇼핑 습관	shopping habit
음력의	lunar	불가피한	inevitable
기리다, 경의를 표하다	pay respects	풍요로움	affluence
조상	ancestor	세계화	globalisation
산소, 무덤	grave	급상승	surge

Day 14 International Relations & Urbanisation
국제관계와 도시화

PART 1

1) Can you read maps?
2) How frequently do you use them?
3) Is there any difference between paper and electronic maps?
4) Do you think city planning is important? Why?
5) Why are there better education offers in cities?
6) What are the main differences between cities and small towns?
7) Would you prefer living in a city or a small town with family?

PART 2

Describe a city you have visited.

You should say:
 what the name is and where it is
 when you visited it
 what the attractive places of this city are
and explain why you liked it.

PART 3

1) What are the advantages and disadvantages of living in a big city?
2) What changes have you observed in your city over the past five years?
3) What are the names of good tourist spots in your city?
4) Why do you think living in your city is a good choice?

보이는 Speaking QR 코드

PART 1

1) Can you read maps? 당신은 지도를 읽을 수 있어요?

Brainstorming	Direct Answer	스마트폰 앱으로 지도를 읽는 것은 정말 쉬움
	Additional Information	구글 지도 오프라인은 해외 여행시 특히 도움이 됨

✏️ 다음 불법포인트를 참고해서 영어 문장을 완성해 보자. (주어와 시제, 품사와 단복수 등을 고려할 것!)

❶ 네, 그리고 스마트폰 앱으로 지도를 읽는 것은 정말 쉽습니다.
Yes, and it is really easy to read maps via _____ .
※ 스마트폰 앱 : smartphone application

❷ 지금 구글 지도 오프라인을 사용하는 것이 가능한데, 이것은 모바일 네트워크 접근 없이 해외 여행을 할 때 특히 도움이 됩니다.
It is now possible to use Google Maps offline, which is especially helpful when _____ without access to a mobile network.
※ 해외 여행을 하다 : travel abroad

Q. Can you read maps?
A. Yes, and it is really easy to read maps via smartphone applications. It is now possible to use Google Maps offline, which is especially helpful when travelling abroad without access to a mobile network.

2) How frequently do you use them? 당신은 얼마나 자주 지도를 사용해요?

Brainstorming	Direct Answer	운전할 때 항상 이용 함
	Additional Information	GPS 없이는 운전할 수 없음

✏️ 다음 불법포인트를 참고해서 영어 문장을 완성해 보자. (주어와 시제, 품사와 단복수 등을 고려할 것!)

❶ 나는 운전할 때 항상 지도를 이용해야 합니다.
I always need to use a map when I am _____ .
※ 운전하다 : drive

❷ 나는 내 GPS 시스템 없이는 운전할 수 없습니다.
I can't drive _____ my GPS system.
※ ~없이 : without

Q. How frequently do you use them?
A. I always need to use a map when I am driving. I can't drive without my GPS system.

3) Is there any difference between paper and electronic maps? 종이 지도와 전자 지도 사이에 차이점이 있어요?

Brainstorming	Direct Answer	작업량의 차이
	Additional Information	종이 지도는 시간이 많이 걸림

✏️ 다음 불법포인트를 참고해서 영어 문장을 완성해 보자. (주어와 시제, 품사와 단복수 등을 고려할 것!)

❶ 네, 주된 차이점은 지도 사용자가 어떤 방향으로 가야 할지 알기 위해 해야 하는 작업량입니다.
Yes, the main difference is _____ that a map user has to do in order to know which _____ to go in. ※ 작업량 : the amount of work / 방향 : direction

❷ 전자 지도는 당신을 위해 자동적으로 경로를 설정하기 때문에 노력이 덜 들지만, 종이 지도는 사람이 어디로 갈 지 수동으로 알아내야 하는데, 이것은 더 많은 시간이 걸립니다.
Electronic maps take less effort as they automatically _____ routes for you, but paper maps require a person to manually work out where to go, which is more _____.
※ 계획을 세우다 : plan out / 시간이 많이 걸리는 : time consuming

Q. Is there any difference between paper and electronic maps?
A. Yes, the main difference is the amount of work that a map user has to do in order to know which direction to go in. Electronic maps take less effort as they automatically plan out routes for you, but paper maps require a person to manually work out where to go, which is more time consuming.

4) Do you think city planning is important? Why? 당신은 도시 계획이 중요하다고 생각해요? 왜?

Brainstorming	Direct Answer	중요한
	Additional Information	효율적으로 운영하고 거주자들을 행복하게 하기 위함

✏️ 다음 불법포인트를 참고해서 영어 문장을 완성해 보자. (주어와 시제, 품사와 단복수 등을 고려할 것!)

❶ 물론입니다. 도시 계획은 중요합니다.
Sure! _____ is important.
※ 도시 계획 : city planning

❷ 효율적으로 운영하고 거주자들을 행복하게 하기 위해 도시가 잘 정비되는 것은 매우 중요합니다.
It is _____ for a city to be well organised in order to run efficiently and keep _____ happy.
※ 매우 중요한 : crucial / 거주자 : resident

Q. Do you think city planning is important? Why?
A. Sure! City planning is important. It is crucial for a city to be well organised in order to run efficiently and keep residents happy.

5) Why are there better education offers in cities? 왜 도시에 더 나은 교육이 제공돼요?

Brainstorming	Direction Answer	더 많은 사람, 기업체, 교육장소가 있음
	Additional Information	다양한 교육을 직접 경험하는 데 더 많은 가능성이 있음

✏️ 다음 불법포인트를 참고해서 영어 문장을 완성해 보자. (주어와 시제, 품사와 단복수 등을 고려할 것!)

❶ 시골보다 도시에 더 많은 사람들, 기업체들 그리고 교육 장소들이 있습니다.
There are more people, businesses and places of education in cities than _____ .
※ 시골에 : in the countryside

❷ 이것은 더 폭넓은 다양한 교육적 기회를 직접적인 경험을 하는 데 더 많은 가능성이 있다는 것을 의미합니다.
It means that there is a better chance to _____ of a wider variety of educational opportunities.
※ 직접적인 경험을 하다 : get hands on experience

Q. Why are there better education offers in cities?
A. There are more people, businesses and places of education in cities than in the countryside. It means that there is a better chance to get hands on experience of a wider variety of educational opportunities.

6) What are the main differences between cities and small towns? 도시와 작은 마을의 주요 차이점은 무엇인가요?

Brainstorming	Direct Answer	생활 편의 시설
	Additional Information	공동체 의식

✏️ 다음 불법포인트를 참고해서 영어 문장을 완성해 보자. (주어와 시제, 품사와 단복수 등을 고려할 것!)

❶ 도시에는 작은 마을과는 대조적으로 쇼핑 센터나 스포츠 시설과 같은 많은 생활 편의 시설이 있습니다.
In cities, there are a lot of _____ such as shopping centres or sports facilities _____ small towns.
※ 생활 편의 시설 : amenity / ~와는 대조적으로 : as opposed to

❷ 다른 주요 차이점은 공동체 의식인데, 작은 마을에 사는 사람들은 도시에서 사는 사람들과 달리 서로 다 알고지내는 경향이 있습니다.
Another difference is _____ , since people who live in small towns tend to all know each other, _____ people who live in cities.
※ 공동체 의식 : a sense of community / ~와 달리 : unlike

Q. What are the main differences between cities and small towns?
A. In cities, there are a lot of amenities such as shopping centres or sports facilities as opposed to small towns. Another difference is the sense of community, since people who live in small towns tend to all know each other, unlike people who live in cities.

7) Would you prefer living in a city or a small town with family?
당신은 가족들과 함께 도시에서 살고 싶어요? 아니면 가족과 함께 작은 마을에서 살고 싶어요?

Brainstorming	Direct Answer	아이들이 생기면 작은 마을에서 살고 싶음
	Additional Information	더 작고 조용한 지역이 아이들을 위해 더 안전함

✏️ 다음 **불법포인트**를 참고해서 영어 문장을 완성해 보자. (주어와 시제, 품사와 단복수 등을 고려할 것!)

❶ 아이들이 생기면 나는 작은 마을에서 살고 싶습니다.
When I have children, I would like to _____ .
※ 작은 마을에서 살다 : live in a small town

❷ 더 작고 조용한 지역에서 사는 것이 그들을 위해 더 안전할 것입니다.
Living in a smaller, _____ area would be safer for them.
※ 더 조용한 : quieter

Q. Would you prefer living in a city or a small town with family?
A. When I have children, I would like to live in a small town. Living in a smaller, quieter area would be safer for them.

PART 2

Describe a city you have visited.

You should say:
    what the name is and where it is
    when you visited it
    what the attractive places of this city are
and explain why you liked it.

당신이 방문했던 도시에 대해 묘사하세요.

당신은 반드시 말해야 합니다.
    그 도시의 이름은 무엇이고 어디에 있는지
    당신이 이 곳을 언제 방문했는지
    이 도시의 매력적인 장소들은 어디인지
그리고 왜 당신이 이 곳을 좋아했는지 설명하세요.

※ 이 질문은 도시에 대해 묘사하는 문제이지만, tourism과도 관련 지어 대답할 수 있다. 내가 여행했던 도시를 떠올리되 구체적으로 관광 명소 등의 이름을 언급하면서 말해야 한다.

주어지는 1분을 어떻게 활용할 것인가? (How to Use Your 1 Minute Preparation Time)

1. 질문 파악 방문했던 도시 묘사에 초점을 맞추는 문제이다.	내가 영어로 잘 설명할 수 있는 도시를 떠올린다.
2. 묘사 대상 결정하기 영어로 가장 자신 있게 묘사할 수 있는 도시를 떠올린다.	마땅히 떠오르는 도시가 없다면, 상상력을 동원해서 가상의 도시를 만들고 거기를 방문한 것처럼 그럴듯하게 설명하자.
3. 하위 질문 확인 + 스토리 작성 하위 질문의 개수를 확인하고, 각각에 대한 답을 적는다.	sub-questions는 3개처럼 보이지만, 마지막 문장의 'and explain why you liked it'을 포함해서 4개이다. 반드시 4개의 질문에 모두 답하되, 답의 길이는 똑같지 않아도 상관없다.
4. 주제 관련 아카데믹 표현 사용 도시와 관련해서 학습한 아카데믹한 표현들을 떠올린다.	London, the capital city of England, many of the famous tourist attractions, Buckingham Palace, the London Eye, Big Ben, famous art galleries, Tate Modern, the National Gallery. markets, browse around, Camden market, Portabello market, massive crowds, dense population, Londoner
5. 주의해야 할 문법 문제의 시제 및 인칭 대명사 등을 확인한다.	방문했던 도시를 묘사하는 문제이기 때문에 주로 과거 시제로 대답해야 하지만, 지금도 그러한 내용, 예를 들어 옷과 액세서리를 판매하는 캠든 시장(Camden market which sells clothes and accessories)이라고 할 때는 현재 시제를 써야 한다.

Brainstorming

Sub-question 1 what the name is and where it is	영국의 수도 런던
Sub-question 2 when you visited it	올 여름 2주 동안
Sub-question 3 what the attractive places of this city are	버킹엄 궁전, 런던 아이, 빅벤, 테이트 모던 미술관, 국립 미술관, 캠든 시장, 포타벨로
Sub-question 4 and explain why you liked it	엄청난 인파와 밀집된 인구에도 불구하고 어떤 런던 사람도 우리를 성가시게 하거나 쳐다보지 않음, 날씨가 맑았음

✏️ 다음 불법포인트를 참고해서 영어 문장을 완성해 보자. (주어와 시제, 품사와 단복수 등을 고려할 것!)

❶ 지금 나는 최근에 방문했던 도시에 대해 이야기하고 싶습니다.
Now, I would like to talk about a city I've visited _____ .
※ 최근에 : lately(lately는 '늦게'라는 뜻이 아니다.)

❷ 내가 선택한 도시는 영국의 수도 런던입니다.
The city I've chosen is London, the _____ city of England.
※ 수도 : capital

❸ 나의 가장 친한 친구 태호와 함께 올 여름 2주 동안 그곳을 갔습니다.
I went there _____ for two weeks with my best friend, Taeho.
※ 올 여름 : this summer(this 앞에는 시간을 나타내는 전치사를 쓰지 않는다. in this summer라고 하지 않는다.)

❹ 우리가 거기에 있는 동안 우리는 왕족이 사는 버킹엄 궁전, 런던 아이 그리고 빅벤과 같은 유명한 관광 명소들을 많이 방문했습니다. 함께 여행했던 내 친구는 정말 예술을 좋아해서 우리는 또한 테이트 모던과 국립 미술관 같은 많은 유명한 미술관들을 방문했습니다. 비록 나는 미술관들을 둘러 보는 것이 즐겁기는 했지만 나는 쇼핑에 더 관심이 있고 런던에는 구경하기에 매력적인 많은 유명한 시장들이 있습니다. 우리는 옷과 액세서리를 판매하는 캠든 마켓과 다양한 골동품들과 빈티지 상품들을 판매하는 포토벨로 로드 마켓에 갔습니다.
While we were there, we visited many of the famous tourist attractions such as Buckingham Palace, where _____ live, the London Eye and Big Ben. My friend who I travelled with really likes art so we also visited many famous art galleries in London, such as the Tate Modern and the National Gallery. Although I enjoyed looking around the galleries, I am more interested in shopping and London has a lot of famous markets that are fascinating to _____ in. We went to Camden Market which sells clothes and accessories and Portobello Road Market which sells various _____ and vintage goods.
※ 왕족 : the Royal Family / 구경하다, 둘러보다 : browse around / 골동품 : antique

❺ 나는 런던을 사랑했는데 엄청난 인파와 밀집된 인구에도 불구하고 어떤 런던 사람도 우리를 성가시게 하거나 쳐다보지 않았기 때문입니다. 운이 좋았던 건 우리가 거기에 있었던 대부분의 시간 동안 날씨가 맑았는데 나는 (런던의) 날씨가 보통 아주 나쁘다고 들었기 때문입니다.
I loved London because despite _____ and a _____ , no Londoner _____ or even looked at us. We were _____ that it was sunny most of the time we were there because I have heard that the weather is usually pretty _____ !
※ 엄청난 인파 : massive crowds / 밀집된 인구 : dense population / 성가시게 하다 : bother / 운 좋은 : fortunate
절망적인, 비참한 : miserable

Sample Answer

Describe a city you have visited.

You should say :
    what the name is and where it is
    when you visited it
    what the attractive places of this city are
and explain why you liked it.

Now, I would like to talk about a city I've visited lately.

The city I've chosen is London, the capital city of England.

I went there this summer for two weeks with my best friend, Taeho.

While we were there, we visited many of the famous tourist attractions such as Buckingham Palace, where the Royal Family live, the London Eye and Big Ben. My friend who I travelled with really likes art so we also visited many famous art galleries in London, such as the Tate Modern and the National Gallery. Although I enjoyed looking around the galleries, I am more interested in shopping and London has a lot of famous markets that are fascinating to browse around in. We went to Camden Market which sells clothes and accessories and Portobello Road Market which sells various antiques and vintage goods.

I loved London because despite massive crowds and a dense population, no Londoner bothered or even looked at us. We were fortunate that it was sunny most of the time we were there because I have heard that the weather is usually pretty miserable!

That's all from me, thank you very much for your attention.

PART 3

1) What are the advantages and disadvantages of living in a big city?
대도시에서 사는 것의 장점과 단점은 무엇인가요?

Brainstorming	Direct Answer	장점은 지루하지 않음
	Supporting Sentence 1	다양한 오락 시설과 식당이 있음
	Supporting Sentence 2	단점도 있음
	Supporting Sentence 3	교통 체증, 많은 사람들, 줄, 무질서한 환경
	Supporting Sentence 4	스트레스가 될 수 있음

✏️ 다음 불법포인트를 참고해서 영어 문장을 완성해 보자. (주어와 시제, 품사와 단복수 등을 고려할 것!)

❶ 대도시에서 사는 것의 장점은 지루해 할 이유가 없다는 것입니다.
An advantage of living in a big city is that _____ to ever be bored.
※ 이유가 없다 : there is no reason

❷ 즐기기 위한 다양한 오락 시설들이나 식당들과 함께 항상 무언가가 있습니다.
_____ with a variety of _____ or restaurants to enjoy.
※ 항상 무언가가 있다 : there is always something going on / 오락 시설 : entertainment facility

❸ 하지만 시가지에서 사는 것은 또한 단점들이 있습니다.
However, living in a _____ also has its _____.
※ 시가지 : built-up area(건물이 많은 지역) / 단점 : disadvantage

❹ 많은 사람들은 도시에서 사는 경향이 있는데 이것은 교통 체증, 많은 사람들, 어디를 가든 줄을 서야 하고 그리고 일반적으로 무질서한 환경을 야기합니다.
Many people tend to live in cities, which causes _____, crowds of people, _____ to get anywhere and a generally _____ environment.
※ 교통 체증 : traffic congestion / 줄 : queue / 무질서한 : chaotic

❺ 누군가에게 이것은 매우 스트레스가 될 수 있습니다.
For some, this can be very _____.
※ 스트레스가 많은 : stressful

Q. What are the advantages and disadvantages of living in a big city?
A. An advantage of living in a big city is that there is no reason to ever be bored. There is always something going on with a variety of entertainment facilities or restaurants to enjoy. However, living in a built-up area also has its disadvantages. Many people tend to live in cities, which causes traffic congestion, crowds of people, queues to get anywhere and a generally chaotic environment. For some, this can be very stressful.

2) **What changes have you observed in your city over the past five years?**
당신은 지난 5년 동안 당신의 도시에서 어떤 변화들을 목격했나요?

Brainstorming		
	Direct Answer	다른 나라에서 온 이주민들이 많아짐
	Supporting Sentence 1	전에는 알려지지 않았던 지역이 개발되고 고급화됨
	Supporting Sentence 2	바쁘고 인기 있는 최신 유행하는 장소가 됨
	Supporting Sentence 3	도시의 평판이 현대적이고 재미있는 장소로 바뀜

✏️ 다음 불법포인트를 참고해서 영어 문장을 완성해 보자. (주어와 시제, 품사와 단복수 등을 고려할 것!)

❶ 다양한 다른 나라에서 온 엄청난 숫자의 이주민들이 지난 5년 간 서울로 이주했습니다.
A huge number of _____ from a variety of different countries have moved into Seoul in the past five years.
※ 이주민 : expatriate

❷ 이 결과로 전에는 조용하고 상대적으로 알려지지 않았던 이 도시의 특정 지역이 개발되고 고급 주택지가 되었습니다.
As a result of this, certain areas of the city that were previously quiet and relatively unknown have been built up and _____ .
※ 고급 주택화하다 : gentrify

❸ 식당들, 술집들 그리고 클럽들을 열면서 이 지역들은 엄청나게 바쁠 뿐만 아니라 인기 있고 최신 유행하는 장소가 되었습니다.
By _____ restaurants, bars and clubs, these areas have become the hot, trendy places as well as incredibly busy.
※ 열다, 개업하다 : open up

❹ 이것은 이 도시의 평판을 거주자들과 이주민들 그리고 관광객들에게 현대적이고 재미있는 장소로 바꾸었습니다.
This has changed the _____ of the city into a modern, fun place for locals, expatriates and tourists.
※ 평판, 명성 : reputation

Q. What changes have you observed in your city over the past five years?
A. A huge number of expatriates from a variety of different countries have moved into Seoul in the past five years. As a result of this, certain areas of the city that were previously quiet and relatively unknown have been built up and gentrified. By opening up restaurants, bars and clubs, these areas have become the hot, trendy places as well as incredibly busy. This has changed the reputation of the city into a modern, fun place for locals, expatriates and tourists.

3) **What are the names of good tourist spots in your city?** 당신의 도시에서 좋은 관광지의 이름들은 무엇인가요?

Brainstorming	Direct Answer	서울에는 많은 관광 명소가 있음
	Supporting Sentence 1	경복궁과 N서울타워
	Supporting Sentence 2	쇼핑을 위해선 명동, 홍대, 강남을 방문함
	Supporting Sentence 3	'강남 스타일' 발매 후 강남역 근처에서 사진을 찍음
	Supporting Sentence 4	강남과 홍대는 밤 문화, 음주, 파티를 위해 좋은 장소

✏️ 다음 **불법포인트**를 참고해서 영어 문장을 완성해 보자. (주어와 시제, 품사와 단복수 등을 고려할 것!)

❶ 서울에는 많은 흥미로운 관광 명소가 있습니다.
In Seoul, there are many interesting _____ .
※ 관광 명소 : tourist attraction

❷ 예를 들어 가장 유명한 관광 명소들 중의 몇몇 곳은 경복궁과 N서울타워입니다.
For example, some of the most famous ones are _____ and the N Seoul Tower.
※ 경복궁 : Gyeongbok Palace

❸ 많은 관광객들이 쇼핑을 위해서 서울을 방문하는데 이와 같은 경우로 그들은 명동, 홍대 그리고 강남과 같은 지역을 갑니다.
A lot of tourists visit Seoul for shopping, _____ they go to areas such as Myeongdong, Hongdae and Gangnam.
※ 이런 경우에 : in which case

❹ 물론, '강남 스타일'이라는 노래가 발매된 이후 많은 관광객들은 강남을 방문하기를 좋아하고 역 근처에 세워진 무대에서 사진을 찍기 위해서 자세를 취합니다.
Of course, after the song 'Gangnam Style' _____ , a lot of tourists like to visit Gangnam and pose for pictures on the stage that has been set up by the station.
※ 발매되다, 나오다 : come out

❺ 강남과 홍대는 또한 밤 문화와 음주 그리고 파티를 즐기는 관광객들에게 좋은 지역입니다.
Gangnam and Hongdae are also good areas for tourists who enjoy _____ , drinking and partying.
※ 밤 문화 : nightlife

Q. What are the names of good tourist spots in your city?
A. In Seoul, there are many interesting tourist attractions. For example, some of the most famous ones are Gyeongbok Palace and the N Seoul Tower. A lot of tourists visit Seoul for shopping, in which case they go to areas such as Myeongdong, Hongdae and Gangnam. Of course, after the song 'Gangnam Style' came out, a lot of tourists like to visit Gangnam and pose for pictures on the stage that has been set up by the station. Gangnam and Hongdae are also good areas for tourists who enjoy nightlife, drinking and partying.

4) Why do you think living in your city is a good choice?
당신은 왜 당신의 도시에서 사는 것이 좋은 선택이라고 생각해요?

Brainstorming	Direct Answer	서울에는 내 기분에 따라 갈 수 있는 다양한 장소들이 있음
	Supporting Sentence 1	쉬거나 자전거를 탈 수 있는 강 옆 공원
	Supporting Sentence 2	쇼핑하거나 술을 마시고 싶으면 갈 수 있는 북적거리는 장소
	Supporting Sentence 3	교통이 저렴하고 편리함

✏️ 다음 불법포인트를 참고해서 영어 문장을 완성해 보자. (주어와 시제, 품사와 단복수 등을 고려할 것!)

❶ 서울에서 사는 것은 좋은 선택인데 내 기분에 따라 갈 수 있는 다양한 장소들이 있습니다.
Living in Seoul is a good choice because there are a variety of places to go depending on my _____ .
※ 기분 : mood

❷ 만약 내가 쉬거나 자전거를 타기 원한다면 강 옆에 공원들이 있습니다.
There are parks by the river if I want to _____ and _____ .
※ 쉬다 : relax / 자전거를 타다 : ride a bike

❸ 또는 내가 쇼핑하거나 술 마시고 싶은 기분이면 매우 북적거리는 장소들이 있습니다.
There are also very _____ areas to go shopping or drinking if I am in that kind of mood.
※ 북적거리는 : bustling

❹ 서울은 또한 살기에 유용한 장소인데 도시 전역의 교통이 저렴하고 편리하기 때문입니다.
Seoul is a practical choice of place to live too because the transport around the city is cheap and _____ .
※ 편리한 : convenient

Q. Why do you think living in your city is a good choice?
A. Living in Seoul is a good choice because there are a variety of places to go depending on my mood. There are parks by the river if I want to relax and ride a bike. There are also very bustling areas to go shopping or drinking if I am in that kind of mood. Seoul is a practical choice of place to live too because the transport around the city is cheap and convenient.

 **Day 14 International Relations & Urbanisation 불법포인트 정리**

스마트폰 앱	smartphone application	성가시게 하다	bother
해외 여행을 하다	travel abroad	운 좋은	fortunate
운전하다	drive	절망적인, 비참한	miserable
~없이	without	이유가 없다	there is no reason
작업량	the amount of work	항상 무언가가 있다	there is always something going on
방향	direction	오락 시설	entertainment facility
계획을 세우다	plan out	시가지	built-up area
시간이 많이 걸리는	time consuming	단점	disadvantage
도시 계획	city planning	교통 체증	traffic congestion
매우 중요한	crucial	줄	queue
거주자	resident	무질서한	chaotic
시골에	in the countryside	스트레스가 많은	stressful
직접적인 경험을 하다	get hands on experience	이주민	expatriate
생활 편의 시설	amenity	고급 주택화하다	gentrify
~와는 대조적으로	as opposed to	열다, 개업하다	open up
공통체 의식	a sense of community	평판, 명성	reputation
~와 달리	unlike	관광 명소	tourist attraction
작은 마을에서 살다	live in a small town	경복궁	Gyeongbok Palace
더 조용한	quieter	이런 경우에	in which case
최근에	lately	발매되다, 나오다	come out
수도	capital	밤 문화	nightlife
올 여름	this summer	기분	mood
왕족	the Royal Family	쉬다	relax
구경하다, 둘러보다	browse around	자전거를 타다	ride a bike
골동품	antique	북적거리는	bustling
엄청난 인파	massive crowds	편리한	convenient
밀집된 인구	dense population		

Day 15 — Environmental Pollution
환경오염

PART 1

1) What is your favourite type of weather?
2) What kind of weather do you dislike?
3) Does the weather influence your mood?
4) What is the climate like in your country?
5) Would you prefer to live in a hot or cold country?
6) What is the best weather for travelling in?
7) What is the worst weather for travelling in?

PART 2

Describe an environmental problem in your city.

You should say:
   what it is
   how long it has existed
   what effect it has brought to people's lives
and explain how you think the problem will develop in the future.

PART 3

1) Which environmental problems are people most concerned about in your country?
2) What should the government and individuals do to protect the environment?
3) How should we educate children to protect the environment?
4) What's the difference between the old and the young as regards environmental protection?

보이는 Speaking QR 코드

PART 1

1) What is your favourite type of weather? 당신이 가장 좋아하는 날씨 유형은 무엇이에요?

Brainstorming	Direct Answer	시원하고 건조하며 맑은 날씨
	Additional Information	섭씨 18도가 나에게 완벽함

✏️ 다음 **불법포인트**를 참고해서 영어 문장을 완성해 보자. (주어와 시제, 품사와 단복수 등을 고려할 것!)

❶ 나는 시원하고 건조하며 맑은 날씨를 엄청 좋아합니다.
_____ cool, dry and sunny weather.
※ 나는 ~을 매우 좋아한다 : I am a big fan of

❷ 약 섭씨 18도의 온도가 나에게는 완벽합니다.
A temperature of about 18 degrees _____ is _____ for me.
※ 섭씨 : Celsius / 완벽한 : perfect

Q. What is your favourite type of weather?

A. I am a big fan of cool, dry and sunny weather. A temperature of about 18 degrees Celsius is perfect for me.

2) What kind of weather do you dislike? 당신은 어떤 유형의 날씨를 싫어해요?

Brainstorming	Direct Answer	고온 다습한 날씨
	Additional Information	끈적거릴 때 정말 불쾌함

✏️ 다음 **불법포인트**를 참고해서 영어 문장을 완성해 보자. (주어와 시제, 품사와 단복수 등을 고려할 것!)

❶ 나는 고온 다습한 날씨를 정말 좋아하지 않습니다.
I don't really like _____ .
※ 고온 다습한 날씨 : humid heat

❷ 나는 맑은 날씨를 좋아하지만 끈적거릴 때 나는 정말 불쾌해집니다.
I like sunny weather but I get very uncomfortable when it gets _____ .
※ 끈적거리는 : sticky

Q. What kind of weather do you dislike?

A. I don't really like humid heat. I like sunny weather but I get very uncomfortable when it gets sticky.

3) Does the weather influence your mood? 날씨가 당신의 기분에 영향을 주나요?

Brainstorming	Direct Answer	물론, 비가 가장 큰 영향을 줌
	Additional Information	우울하고 침울하게 만듦

✏️ 다음 불법포인트를 참고해서 영어 문장을 완성해 보자. (주어와 시제, 품사와 단복수 등을 고려할 것!)

❶ 물론입니다. 비가 나의 기분에 가장 영향을 줍니다.
Certainly, and it's rain that _____ my mood the most.
※ 영향을 미치다 : affect(=impact / influence)

❷ 비는 나를 너무 우울하고 침울하게 합니다.
It makes me feel so _____ .
※ 우울하고 침울한 : down and gloomy

Q. Does the weather influence your mood?
A. Certainly, and it's rain that affects my mood the most. It makes me feel so down and gloomy.

4) What is the climate like in your country? 당신의 나라의 기후는 어때요?

Brainstorming	Direct Answer	뚜렷한 4계절
	Additional Information	여름은 매우 덥고 습함, 겨울은 눈이 많이 옴

✏️ 다음 불법포인트를 참고해서 영어 문장을 완성해 보자. (주어와 시제, 품사와 단복수 등을 고려할 것!)

❶ 우리나라에는 뚜렷한 4 계절이 있어서 기후는 연중 달라집니다.
There are _____ in my country so the climate varies depending on the time of year.
※ 뚜렷한 4계절 : four distinct seasons

❷ 여름에는 매우 덥고 습하지만 겨울에는 눈이 많이 옵니다.
In the summer, it can be very _____ , whereas in the winter it snows a lot.
※ 덥고 습한 : hot and humid

Q. What is the climate like in your country?
A. There are four distinct seasons in my country so the climate varies depending on the time of year. In the summer, it can be very hot and humid, whereas in the winter it snows a lot.

5) Would you prefer to live in a hot or cold country?
당신은 더운 나라에서 살고 싶어요? 아니면 추운 나라에서 살고 싶어요?

Brainstorming	Direction Answer	더운 나라
	Additional Information	더운 나라에서 사는 사람들이 훨씬 더 행복함

✏️ 다음 불법포인트를 참고해서 영어 문장을 완성해 보자. (주어와 시제, 품사와 단복수 등을 고려할 것!)

❶ 나는 더운 나라에서 사는 것을 더 좋아합니다.
I would prefer to live in a _____ .
※ 더운 나라 : hot country

❷ 더운 나라에서 사는 사람들은 보통 추운 나라에서 사는 사람들보다 훨씬 더 행복합니다.
People who live in hot countries are usually _____ than those who live in cold countries.
※ 훨씬 더 행복한 : much happier

Q. Would you prefer to live in a hot or cold country?
A. I would prefer to live in a hot country. People who live in hot countries are usually much happier than those who live in cold countries.

6) What is the best weather for travelling in? 여행하기에 최상의 날씨는 어떤 날씨에요?

Brainstorming	Direct Answer	맑고 약간 더운 날씨
	Additional Information	여름 옷은 가벼워서 무거운 여행 가방으로 애를 먹을 필요가 없음

✏️ 다음 불법포인트를 참고해서 영어 문장을 완성해 보자. (주어와 시제, 품사와 단복수 등을 고려할 것!)

❶ 여행하기에 최상의 날씨는 맑고 약간 더운 날씨입니다.
_____ to travel in is sunny and a bit hot.
※ 최상의 날씨 : the best weather

❷ 대부분의 여름 옷들은 꽤 가볍기 때문에 나는 무거운 여행 가방으로 애를 먹을 필요가 없습니다.
As most summer clothes are quite light, I don't have to _____ a heavy suitcase.
※ 애를 쓰다 : struggle with

Q. What is the best weather for travelling in?
A. The best weather to travel in is sunny and a bit hot. As most summer clothes are quite light, I don't have to struggle with a heavy suitcase.

7) What is the worst weather for travelling in? 여행하기에 최악의 날씨는 어떤 날씨에요?

Brainstorming	Direct Answer	지나치게 덥고 습한 날씨
	Additional Information	쉽게 지치고 불쾌 지수 높음

✏️ 다음 불법포인트를 참고해서 영어 문장을 완성해 보자. (주어와 시제, 품사와 단복수 등을 고려할 것!)

❶ 여행하기에 최악의 날씨는 지나치게 덥고 습한 날씨입니다.
The worst weather to travel in is _____ hot and humid weather.
※ 지나치게 : excessively

❷ 이런 날씨에 사람들은 쉽게 지치고 그들의 불쾌 지수도 높습니다.
In this weather, people tire easily and their _____ is also high.
※ 불쾌 지수 : discomfort index

Q. What is the worst weather for travelling in?
A. The worst weather to travel in is excessively hot and humid weather. In this weather, people tire easily and their discomfort index is also high.

PART 2

Describe an environmental problem in your city.

You should say:
　　what it is
　　how long it has existed
　　what effect it has brought to people's lives
and explain how you think the problem will develop in the future.

당신 도시의 환경 문제 대해 묘사하세요.

당신은 반드시 말해야 합니다.
　　그것이 무엇인지
　　그것은 얼마나 오랫 동안 존재했는지
　　사람들의 삶에 어떤 영향을 미치는지
그리고 당신은 미래에 이 문제가 어떻게 될 거라고 생각하는지 설명하세요.

주어지는 1분을 어떻게 활용할 것인가? (How to Use Your 1 Minute Preparation Time)

1. 질문 파악 내가 살고 있는 도시의 환경 문제에 초점을 맞추는 문제이다.	내가 영어로 잘 설명할 수 있는 환경 문제를 떠올린다.
2. 묘사 대상 결정하기 영어로 가장 자신 있게 묘사할 수 있는 환경 문제를 떠올린다.	반드시 아카데믹한 단어로 자신 있게 설명할 수 있는 환경 문제를 묘사해야 한다.
3. 하위 질문 확인 + 스토리 작성 하위 질문의 개수를 확인하고, 각각에 대한 답을 적는다.	sub-questions는 3개처럼 보이지만, 마지막 문장의 'and explain how you think the problem will develop in the future'를 포함해서 4개이다. 반드시 4개의 질문에 모두 답하되, 답의 길이는 똑같지 않아도 상관없다.
4. 주제 관련 아카데믹 표현 사용 환경 오염과 관련해서 학습한 아카데믹한 표현들을 떠올린다.	a serious environmental problem, air pollution, South Korea's geographical location, yellow dust, the Gobi Desert in China, a huge amount of traffic, carbon monoxide, exhaust fumes, get worse, affect, the polluted air, respiratory problems, emphysema, asthma, use public transportation
5. 주의해야 할 문법 문제의 시제 및 인칭 대명사 등을 확인한다.	과거부터 지금까지도 계속 발생하는 일은 현재 완료, 시간에 상관없이 늘 사실인 내용은 현재, 그리고 앞으로 발생할 일은 미래 시제로 적절하게 표현한다.

Brainstorming

Sub-question 1 what it is	서울의 환경 문제는 대기 오염, 중국의 고비사막으로부터의 황사, 서울의 엄청난 교통량으로 인한 일산화탄소와 배기 가스로 공기가 오염됨
Sub-question 2 how long it has existed	지난 몇 십 년 동안 문제, 계속해서 더 나빠지고 있음
Sub-question 3 what effect it has brought to people's lives	도시의 심미적인 매력과 사람들의 건강에도 영향을 미침, 폐기종과 천식 같은 호흡기 질환을 야기
Sub-question 4 and explain how you think the problem will develop in the future	자동차에 대한 의존도 낮추고 대중 교통을 더 많이 이용

✏️ 다음 불법포인트를 참고해서 영어 문장을 완성해 보자. (주어와 시제, 품사와 단복수 등을 고려할 것!)

❶ 지금 나는 심각한 환경 문제에 대해 이야기하고 싶습니다.
Now, I would like to talk about a serious _____ .
※ 환경 문제 : environmental problem

❷ 내가 선택한 서울의 환경 문제는 대기 오염입니다. 공해는 전 세계적인 문제이지만 대한민국의 지리적 위치 때문에 중국의 고비사막으로부터 황사가 날아옵니다. 또한 서울의 엄청난 교통량은 일산화탄소와 배기 가스를 만들기 때문에 공기는 눈에 띄게 오염됩니다.
The environmental problem that I've chosen in Seoul is its _____ . Pollution is a problem all over the world but due to South Korea's _____ , _____ blows over from the Gobi Desert in China. Also, as _____ in Seoul produces _____ and _____ , the air is _____ polluted.
※ 대기 오염 : air pollution / 지리학적 위치 : geographical location / 황사 : yellow dust
엄청난 교통량 : a huge amount of traffic / 일산화탄소 : carbon monoxide(CO) / 배기 가스 : exhaust fumes
눈에 띄게 : visibly

❸ 이것은 지난 몇 십 년 동안 문제였고 계속해서 더 나빠지고 있습니다.
This has been a problem _____ and continues to get worse.
※ 지난 몇 십 년 동안 : over the last few decades

❹ 이것은 도시의 심미적인 매력에 영향을 미칠 뿐만 아니라 사람들의 건강에도 영향을 미치는데 오염된 대기에서 숨을 쉬는 것은 폐기종과 천식 같은 호흡기 질환을 야기할 수 있습니다.
It not only affects the _____ appeal of the city but also impacts on people's health since breathing in the polluted air can cause _____ such as _____ and _____ .
※ 심미적인 : aesthetic / 호흡기 질환 : respiratory problem / 폐기종 : emphysema / 천식 : asthma

❺ 나는 미래에는 자동차를 이용하는 것에 의존하는 사람들은 (더) 거의 없고, 더 많은 사람들이 대중 교통을 이용하기를 희망합니다.
I hope that in the future, fewer people will _____ to using cars and more people will use public transportation.
※ 의존하다 : resort

Sample Answer

> Describe an environmental problem in your city.
>
> You should say :
>   what it is
>   how long it has existed
>   what effect it has brought to people's lives
> and explain how you think the problem will develop in the future.

Now, I would like to talk about a serious environmental problem.

The environmental problem that I've chosen in Seoul is its air pollution. Pollution is a problem all over the world but due to South Korea's geographical location, yellow dust blows over from the Gobi Desert in China. Also, as a huge amount of traffic in Seoul produces carbon monoxide and exhaust fumes, the air is visibly polluted.

This has been a problem over the last few decades and continues to get worse.

It not only affects the aesthetic appeal of the city but also impacts on people's health since breathing in the polluted air can cause respiratory problems such as emphysema and asthma.

I hope that in the future, fewer people will resort to using cars and more people will use public transportation.

That's all from me, thank you very much for your attention.

PART 3

1) Which environmental problems are people most concerned about in your country?
당신의 나라에서 사람들이 가장 걱정하는 환경 문제는 무엇이에요?

Brainstorming		
	Direct Answer	공해 문제
	Supporting Sentence 1	지구 온난화
	Supporting Sentence 2	봄과 가을이 짧아짐
	Supporting Sentence 3	여름과 겨울은 더 길고 극심해짐

✏️ 다음 **불법포인트**를 참고해서 영어 문장을 완성해 보자. (주어와 시제, 품사와 단복수 등을 고려할 것!)

❶ 한국 사람들은 특히 그들의 건강에 영향을 주고 호흡 문제를 야기하고 때때로 사람들의 눈을 자극하는 공해 문제를 걱정합니다.
Koreans are particularly worried about the problem of pollution, which is affecting their health, causing problems with breathing and sometimes _____ people's eyes.
※ 자극하다 : irritate

❷ 우리나라에서 걱정이 우려되는 또 다른 문제는 지구 온난화의 영향입니다.
Another problem that is cause for concern in my country is _____
_____ .
※ 지구 온난화의 영향 : the impact of global warming

❸ 과거에 한국은 매우 뚜렷한 4계절이 있었지만 지금은 봄과 가을이 단지 2주 정도 지속됩니다.
In the past, Korea had four very distinct seasons but now, the spring and autumn only last _____ .
※ 2주 : a couple of weeks(정확하게 2주를 말하는 것이 아니라 '2주 정도', '2~3주 정도'의 뜻)

❹ 이것은 여름과 겨울이 훨씬 더 길고 더 극심하다는 것을 의미합니다.
This means that the summer and winter are much longer and more _____ .
※ 극심한 : extreme

Q. Which environmental problems are people most concerned about in your country?
A. Koreans are particularly worried about the problem of pollution, which is affecting their health, causing problems with breathing and sometimes irritating people's eyes. Another problem that is cause for concern in my country is the impact of global warming. In the past, Korea had four very distinct seasons but now, the spring and autumn only last a couple of weeks. This means that the summer and winter are much longer and more extreme.

2) What should the government and individuals do to protect the environment?
환경을 보호하기 위해서 정부와 개인들은 무엇을 해야 하나요?

Brainstorming		
	Direct Answer	정부는 법률 시행과 위반 처벌에 더 엄격해야 함
	Supporting Sentence 1	회사들은 특정 온도 이상 에어컨을 켜서는 안 되는 법이 있음
	Supporting Sentence 2	재활용법에 대한 좀 더 철저한 모니터가 필요함
	Supporting Sentence 3	자동차에 더 많은 세금을 부과해서 대도시 교통량을 줄여야 함

✏️ 다음 **불법포인트**를 참고해서 영어 문장을 완성해 보자. (주어와 시제, 품사와 단복수 등을 고려할 것!)

❶ 정부는 법률을 시행하고 위반을 처벌하는 데 더 엄격해야 합니다.
The government should be stricter with _____ and _____ .
※ 법을 시행하다 : impose laws / 위반을 처벌하다 : punish violations

❷ 예를 들면 회사들은 특정 온도 이상으로 에어컨을 켤 수 없다는 것을 명시한 법이 있습니다.
For example, there are laws _____ that companies cannot _____ their air conditioner over a certain temperature.
※ 명시하다 : state / 켜다 : turn on

❸ 모든 사람이 재활용을 하도록 만든 법이 있는데 좀 더 철저히 모니터 될 필요가 있습니다.
There are also laws making it necessary for everyone to _____ , which need to be more _____ monitored.
※ 재활용하다 : recycle / 철저히, 면밀히 : closely

❹ 이것들은 긍정적인 움직임이지만, 정부가 취해야 하는 다음으로 중요한 조치는 자동차에 더 많은 세금을 부과함으로써 대도시의 교통량을 줄이는 것이라고 생각합니다.
These are positive moves but the next major step I believe that the government needs to take is to reduce the amount of traffic in major cities by _____ private cars.
※ ~에 더 많은 세금을 부과하다 : impose more taxes on

Q. What should the government and individuals do to protect the environment?

A. The government should be stricter with imposing laws and punishing violations. For example, there are laws stating that companies cannot turn on their air conditioner over a certain temperature. There are also laws making it necessary for everyone to recycle, which need to be more closely monitored. These are positive moves but the next major step I believe that the government needs to take is to reduce the amount of traffic in major cities by imposing more taxes on private cars.

3) How should we educate children to protect the environment?
환경을 보호하기 위해서 어린이들은 어떻게 교육해야 할까요?

Brainstorming	Direct Answer	지구 온난화의 영향에 대해 교육해야 함
	Supporting Sentence 1	북극 지역이 더 따뜻해지고 있다는 것을 알아야 함
	Supporting Sentence 2	전 세계 사람들과 동물에 관심을 갖고 도미노 효과의 중요성을 가르쳐야 함
	Supporting Sentence 3	작은 탄소 발자국을 유지하도록 격려해야 함

✏️ 다음 불법포인트를 참고해서 영어 문장을 완성해 보자. (주어와 시제, 품사와 단복수 등을 고려할 것!)

❶ 우리는 지구 온난화의 영향에 대해서 아이들에게 교육을 해야 합니다.
We should educate children about the _____ of global warming.
※ 영향 : impact(=effect / influence)

❷ 그들은 북극 지역이 과거에 그랬던 것보다 더 따뜻하고, 계속해서 더 따뜻해지고 있다는 사실을 알아야 합니다.
They should know that _____ is warmer than it used to be and it continues to get warmer.
※ 북극 지역 : the Arctic region

❸ 또한 전 세계의 사람들과 동물들에 관심을 갖도록 아이들을 장려하고 도미노 효과의 중요성을 가르치는 것은 필수적입니다.
Also, encouraging children to _____ people and animals all over the world and teaching them the importance of _____ are essential.
※ 관심을 갖다, 마음을 쓰다 : care about
　도미노 효과 : the domino effect(한 가지 일이 일어나면 같은 일이 뒤를 이어 일어나는 누적 효과)

❹ 이것은 그들이 할 수 있을 만큼 작은 자신의 탄소 발자국을 유지하도록 그들을 격려할 것입니다.
It will encourage them to keep their own _____ as small as they can.
※ 탄소 발자국 : carbon footprint

Q. How should we educate children to protect the environment?
A. We should educate children about the impact of global warming. They should know that the Arctic region is warmer than it used to be and it continues to get warmer. Also, encouraging children to care about people and animals all over the world and teaching them the importance of the domino effect are essential. It will encourage them to keep their own carbon footprint as small as they can.

4) **What's the difference between the old and the young as regards environmental protection?**
환경 보호에 관해서 나이든 사람들과 젊은 사람들 사이에 차이점은 무엇인가요?

Brainstorming	Direct Answer	젊은 세대가 더 진지하게 환경을 보호함
	Supporting Sentence 1	나이든 사람들은 그들의 행동이 만들 수 있는 차이를 인식 못함
	Supporting Sentence 2	젊은 사람들은 환경에 이로운 생활방식의 변화에 더 열정적임

✏️ 다음 불법포인트를 참고해서 영어 문장을 완성해 보자. (주어와 시제, 품사와 단복수 등을 고려할 것!)

❶ 젊은 세대가 나이든 세대보다 더 진지하게 환경을 보호합니다.
The younger generations take _____ more seriously than the older ones.
※ 환경 보호 : environmental protection

❷ 나이든 사람들은 그들의 방식을 더 고수하고 그들의 행동이 만들 수 있는 차이를 거의 인식하지 못합니다.
Older people are more _____ and they hardly _____ the difference that their actions can make.
※ ~의 방식을 고수하다 : set in one's ways / 인식하다 : recognise

❸ 하지만 젊은 사람들은 환경에 이로운 생활방식의 변화에 대해 더 열정적입니다.
However, younger people are more _____ about making lifestyle changes that benefit the environment.
※ 열정적인, 열렬한 : enthusiastic

Q. What's the difference between the old and the young as regards environmental protection?
A. The younger generations take environmental protection more seriously than the older ones. Older people are more set in their ways and they hardly recognise the difference that their actions can make. However, younger people are more enthusiastic about making lifestyle changes that benefit the environment.

Day 15 Environmental Pollution 불법포인트 정리

나는 ~을 매우 좋아한다	I am a big fan of	호흡기 질환	respiratory problem
섭씨	Celsius	폐기종	emphysema
완벽한	perfect	천식	asthma
고온 다습한 날씨	humid heat	의존하다	resort
끈적거리는	sticky	자극하다	irritate
영향을 미치다	affect / impact / influence	지구 온난화의 영향	the impact of global warming
우울하고 침울한	down and gloomy	2주	a couple of weeks
뚜렷한 4계절	four distinct seasons	극심한	extreme
덥고 습한	hot and humid	법을 시행하다	impose laws
더운 나라	hot country	위반을 처벌하다	punish violations
훨씬 더 행복한	much happier	명시하다	state
최상의 날씨	the best weather	켜다	turn on
애를 쓰다	struggle with	재활용하다	recycle
지나치게	excessively	철저히, 면밀히	closely
불쾌 지수	discomfort index	~에 더 많은 세금을 부과하다	impose more taxes on
환경 문제	environmental problem	영향	impact / effect / influence
대기 오염	air pollution	북극 지역	the Arctic region
지리학적 위치	geographical location	관심을 갖다, 마음을 쓰다	care about
황사	yellow dust	도미노 효과	the domino effect
엄청난 교통량	a huge amount of traffic	탄소 발자국	carbon footprint
일산화탄소	carbon monoxide / CO	환경 보호	environmental protection
배기 가스	exhaust fumes	~의 방식을 고수하다	set in one's ways
눈에 띄게	visibly	인식하다	recognise
지난 몇 십 년 동안	over the last few decades	열정적인, 열렬한	enthusiastic
심미적인	aesthetic		

Day 16 The Energy Crisis
에너지 위기

PART 1

1) How often do you recycle?
2) What are the advantages of recycling?
3) Are there any disadvantages to recycling?
4) Is it easy in your country to recycle?
5) Would you like to recycle more?
6) How important is recycling in your opinion?
7) Do you think that banning plastic bags is a good idea?

PART 2

Describe something that you have bought and never used.

You should say :
   what the item is
   when you bought it
   where you bought it
and explain the reason you did not use the item.

PART 3

1) What are the advantages and disadvantages of hybrid cars?
2) In what ways do alternative fuels benefit society?
3) Why do some people resist nuclear energy?
4) How has people's awareness of green issues changed over the last 50 years in your country?

보이는 Speaking QR 코드

PART 1

1) How often do you recycle? 당신은 얼마나 자주 재활용해요?

Brainstorming	Direct Answer	항상
	Additional Information	한국에는 쓰레기 분리수거 정책이 있음

✏️ 다음 **불법포인트**를 참고해서 영어 문장을 완성해 보자. (주어와 시제, 품사와 단복수 등을 고려할 것!)

❶ 나는 항상 재활용해야 합니다.
I have to recycle _____ .
※ 항상 : all the time

❷ 한국에는 내가 준수해야 하는 쓰레기 분리수거 정책이 있습니다.
In Korea there is _____ which I should _____ .
※ 쓰레기 분리수거 정책 : a separate garbage collection policy / (법을) 준수하다, 따르다 : abide by

Q. How often do you recycle?
A. I have to recycle all the time. In Korea there is a separate garbage collection policy which I should abide by.

2) What are the advantages of recycling? 재활용의 장점은 무엇인가요?

Brainstorming	Direct Answer	환경에 이로움
	Additional Information	쓰레기 매립지가 넘쳐나지 않음

✏️ 다음 **불법포인트**를 참고해서 영어 문장을 완성해 보자. (주어와 시제, 품사와 단복수 등을 고려할 것!)

❶ 재활용의 주요한 장점은 환경에 이롭다는 것입니다.
The main advantage is that it _____ the environment.
※ 이롭다, 유익하다 : benefit

❷ 재활용 덕택에 쓰레기 매립지는 분해되지 않고 독성 화학 물질을 배출하는 제품들로 넘쳐나지 않습니다.
Thanks to recycling, _____ are not being _____ with products that won't break down and which _____ .
※ 쓰레기 매립지 : landfill / 과적하다, 과부하게 걸리게 하다 : overload / 독성화학 물질을 배출하다 : release toxic chemicals

Q. What are the advantages of recycling?
A. The main advantage is that it benefits the environment. Thanks to recycling, landfills are not being overloaded with products that won't break down and which release toxic chemicals.

3) Are there any disadvantages to recycling? 재활용에는 어떤 단점이 있어요?

Brainstorming	Direct Answer	시간이 많이 걸림
	Additional Information	같은 장소에 모든 것을 내다 버리는 것보다 더 오랜 시간이 걸림

✏️ 다음 불법포인트를 참고해서 영어 문장을 완성해 보자. (주어와 시제, 품사와 단복수 등을 고려할 것!)

❶ 재활용의 단점은 시간이 많이 걸린다는 것입니다.
One disadvantage is that it is _____ .
※ 시간이 많이 걸리는 : time consuming

❷ 쓰레기를 분리하는 방법을 아는 것과 그렇게 할 것을 기억하는 것은 같은 장소에 모든 것을 내다 버리는 것보다 더 오랜 시간이 걸립니다.
Knowing how to _____ rubbish and remembering to do so takes longer than throwing everything out in the same place.
※ 분리하다 : separate

Q. Are there any disadvantages to recycling?
A. One disadvantage is that it is time consuming. Knowing how to separate rubbish and remembering to do so takes longer than throwing everything out in the same place.

4) Is it easy in your country to recycle? 당신의 나라에서 재활용 하는 것은 쉬워요?

Brainstorming	Direct Answer	꽤 쉬움
	Additional Information	쓰레기 종류에 따른 다른 색상의 쓰레기 봉투가 있음

✏️ 다음 불법포인트를 참고해서 영어 문장을 완성해 보자. (주어와 시제, 품사와 단복수 등을 고려할 것!)

❶ 네, 우리나라에서 재활용하는 것은 꽤 쉽습니다.
Yes, it is quite easy to _____ in my country.
※ 재활용하다 : recycle

❷ 각각의 봉투에 어떤 종류의 쓰레기가 들어가야 하는지 분명하게 명시된 다른 색상의 쓰레기 봉투들이 있습니다.
There are different coloured rubbish bags that clearly _____ what kind of _____ should go into each bag.
※ 명시하다 : state / 쓰레기 : waste(=rubbish)

Q. Is it easy in your country to recycle?
A. Yes, it is quite easy to recycle in my country. There are different coloured rubbish bags that clearly state what kind of waste should go into each bag.

5) Would you like to recycle more? 당신은 재활용을 더 하고 싶어요?

Brainstorming	Direction Answer	환경 애호가로서 재활용을 더 하려고 노력함
	Additional Information	탄소 발자국을 자각하는 것은 개인들에게 중요함

✏️ 다음 **불법포인트**를 참고해서 영어 문장을 완성해 보자. (주어와 시제, 품사와 단복수 등을 고려할 것!)

❶ 물론입니다. 환경 애호가로서 나는 이미 재활용을 더 하려고 노력하고 있습니다.
Sure, as _____ , I am already trying to recycle more.
※ 환경 애호가 : an environment lover

❷ 자신의 탄소 발자국을 자각하는 것은 개인들에게 중요합니다.
It is important for individuals to _____ their own carbon footprint.
※ ~을 자각하다, 알고 있다 : be conscious of

Q. Would you like to recycle more?
A. Sure, as an environment lover, I am already trying to recycle more. It is important for individuals to be conscious of their own carbon footprint.

6) How important is recycling in your opinion? 당신 생각에 재활용은 얼마나 중요한가요?

Brainstorming	Direct Answer	엄청나게 중요함
	Additional Information	모든 사람들의 기여가 쌓일 것임

✏️ 다음 **불법포인트**를 참고해서 영어 문장을 완성해 보자. (주어와 시제, 품사와 단복수 등을 고려할 것!)

❶ 재활용은 엄청나게 중요합니다.
Recycling is _____ important.
※ 엄청나게, 믿을 수 없을 정도로 : incredibly

❷ 이것은 우리 지구를 돕는데 작은 기여이지만 만약 모든 사람들이 그런 노력을 한다면 이것은 쌓일 것입니다.
It is a small _____ towards helping our planet but it _____ if everyone makes that effort.
※ 기여 : contribution / 쌓이다 : add up

Q. How important is recycling in your opinion?
A. Recycling is incredibly important. It is a small contribution towards helping our planet but it adds up if everyone makes that effort.

7) Do you think that banning plastic bags is a good idea?
당신은 비닐 봉지를 금지하는 것이 좋은 생각이라고 생각해요?

Brainstorming	Direct Answer	지금은 비닐 봉지 사용이 불가피함
	Additional Information	튼튼하고 값은 싸지만 환경에 더 나은 대체품을 만들기 쉽지 않음

✏️ 다음 **불법포인트**를 참고해서 영어 문장을 완성해 보자. (주어와 시제, 품사와 단복수 등을 고려할 것!)

❶ 아니요, 지금은 비닐 봉지를 사용하는 것이 불가피합니다.
No, using plastic bags is _____ at the moment.
※ 불가피한 : inevitable

❷ 비닐 봉지만큼 튼튼하고 값은 싸지만 환경에는 더 나은 대체품을 만들어 내기 쉽지 않기 때문입니다.
This is because it is not easy to create an _____ that is as strong and as cheap as a _____ while also being any better for the environment.
※ 대체품 : alternative / 비닐 봉지 : plastic bag

Q. Do you think that banning plastic bags is a good idea?
A. No, using plastic bags is inevitable at the moment. This is because it is not easy to create an alternative that is as strong and as cheap as a plastic bag while also being any better for the environment.

PART 2

Describe something that you have bought and never used.

You should say:
- what the item is
- when you bought it
- where you bought it

and explain the reason you did not use the item.

당신이 구입했지만 한 번도 사용한 적이 없는 것에 대해 묘사하세요.

당신은 반드시 말해야 합니다.
- 그 상품이 무엇인지
- 당신은 그것을 언제 샀는지
- 당신은 그것을 어디에서 샀는지

그리고 그 상품을 사용하지 않았던 이유를 설명하세요.

※ 어느 상품을 선정해도 좋다. 실제로 구매 후 사용하지 않고 있는 상품을 떠올리기 보다는 내가 영어로 잘 표현할 수 있는 상품을 선정해야 한다. 여기서는 하얀 털 칼라가 있는 핫 핑크 코트를 선정했는데, 남학생이라면 내가 이 답안을 외워야 하나? 약간의 의구심이 들지도 모른다. 하지만 이 코트는 줄리정이 런던 유학 당시 버스 정류장에서 이 코트를 입었던 영국인 남자를 떠올리며 작성한 것이다! 시험관은 나의 개성이 아닌, 아카데믹한 영어 실력만을 체크할 뿐이다.

주어지는 1분을 어떻게 활용할 것인가? (How to Use Your 1 Minute Preparation Time)

1. 질문 파악 상품 묘사에 초점을 맞추는 문제이다.	내가 영어로 잘 설명할 수 있는 상품을 떠올린다.
2. 묘사 대상 결정하기 영어로 가장 자신 있게 묘사할 수 있는 상품을 떠올린다.	시험관이 그 상품을 상상할 수 있도록 상품의 이름과 색상, 특징, 가격 등 최대한 구체적으로 정보를 전달해야 한다.
3. 하위 질문 확인 + 스토리 작성 하위 질문의 개수를 확인하고, 각각에 대한 답을 적는다.	sub-questions는 3개처럼 보이지만, 마지막 문장의 'and explain the reason you did not use the item'를 포함해서 4개이다. 반드시 4개의 질문에 모두 답하되, 답의 길이는 똑같지 않아도 상관없다.
4. 주제 관련 아카데믹 표현 사용 상품 묘사와 관련해서 학습한 아카데믹한 표현들을 떠올린다.	an item I have purchased, a winter coat. a hot pink coat with a white fur collar, wear on nights out, outfits, look more exciting, be drawn to, during a going-out-of-business sale from a vintage store, cut the price by half, unique items, shut down, a regular customer, go out in public places, conspicuous, wardrobe, wear it out with pride
5. 주의해야 할 문법 문제의 시제 및 인칭 대명사 등을 확인한다.	상품을 샀던 시점에 초점을 맞출 때는 과거 시제, 상품의 특징에 대해 묘사할 때는 현재 시제로 적절하게 표현한다.

Brainstorming

Sub-question 1 what the item is	겨울 코트, 흰색 털 칼라가 있는 선명한 핑크색 코트
Sub-question 2 when you bought it	지난 여름, 점포 정리 세일 동안
Sub-question 3 where you bought it	'블루문', 빈티지 가게
Sub-question 4 and explain the reason you did not use the item	그것을 입고 공공장소에 나갈 정도로 충분히 용감하지 못함. 너무 눈에 띄기를 원하지 않았기 때문

✏️ 다음 불법포인트를 참고해서 영어 문장을 완성해 보자. (주어와 시제, 품사와 단복수 등을 고려할 것!)

❶ 지금 나는 구매했지만 한 번도 사용한 적이 없는 상품에 대해 이야기하고 싶습니다.
Now, I would like to talk about a product that I _____ but have never used.
※ 구입하다 : purchase

❷ 내가 선택한 상품은 겨울 코트입니다. 흰색 털 칼라가 있는 선명한 핑크색 코트입니다. 나는 밤에 외출할 때 더 멋지게 보이기 위해 이 옷을 입을 수 있을 거라고 생각했습니다. 이것은 길고 정말 밝아서 내가 이 코트를 봤을 때 즉각 마음이 끌렸습니다.
The item which I've chosen is a winter coat. It is a hot pink coat with a white fur collar. I thought I could wear it _____ to make my outfits look more exciting. It is long and very bright so I _____ immediately _____ the coat when I saw it.
※ 밤에 외출할 때 : on nights out / ~에 끌리다 : be drawn to

❸ 나는 빈티지 가게에서 지난 여름 점포 정리 세일 동안 샀습니다. 그들은 할인기간 동안 가격을 절반으로 내렸고 나는 그 코트에 35만원만 지불했습니다.
I bought it last summer during _____ from a vintage store. They cut the price by half during the sale and I paid only 350,000 won for the coat.
※ 점포 정리 세일 : a going-out-of-business sale

❹ '블루문'이라는 빈티지 가게는 독특한 물건을 살 수 있어서 내가 가장 좋아하는 곳들 중의 하나입니다. 하지만 작년에 가게는 문을 닫았는데, 주인인 미즈 정이 결혼하기 위해서 영국에 가야만 했기 때문입니다. 이 가게의 단골 손님으로서 나는 슬펐습니다.
The vintage shop, 'Blue Moon', was one of my favourites where I could buy _____ items. But last year the shop _____ because the owner, Ms. Jung, had to go to England to _____. As _____ at the shop, I felt sad.
※ 독특한 : unique / (가게가) 문을 닫다 : shut down / 결혼하다 : get married / 단골 손님 : a regular customer

❺ 나는 코트를 산 후에 종종 이 코트를 입는 것을 생각했습니다. 하지만 그것을 입고 공공장소에 나갈 정도로 충분히 용감하지 못했는데 나는 너무 눈에 띄기를 원하지 않았기 때문입니다. 나는 옷장에 걸려 있는 코트를 볼 때마다 여전히 좋지만 나는 조금 더 용감해져서 자신 있게 그것을 입고 나가야 합니다.
After I bought it, I often considered wearing the coat. But I didn't feel _____ enough to go out _____ wearing it because I didn't want to be too _____. I still love it whenever I see it hanging up in my _____ but I need to be a bit braver and wear it out with pride!
※ 용감한 : brave / 공공장소에서 : in public places / 눈에 띄는 : conspicuous / 옷장 : wardrobe

Sample Answer

> Describe something that you have bought and never used.
>
> You should say:
>   what the item is
>   when you bought it
>   where you bought it
> and explain the reason you did not use the item.

Now, I would like to talk about a product that I purchased but have never used.

The item which I've chosen is a winter coat. It is a hot pink coat with a white fur collar. I thought I could wear it on nights out to make my outfits look more exciting. It is long and very bright so I was immediately drawn to the coat when I saw it.

I bought it last summer during a going-out-of-business sale from a vintage store. They cut the price by half during the sale and I paid only 350,000 won for the coat.

The vintage shop, 'Blue Moon', was one of my favourites where I could buy unique items. But last year the shop shut down because the owner, Ms. Jung, had to go to England to get married. As a regular customer at the shop, I felt sad.

After I bought it, I often considered wearing the coat. But I didn't feel brave enough to go out in public places wearing it because I didn't want to be too conspicuous. I still love it whenever I see it hanging up in my wardrobe but I need to be a bit braver and wear it out with pride!

That's all from me, thank you very much for your attention.

PART 3

1) What are the advantages and disadvantages of hybrid cars?
하이브리드 차량의 장점과 단점은 무엇인가요?

Brainstorming		
	Direct Answer	장점 - 더 적은 공해 발생
	Supporting Sentence 1	연료에 돈을 덜 씀
	Supporting Sentence 2	단점 – 휘발유 차량보다 더 비쌈
	Supporting Sentence 3	추가 비용은 더 낮은 유지비와 면세로 상쇄될 수 있음

✏️ 다음 **불법포인트**를 참고해서 영어 문장을 완성해 보자. (주어와 시제, 품사와 단복수 등을 고려할 것!)

❶ 하이브리드 차량의 장점은 전기 엔진 때문에 일반 차량보다 훨씬 더 적은 공해를 발생시키는 것입니다.
An advantage of hybrid cars is that they produce much less _____ than regular cars due to their electric engine.
※ 공해, 오염 : pollution

❷ 이것은 또한 하이브리드 차량을 소유한 사람들은 일반 차량을 소유한 사람보다 연료에 돈을 훨씬 덜 쓴 다는 것을 의미합니다.
This also means that people who own hybrid cars spend much less money on _____ than those who own regular cars.
※ 연료 : fuel

❸ 하지만 하이브리드 차량의 단점은 일반 휘발유 차량보다 더 비싸다는 것입니다.
On the other hand, a disadvantage of hybrid cars is that they are more expensive to buy than a regular _____ vehicle.
※ 휘발유 : petrol(petrol은 영국식, gasoline은 미국식)

❹ 그러나 추가적인 비용은 더 낮은 유지비와 면세로 상쇄될 수 있습니다.
However, the extra amount can be _____ by lower _____ and _____.
※ 상쇄하다 : offset / 유지비 : running cost / 면세 : tax exemptions

Q. What are the advantages and disadvantages of hybrid cars?
A. An advantage of hybrid cars is that they produce much less pollution than regular cars due to their electric engine. This also means that people who own hybrid cars spend much less money on fuel than those who own regular cars. On the other hand, a disadvantage of hybrid cars is that they are more expensive to buy than a regular petrol vehicle. However, the extra amount can be offset by lower running costs and tax exemptions.

2) In what ways do alternative fuels benefit society? 어떤 면에서 대체 연료가 사회에 유익해요?

Brainstorming	Direct Answer	배기 가스를 덜 배출함으로써 탄소 발자국을 줄임
	Supporting Sentence 1	화석 연료의 고갈로 대체 연료 개발은 유익함
	Supporting Sentence 2	더 건강하고 더 친환경적인 미래를 위해서 필요함

✏️ 다음 **불법포인트**를 참고해서 영어 문장을 완성해 보자. (주어와 시제, 품사와 단복수 등을 고려할 것!)

❶ 바이오 디젤과 같은 대체 연료는 사회에 유익한데, 이것은 배기 가스를 덜 배출함으로써 세계의 탄소 발자국을 줄이기 때문입니다.

_____ such as biodiesel benefit society because they reduce the world's carbon footprint by producing less _____ .

※ 대체 연료 : alternative fuels / 배기 가스 : exhaust gas

❷ 석탄과 휘발유와 같은 화석 연료는 고갈되고 있기 때문에 대체 연료와 에너지원을 개발하는 것이 유익합니다.

Since _____ such as coal and petrol are being _____ , it is beneficial for society to develop alternative fuels and sources of energy.

※ 화석 연료 : fossil fuels / 다 써버리다, 고갈시키다 : deplete

❸ 이것은 더 건강하고 더 친환경적인 미래를 위해서 계속해서 필요할 것입니다.

They will continue to be needed for a healthier and more _____ future.

※ 친환경적인 : eco-friendly

Q. In what ways do alternative fuels benefit society?

A. Alternative fuels such as biodiesel benefit society because they reduce the world's carbon footprint by producing less exhaust gas. Since fossil fuels such as coal and petrol are being depleted, it is beneficial for society to develop alternative fuels and sources of energy. They will continue to be needed for a healthier and more eco-friendly future.

3) **Why do some people resist nuclear energy?** 왜 어떤 사람들은 원자력 에너지를 반대해요?

Brainstorming	Direct Answer	위험함
	Supporting Sentence 1	폐기물에는 방사능이 있고 유출될 수 있음
	Supporting Sentence 2	사람의 건강에 영향을 주고 핵무기 제조에 사용될 수 있음

✏️ 다음 불법포인트를 참고해서 영어 문장을 완성해 보자. (주어와 시제, 품사와 단복수 등을 고려할 것!)

❶ 일부 사람들은 원자력 에너지를 반대하는데 이것은 위험할 수 있기 때문입니다.
Some people _____ nuclear energy because it can be dangerous.
※ 반대하다, 저항하다 : resist

❷ 생산된 폐기물에는 방사능이 있고 만약 적절하게 처리되지 않으면 유출될 수 있습니다.
The waste produced is _____ and can _____ if it is not properly _____ .
※ 방사능의 : radioactive / 유출되다, 새다 : leak / 처리하다 : dispose of

❸ 이것은 사람들의 건강에 영향을 줄 수 있고 또한 핵무기를 만드는 데 사용될 수 있습니다.
This can affect people's health and can also be used to make _____ .
※ 핵무기 : nuclear weapon

Q. Why do some people resist nuclear energy?
A. Some people resist nuclear energy because it can be dangerous. The waste produced is radioactive and can leak if it is not properly disposed of. This can affect people's health and can also be used to make nuclear weapons.

4) How has people's awareness of green issues changed over the last 50 years in your country?
지난 50년 동안 당신의 나라에서는 환경 문제에 대한 사람들의 인식이 바뀌었나요?

Brainstorming	Direct Answer	환경 문제를 더 인식함
	Supporting Sentence 1	정부, 환경단체, 개인들의 노력
	Supporting Sentence 2	특히 젊은 사람들은 더 친환경적, 세계를 보호하려고 함

✎ 다음 불법포인트를 참고해서 영어 문장을 완성해 보자. (주어와 시제, 품사와 단복수 등을 고려할 것!)

❶ 지난 50년 동안, 사람들은 갈수록 더 환경 문제를 인식하게 되었습니다.
Over the last 50 years, people have become increasingly aware of _____ .
※ 환경적인 문제들 : environmental issues

❷ 이것은 부분적으로 환경을 보호하려고 새 법률을 시행하는 정부들, 말을 퍼뜨리는 환경 단체들 그리고 그들 자신의 삶에서 지구 온난화의 영향을 목격하는 개인들 때문입니다.
This is _____ due to governments imposing new laws to protect the environment, _____ spreading the word and individuals seeing the impact of global warming in their own lives.
※ 부분적으로 : partially / 환경 단체 : environmentalist group

❸ 특히 젊은 사람들은 더 친환경적이 되려고 하고 세계를 보호하는데 자신들의 본분을 하려고 합니다.
Especially young people try to be greener and _____ in protecting the world.
※ 자신의 본분을 하다 : do one's part

Q. How has people's awareness of green issues changed over the last 50 years in your country?
A. Over the last 50 years, people have become increasingly aware of environmental issues. This is partially due to governments imposing new laws to protect the environment, environmentalist groups spreading the word and individuals seeing the impact of global warming in their own lives. Especially young people try to be greener and do their part in protecting the world.

# Day 16 The Energy Crisis 불법포인트 정리

항상	all the time	결혼하다	get married
쓰레기 분리수거 정책	a separate garbage collection policy	단골 손님	a regular customer
(법을) 준수하다, 따르다	abide by	용감한	brave
이롭다, 유익하다	benefit	공공장소에서	in public places
쓰레기 매립지	landfill	눈에 띄는	conspicuous
과적하다, 과부하게 걸리게 하다	overload	옷장	wardrobe
독성화학 물질을 배출하다	release toxic chemicals	공해, 오염	pollution
시간이 많이 걸리는	time consuming	연료	fuel
분리하다	separate	휘발유	petrol
재활용하다	recycle	상쇄하다	offset
명시하다	state	유지비	running cost
쓰레기	waste / rubbish	면세	tax exemptions
환경 애호가	an environment lover	대체 연료	alternative fuels
~을 자각하다, 알고 있다	be conscious of	배기 가스	exhaust gas
엄청나게, 믿을 수 없을 정도로	incredibly	화석 연료	fossil fuels
기여	contribution	다 써버리다, 고갈시키다	deplete
쌓이다	add up	친환경적인	eco-friendly
불가피한	inevitable	반대하다, 저항하다	resist
대체품	alternative	방사능의	radioactive
비닐 봉지	plastic bag	유출되다, 새다	leak
구입하다	purchase	처리하다	dispose of
밤에 외출할 때	on nights out	핵무기	nuclear weapon
~에 끌리다	be drawn to	환경적인 문제들	environmental issues
점포 정리 세일	a going-out-of-business sale	부분적으로	partially
독특한	unique	환경 단체	environmentalist group
(가게가) 문을 닫다	shut down	자신의 본분을 하다	do one's part

Day 17 — Economy & Business
경제와 산업

PART 1

1) What work do you do?
2) What do you enjoy most about your work?
3) What are your main duties?
4) Are you satisfied with your job?
5) Is there any other work you would like to do in the future?
6) What skills and qualifications are required for this job?
7) Are there good job opportunities in your home country?

PART 2

Describe a job that you consider highly important.

You should say:
    what the job is
    what the job involves
    why it is important
and explain if people who do this job are appreciated enough by society.

PART 3

1) What jobs are most popular among young people these days?
2) Is it easier to change jobs now than in the past?
3) Is it a good idea to leave a secure job in order to pursue a dream?
4) What career advice should be given to young people?

보이는 Speaking QR 코드

PART 1

1) What work do you do? 당신은 무슨 일을 해요?

Brainstorming	Direct Answer	선생님
	Additional Information	홍대에 있는 미술학원에서 미술을 가르침

✏️ 다음 **불법포인트**를 참고해서 영어 문장을 완성해 보자. (주어와 시제, 품사와 단복수 등을 고려할 것!)

❶ 나는 선생님으로서 일합니다.
I work _____ .
※ 선생님으로서 : as a teacher

❷ 나는 홍대에 있는 미술학원에서 학생들과 성인들에게 미술 (수업)을 가르칩니다.
I teach art classes to students and adults at an _____ in Hongdae.
※ 미술학원 : art institution

Q. What work do you do?
A. I work as a teacher. I teach art classes to students and adults at an art institution in Hongdae.

2) What do you enjoy most about your work? 당신의 업무에서 가장 좋아하는 것은 무엇이에요?

Brainstorming	Direct Answer	창의적인 사람들로 둘러쌓인 것
	Additional Information	학생들의 대부분은 재능이 있고 마음이 따뜻함

✏️ 다음 **불법포인트**를 참고해서 영어 문장을 완성해 보자. (주어와 시제, 품사와 단복수 등을 고려할 것!)

❶ 나는 창의적인 사람들로 둘러쌓인 것에 행복(감)을 느낍니다.
I feel _____ from being surrounded by creative people.
※ 행복감 : a sense of happiness

❷ 내 학생들의 대부분은 재능이 있고 마음이 따뜻합니다.
Most of my students are really _____ and _____ .
※ 재능이 있는 : talented / 마음이 따뜻한 : warm-hearted

Q. What do you enjoy most about your work?
A. I feel a sense of happiness from being surrounded by creative people. Most of my students are really talented and warm-hearted.

3) What are your main duties? 당신의 중요 업무는 무엇이에요?

Brainstorming	Direct Answer	학생들이 예술적인 재능을 개발하도록 돕는 것
	Additional Information	수업 계획을 짜고, 누드 모델을 예약함

✏️ 다음 **불법포인트**를 참고해서 영어 문장을 완성해 보자. (주어와 시제, 품사와 단복수 등을 고려할 것!)

❶ 나의 주요 업무는 학생들이 예술적인 재능을 개발하도록 그들을 돕는 것입니다.
My main duty is to help the students develop their _____ .
※ 예술적 재능 : artistic skill

❷ 나는 또한 수업 계획을 짜고 누드 모델들을 예약해야 합니다.
I also need to organise lesson plans and _____ nude models.
※ 예약하다 : book(=reserve)

Q. What are your main duties?
A. My main duty is to help the students develop their artistic skills. I also need to organise lesson plans and book nude models.

4) Are you satisfied with your job? 당신은 당신의 직업에 만족해요?

Brainstorming	Direct Answer	매우 만족함
	Additional Information	바꾸지 않을 것임

✏️ 다음 **불법포인트**를 참고해서 영어 문장을 완성해 보자. (주어와 시제, 품사와 단복수 등을 고려할 것!)

❶ 나는 나의 직업에 매우 만족합니다.
I _____ my job.
※ ~에 매우 만족하다 : be very satisfied with

❷ 무슨 일이 있어도 직업을 결코 바꾸지 않을 것입니다.
I wouldn't change it _____ .
※ 무슨 일이 있어도, 결코 : for all the world

Q. Are you satisfied with your job?
A. I am very satisfied with my job. I wouldn't change it for all the world.

5) Is there any other work you would like to do in the future?
미래에 당신이 하고 싶은 어떤 다른 일이 있어요?

Brainstorming	Direction Answer	미술 학원 운영
	Additional Information	창의적인 분위기를 만들고 장애인에게 무료 수업 제공

✏️ 다음 불법포인트를 참고해서 영어 문장을 완성해 보자. (주어와 시제, 품사와 단복수 등을 고려할 것!)

❶ 나는 5년 안에 내 소유의 미술 학원을 운영하고 싶습니다.
I would like to _____ my own art institution in five years.
※ 운영하다 : run

❷ 미래의 피카소를 위해 좀 더 창의적인 분위기를 만들고 장애인들에게 무료 수업을 제공하는 것이 나의 목표입니다.
Developing a more _____ for a future Picasso and offering _____ to _____ are my goals.
※ 창의적인 분위기 : creative atmosphere / 무료 수업, 학비 면제 : free tuition / 장애인들 : disabled people

Q. Is there any other work you would like to do in the future?
A. I would like to run my own art institution in five years. Developing a more creative atmosphere for a future Picasso and offering free tuition to disabled people are my goals.

6) What skills and qualifications are required for this job? 이 직업에는 어떤 기술과 자격 요건이 요구돼요?

Brainstorming	Direct Answer	참을성
	Additional Information	미술 석사 학위

✏️ 다음 불법포인트를 참고해서 영어 문장을 완성해 보자. (주어와 시제, 품사와 단복수 등을 고려할 것!)

❶ 학생들은 매우 민감할 수 있기 때문에 학생들을 대할 때 참을성이 필요합니다.
It is necessary to be _____ with the students since they can be very _____ .
※ 참을성이 있는 : patient / 민감한, 섬세한 : sensitive

❷ 비록 이 직업에 필수적인 자격 요건은 아니지만 나는 또한 미술 석사 학위를 가지고 있습니다.
I also have a _____ in fine art, although that is not an essential _____ for this job.
※ 석사 학위 : masters degree / 자격 요건 : qualification

Q. What skills and qualifications are required for this job?
A. It is necessary to be patient with the students since they can be very sensitive. I also have a masters degree in fine art, although that is not an essential qualification for this job.

7) Are there good job opportunities in your home country? 당신의 고국에는 좋은 일자리가 있어요?

Brainstorming	Direct Answer	불경기 이후 채용공고가 더 적음
	Additional Information	최근에 젊은이들은 직업을 구하려고 고생함

✏️ 다음 **불법포인트**를 참고해서 영어 문장을 완성해 보자. (주어와 시제, 품사와 단복수 등을 고려할 것!)

❶ 불행히도 불경기 이후, 전보다 채용공고가 더 적습니다.
Unfortunately, after the ＿＿＿＿＿＿ , there have been fewer ＿＿＿＿＿＿ than before.
※ 불경기 : recession / 채용공고, 구인 : job openings

❷ 그래서 최근에 많은 젊은이들은 직업을 구하려고 할 때 고생을 합니다.
So nowadays many young adults suffer when trying to ＿＿＿＿＿＿ .
※ 직업을 구하다 : get a job

Q. Are there good job opportunities in your home country?
A. Unfortunately, after the recession, there have been fewer job openings than before. So nowadays many young adults suffer when trying to get a job.

PART 2

Describe a job that you consider highly important.

You should say:
 what the job is
 what the job involves
 why it is important
and explain if people who do this job are appreciated enough by society.

당신이 매우 중요하게 생각하는 일을 묘사하세요.

당신은 반드시 말해야 합니다.
 그 일은 무엇인지
 그 일은 무엇을 포함하는지
 왜 그 일이 중요한지
그리고 이 일을 하는 사람들은 사회로부터 충분히 평가되는지 아닌지 설명하세요.

※ 어떤 직업이 중요한 직업일까? 흔히들 떠올리는 소방관, 경찰, 의사, 간호사, 교사 등에 대해 영어로 잘 설명할 수 없다면 지금 본인이 하고 있는 일을 중요한 직업이라고 생각하자. 직업에는 귀천이 없고 모든 직업은 중요하다. 만약 내가 IT 전문가라면 IT의 발달 없이는 사람들이 편리한 생활을 계속 이어갈 수 없기 때문에 중요하다고 말하면서 영어로 된 IT 전문용어를 마음껏 답변에 넣는다. 중요한 직업을 선택하기 보다는 내가 영어로 잘 설명할 수 있는 직업을 중요한 직업이라고 생각하면서 말하는 것이 중요하다.

주어지는 1분을 어떻게 활용할 것인가? (How to Use Your 1 Minute Preparation Time)

1. 질문 파악 중요한 직업 묘사에 초점을 맞추는 문제이다.	내가 영어로 잘 설명할 수 있는 직업을 떠올린다.
2. 묘사 대상 결정하기 영어로 가장 자신 있게 묘사할 수 있는 직업을 떠올린다.	마땅히 떠오르는 직업이 없다면 직장인인 경우 본인의 직업을 떠올리자. 영어로 잘 설명할 수 있는 직업을 선택하는 것이 가장 중요하다.
3. 하위 질문 확인 + 스토리 작성 하위 질문의 개수를 확인하고, 각각에 대한 답을 적는다.	sub-questions는 3개처럼 보이지만, 마지막 문장의 'and explain if people who do this job are appreciated enough by society'를 포함해서 4개이다. 반드시 4개의 질문에 모두 답하되, 답의 길이는 똑같지 않아도 상관없다.
4. 주제 관련 아카데믹 표현 사용 직업 묘사와 관련해서 학습한 아카데믹한 표현들을 떠올린다.	a firefighter, extinguishing fires, a burning building, safely, be called upon to rescue, a serious accident, a very important job, a public service, dangerous, require bravery, save people's lives, gratitude, not a well-paid job, risk involved, has a lot of respect for, a profession
5. 주의해야 할 문법 문제의 시제 및 인칭 대명사 등을 확인한다.	firefighter라고 여러 번 반복하기 보다는, job, profession, these men and women 등의 동의어를 활용하자. 또한 소방관이 하는 일을 묘사하는 문제이기 때문에 현재 시제를 주로 사용한다.

Brainstorming

Sub-question 1 what the job is	소방관
Sub-question 2 what the job involves	불을 끄고 모든 사람들이 안전하게 불타는 건물에서 빠져 나오게 하는 것, 키 큰 나무에서 동물을 구하는 것, 심각한 (교통)사고가 났을 때 누군가를 차량으로부터 꺼내는 것
Sub-question 3 why it is important	위험하고 용기가 요구되는 공공 서비스
Sub-question 4 and explain if people who do this job are appreciated enough by society	마땅히 받아야 할 감사를 받지 못함, 위험이 포함되는데도 불구하고 보수가 좋은 직업은 아님, 사회가 많은 존경심을 갖고 있음, 멸시당하는 직업은 아님

✏️ **다음 불법포인트를 참고해서 영어 문장을 완성해 보자. (주어와 시제, 품사와 단복수 등을 고려할 것!)**

❶ 지금 나는 내가 가치 있게 여기는 직업에 대해 이야기하고 싶습니다.
Now, I would like to talk about a job that I particularly _____ .
※ 가치 있게 여기다 : value

❷ 내가 선택한 직업은 소방관입니다.
The job that I've chosen is that of a _____ .
※ 소방관 : firefighter

❸ 이 직업은 주로 불을 끄고 모든 사람들이 안전하게 불타는 건물에서 빠져 나오게 하는 것입니다. 하지만 소방관은 키 큰 나무에서 동물을 구하거나 심각한 (교통)사고가 났을 때 누군가를 차량으로부터 꺼내달라고 요청을 받을지도 모릅니다.
This profession mainly involves _____ and making sure that everyone gets out of burning buildings safely. However, a firefighter may also be called upon to _____ animals out of tall trees or to cut someone free from a car when there has been a serious _____ .
※ 불을 끄다, 화재를 진압하다 : extinguish fires / 구하다 : rescue / 사고 : accident

❹ 이것은 매우 중요한 직업인데 위험하고 용기가 요구되는 공공 서비스이기 때문입니다.
It is a very important job because it is a _____ that is dangerous and requires _____ .
※ 공공 서비스 : public service / 용기 : bravery

❺ 이 남성들과 여성들은 사람들의 목숨을 구하고 그들이 마땅히 받아야 할 만큼 감사를 받지 못합니다. 소방관이 되는 것은 위험이 포함되는데도 불구하고 보수가 좋은 직업은 아닙니다. 하지만 나는 사회가 이 직업을 수행하는 사람들에 대해 많은 존경심을 갖고 있고 이것은 멸시당하는 직업은 아니라고 생각합니다.
These men and women save people's lives and don't receive as much _____ as they ought to. Being a firefighter is not _____ , despite the risks involved. However, I do think that society has a lot of respect for people who do this job and it isn't a _____ that is _____ .
※ 감사 : gratitude / 보수가 좋은 직업 : a well-paid job / 직업 : profession / 멸시하다, 깔보다 : look down upon

Sample Answer

> Describe a job that you consider highly important.
>
> You should say:
>   what the job is
>   what the job involves
>   why it is important
> and explain if people who do this job are appreciated enough by society.

Now, I would like to talk about a job that I particularly value.

The job that I've chosen is that of a firefighter.

This profession mainly involves extinguishing fires and making sure that everyone gets out of burning buildings safely. However, a firefighter may also be called upon to rescue animals out of tall trees or to cut someone free from a car when there has been a serious accident.

It is a very important job because it is a public service that is dangerous and requires bravery.

These men and women save people's lives and don't receive as much gratitude as they ought to. Being a firefighter is not a well-paid job, despite the risks involved. However, I do think that society has a lot of respect for people who do this job and it isn't a profession that is looked down upon.

That's all from me, thank you very much for your attention.

PART 3

1) What jobs are most popular among young people these days?
요즘 젊은이들 사이에서 어떤 직업이 가장 인기 있어요?

Brainstorming	Direct Answer	창의적인 직업
	Supporting Sentence 1	그래픽 디자인
	Supporting Sentence 2	회사 로고부터 마케팅 자료를 만드는 데까지 디자인 수요가 있음

✏️ 다음 불법포인트를 참고해서 영어 문장을 완성해 보자. (주어와 시제, 품사와 단복수 등을 고려할 것!)

❶ 창의적인 직종의 직업이 최근에 젊은 사람들 사이에서 더 인기가 있습니다.
Jobs in _____ have become more popular among young people recently.
※ 창의적인 직종 : creative professions

❷ 예를 들면, 요즘 많은 사람들이 그래픽 디자인을 공부하고 광고 대행사, 패션 업체의 디자이너로 일하거나 심지어 자기 사업을 시작합니다.
For example, many people these days study graphic design and work as designers for _____ , fashion companies or even _____ their own businesses.
※ 광고 대행사 : advertising agency / 시작하다 : set up

❸ 기술이 오늘날 각종 사업에서 흔히 사용되기 때문에 회사 로고부터 마케팅 자료를 만드는 데까지 항상 디자인 측면에 대한 수요가 있습니다.
Since technology is commonly used today by _____ , there is always a need for a design aspect, from creating a company logo to all their marketing material.
※ 각종 사업들 : all sorts of businesses

Q. What jobs are most popular among young people these days?
A. Jobs in creative professions have become more popular among young people recently. For example, many people these days study graphic design and work as designers for advertising agencies, fashion companies or even set up their own businesses. Since technology is commonly used today by all sorts of businesses, there is always a need for a design aspect, from creating a company logo to all their marketing material.

2) Is it easier to change jobs now than in the past? 과거보다 지금 직업을 바꾸는 것이 더 쉬워요?

Brainstorming	Direct Answer	더 쉬움
	Supporting Sentence 1	젊은 사람들은 다른 진로를 경험하기 원함
	Supporting Sentence 2	많은 사람들이 직장을 떠나고 빈자리 발생함
	Supporting Sentence 3	세계화 시대에 해외에서 직업을 구하기 위해 떠남
	Supporting Sentence 4	다른 나라에서 일하는 것이 더 나은 복지혜택과 높은 연봉을 보장함

✏️ 다음 **불법포인트**를 참고해서 영어 문장을 완성해 보자. (주어와 시제, 품사와 단복수 등을 고려할 것!)

❶ 네, 과거와 비교해서 지금은 직업을 바꾸는 것이 더 쉽습니다.
Yes, it is easier to change jobs now _____ in the past.
※ ~와 비교해서 : compared to

❷ 이것은 많은 젊은 사람들이 다른 진로를 경험하기를 원하기 때문입니다.
This is because many young people want to experience different _____ .
※ 진로 : career path

❸ 그것은 결국 많은 직장인들이 직장을 떠나고 있다는 것을 의미하고 그러므로 빈자리가 발생합니다.
That in turn means a lot of employees are leaving jobs, therefore creating _____ .
※ 빈자리, 공석 : vacancy

❹ 또한 세계화 시대에 많은 젊은 사람들이 해외에서 직업을 구하기 위해서 그들의 나라를 떠납니다.
Also, _____ , a number of young people leave their country to _____ a job abroad.
※ 세계화 시대에 : in this era of globalisation / 찾다 : look for

❺ 다른 나라에서 일하는 것은 꽤 더 나은 복지혜택과 함께 높은 연봉을 보장합니다.
Working in other countries often _____ a higher salary with better _____ .
※ 보장하다 : guarantee / 복지 : benefits

Q. Is it easier to change jobs now than in the past?
A. Yes, it is easier to change jobs now compared to in the past. This is because many young people want to experience different career paths. That in turn means a lot of employees are leaving jobs, therefore creating vacancies. Also, in this era of globalisation, a number of young people leave their country to look for a job abroad. Working in other countries often guarantees a higher salary with better benefits.

3) Is it a good idea to leave a secure job in order to pursue a dream?
꿈을 추구하기 위해서 안정된 직장을 떠나는 것이 좋은 생각이에요?

Brainstorming	Direct Answer	각자의 상황에 달려 있음
	Supporting Sentence 1	젊고 책임져야 할 대상이 없다면 잃을 것이 없음
	Supporting Sentence 2	꿈을 추구해야 함
	Supporting Sentence 3	나이가 들거나 부양가족이 있다면 안정된 직업을 유지해야 함

✏️ 다음 불법포인트를 참고해서 영어 문장을 완성해 보자. (주어와 시제, 품사와 단복수 등을 고려할 것!)

❶ 이것은 좋은 생각처럼 들리지만 나는 각자의 상황에 달려 있다고 생각합니다.
It sounds like a good idea but I think that it does depend on an individual's _____.
※ 상황, 환경 : circumstances

❷ 만약 어떤 사람이 젊고 책임져야할 대상이 없다면, 그들은 잃을 것이 없습니다.
If a person is young and has no responsibilities, then they _____.
※ 잃을 것이 없다 : have nothing to lose

❸ 그러므로, 그들은 분명히 그들의 꿈을 추구하기 위해서 노력해야 합니다.
Therefore, they should definitely try to _____.
※ ~의 꿈을 추구하다 : pursue one's dream

❹ 하지만 만약 어떤 사람이 나이가 들거나 아이들과 같은 부양가족이 있다면, 그들에게는 더 힘들 수도 있고 아마도 그들은 그들의 안정된 직업을 유지해야 합니다.
However, if a person is older or has _____ such as children, it can be more difficult for them and perhaps they should keep their _____.
※ 부양가족 : dependents / 안정된 직업 : secure job

Q. Is it a good idea to leave a secure job in order to pursue a dream?
A. It sounds like a good idea but I think that it does depend on an individual's circumstances. If a person is young and has no responsibilities, then they have nothing to lose. Therefore, they should definitely try to pursue their dream. However, if a person is older or has dependents such as children, it can be more difficult for them and perhaps they should keep their secure job.

4) What career advice should be given to young people?
어떤 직업에 관한 조언이 젊은이들에게 주어져야 할까요?

Brainstorming	Direct Answer	높은 포부를 가질 것
	Supporting Sentence 1	마음먹고 노력하면 성취할 수 있다고 믿는 것
	Supporting Sentence 2	성장 중이므로 잠재력을 저평가하면 안됨

✏️ 다음 불법포인트를 참고해서 영어 문장을 완성해 보자. (주어와 시제, 품사와 단복수 등을 고려할 것!)

❶ 젊은 사람들은 높은 포부를 갖도록 격려 받아야 합니다.
Young people should be encouraged to have high _____ .
※ 포부 : aspirations

❷ 그들에게는 목표를 높게 갖도록 격려 받고 그들이 마음먹고 노력하면 성취할 수 있다고 믿는 것이 중요합니다.
It is important for them to be encouraged to aim high and believe that they can _____ anything that they _____ .
※ 성취하다 : accomplish / 마음먹고 노력하다, 전력을 다하다 : put one's mind to

❸ 사람들이 나이가 들수록 그들은 그들 자신의 결점들과 강점들을 인식하지만 젊은이들은 여전히 성장 중이어서 그들의 잠재력을 저평가해서는 안됩니다.
As people grow older, they realise their own _____ but young people are still developing so they should not _____ their potential.
※ 결점들과 강점들 : shortcomings and strengths / 저평가하다 : underestimate

Q. What career advice should be given to young people?
A. Young people should be encouraged to have high aspirations. It is important for them to be encouraged to aim high and believe that they can accomplish anything that they put their mind to. As people grow older, they realise their own shortcomings and strengths but young people are still developing so they should not underestimate their potential.

Day 17 Economy & Business 불법포인트 정리

선생님으로서	as a teacher	용기	bravery
미술학원	art institution	감사	gratitude
행복감	a sense of happiness	보수가 좋은 직업	a well-paid job
재능이 있는	talented	직업	profession
마음이 따뜻한	warm-hearted	멸시하다, 깔보다	look down upon
예술적 재능	artistic skill	창의적인 직종	creative professions
예약하다	book / reserve	광고 대행사	advertising agency
~에 매우 만족하다	be very satisfied with	시작하다	set up
무슨 일이 있어도, 결코	for all the world	각종 사업들	all sorts of businesses
운영하다	run	~와 비교해서	compared to
창의적인 분위기	creative atmosphere	진로	career path
무료 수업, 학비 면제	free tuition	빈자리, 공석	vacancy
장애인들	disabled people	세계화 시대에	in this era of globalisation
참을성이 있는	patient	찾다	look for
민감한, 섬세한	sensitive	보장하다	guarantee
석사 학위	masters degree	복지	benefits
자격 요건	qualification	상황, 환경	circumstances
불경기	recession	잃을 것이 없다	have nothing to lose
채용공고, 구인	job openings	~의 꿈을 추구하다	pursue one's dream
직업을 구하다	get a job	부양가족	dependents
가치 있게 여기다	value	안정된 직업	secure job
소방관	firefighter	포부	aspirations
불을 끄다 화재를 진압하다	extinguish fires	성취하다	accomplish
구하다	rescue	마음먹고 노력하다, 전력을 다하다	put one's mind to
사고	accident	결점들과 장점들	shortcomings and strengths
공공 서비스	public service	저평가하다	underestimate

Day 18 ▶ The Government & Law
정부와 법

PART 1

1) What is the legal age of voting and marriage in your country?
2) Is it the right age or would you like to make some changes?
3) If you could introduce a new law in your country, what would it be?
4) What are the criteria to be a police officer?
5) What are the criteria to be a lawyer?
6) Do you abide by the law?
7) Do most people in your country abide by the law?

PART 2

Talk about a new law you would implement where you live to make it a better place.

You should say :
   what law it would be
   how easy it would be to introduce such a law
   how popular it would be
and explain what the benefits of such a new law would be.

PART 3

1) Are lawyers respected in your country? [Why?/Why not?]
2) In your opinion is it fair that lawyers are paid very well?
3) Do you think that being a police officer is a good career choice?
   What are some of the advantages of this profession?
4) Do you agree that all police officers should have guns?

보이는 Speaking QR 코드

PART 1

1) What is the legal age of voting and marriage in your country?
당신의 나라에서 투표와 결혼을 하기 위한 법정 연령은 몇 살이에요?

Brainstorming	Direct Answer	결혼 - 18세 / 투표 - 19세
	Additional Information	정부는 투표 법정 연령을 더 낮추려고 함

✏️ 다음 불법포인트를 참고해서 영어 문장을 완성해 보자. (주어와 시제, 품사와 단복수 등을 고려할 것!)

❶ 결혼과 투표를 위한 법적 나이는 각각 18살과 19살입니다.
_____ for marrying and voting is 18 and 19 years old _____ .
※ 법적 나이, 법정 연령 : the legal age / 각각 : respectively

❷ 하지만 우리 정부는 더 많은 표를 얻기 위해 투표를 위한 법적 나이를 낮추려고 합니다.
However, our government has been trying to lower the legal age for voting to get more _____ . ※ 표 : vote

Q. What is the legal age of voting and marriage in your country?
A. The legal age for marrying and voting is 18 and 19 years old respectively. However, our government has been trying to lower the legal age for voting to get more votes.

2) Is it the right age or would you like to make some changes?
이것은 알맞은 나이인가요? 아니면 당신은 바꾸고 싶어요?

Brainstorming	Direct Answer	결혼하기에는 너무 어림
	Additional Information	투표하는 나이는 문제 없음

✏️ 다음 불법포인트를 참고해서 영어 문장을 완성해 보자. (주어와 시제, 품사와 단복수 등을 고려할 것!)

❶ 법적 이유로는 적령기이지만 나는 개인적으로 실제로 결혼하기에는 너무 어리다고 생각합니다.
It is the right age for legal reasons but I _____ think that it is too young for a person to actually _____ .
※ 개인적으로 : personally / 결혼하다 : get married

❷ 투표의 경우에는, 사람들이 그 나이에 투표를 하는 데에는 문제가 없습니다.
In the case of _____ , there is no problem with people voting at that age.
※ 투표, 선거 : voting

Q. Is it the right age or would you like to make some changes?
A. It is the right age for legal reasons but I personally think that it is too young for a person to actually get married. In the case of voting, there is no problem with people voting at that age.

3) **If you could introduce a new law in your country, what would it be?**
당신이 당신의 나라에 새로운 법을 도입한다면 그것이 무엇이예요?

Brainstorming	Direct Answer	아이들이 방과 후 학원에서 보내는 시간을 제한하는 법
	Additional Information	너무 많은 학원을 가는 건 아이들의 스트레스를 가중시킴

✎ 다음 불법포인트를 참고해서 영어 문장을 완성해 보자. (주어와 시제, 품사와 단복수 등을 고려할 것!)

❶ 나는 아이들을 방과후 학원에서 보내는 시간을 제한하는 법을 도입할 것입니다.
I would _____ that restricts the number of hours that children spend at after school academies.   ※ 법을 도입하다 : introduce a law

❷ 일부 아이들은 정규 학교에 출석한 후에 너무 많은 학원에 가는데, 이것은 많은 스트레스를 가중시킵니다.
Some children go to so many academies after they have attended regular school, which adds _____ .
※ 많은 스트레스 : a lot of stress

Q. If you could introduce a new law in your country, what would it be?
A. I would introduce a law that restricts the number of hours that children spend at after school academies. Some children go to so many academies after they have attended regular school, which adds a lot of stress.

4) **What are the criteria to be a police officer?** 경찰관이 되기 위한 기준들은 무엇이예요?

Brainstorming	Direct Answer	대학에 전공 과정이 있음
	Additional Information	건강하고 용감하며 법을 준수하는 것이 중요함

✎ 다음 불법포인트를 참고해서 영어 문장을 완성해 보자. (주어와 시제, 품사와 단복수 등을 고려할 것!)

❶ 경찰관이 되고 싶은 사람들을 위한 전공 과정이 대학에 있습니다.
There is a course at university for people to be _____ .
※ 경찰관 : a police officer

❷ 그러나 경찰에 지원하는 사람들은 건강하고 용감하며 법을 준수하는 것이 중요합니다.
But it is important for those _____ the police force to be healthy, brave and _____ .
※ 지원하다 : apply for / 법을 준수하는 : law abiding

Q. What are the criteria to be a police officer?
A. There is a course at university for people to be a police officer. But it is important for those applying for the police force to be healthy, brave and law abiding.

5) What are the criteria to be a lawyer? 변호사가 되기 위한 기준들은 무엇이에요?

Brainstorming	Direction Answer	법과 법의 특정 분야를 전공해야 함
	Additional Information	논리적이고 토론 기술을 갖춰야 함

✏️ 다음 불법포인트를 참고해서 영어 문장을 완성해 보자. (주어와 시제, 품사와 단복수 등을 고려할 것!)

❶ 변호사가 되기 위해서는 법을 공부하고 법의 특정 분야를 전공해야 하는 것은 필요합니다.
To be a lawyer, it is _____ to have studied law and majored in a particular field of law.
※ 필요한 : necessary

❷ 변호사는 또한 논리적이고 토론 기술을 갖춰야 합니다.
A lawyer also should be _____ and _____ strong _____ .
※ 논리적인 : logical / 갖추다, 소유하다 : possess / 토론 기술 : debating skills

Q. What are the criteria to be a lawyer?
A. To be a lawyer, it is necessary to have studied law and majored in a particular field of law. A lawyer also should be logical and possess strong debating skills.

6) Do you abide by the law? 당신은 법을 준수해요?

Brainstorming	Direct Answer	준수함
	Additional Information	곤란해지는 것을 피하기 위해 법에 주의를 기울여야 함

✏️ 다음 불법포인트를 참고해서 영어 문장을 완성해 보자. (주어와 시제, 품사와 단복수 등을 고려할 것!)

❶ 네, 준수합니다. 법은 우리들을 보호하기 위해 존재합니다.
Yes, I do. Laws are in place for our _____ .
※ 보호 : protection

❷ 그래서 나는 곤란해지는 것을 피하기 위해서 법에 주의를 기울이는 것이 중요하다고 생각합니다.
So I believe it is important to _____ laws to avoid _____ .
※ 주의를 기울이다 : pay attention to / 곤란해지다, 문제가 생기다 : get into trouble

Q. Do you abide by the law?
A. Yes, I do. Laws are in place for our protection. So I believe it is important to pay attention to laws to avoid getting into trouble.

7) Do most people in your country abide by the law?
당신의 나라에서 대부분의 사람들은 법을 준수해요?

Brainstorming	Direct Answer	대부분의 사람들이 법을 준수함
	Additional Information	한국이 안전한 나라인 것은 법을 준수하는 시민들을 반영한 것

✏️ 다음 불법포인트를 참고해서 영어 문장을 완성해 보자. (주어와 시제, 품사와 단복수 등을 고려할 것!)

❶ 네, 나는 우리나라에서 대부분의 사람들은 법을 준수한다고 대답할 것입니다.
I would say, yes, most people in my country _____ .
※ 법을 준수하다 : abide by the law

❷ 한국은 안전한 나라라고 여겨지는데, 이것은 법을 준수하는 시민들을 반영하는 것입니다.
Korea is considered a safe country, which is a _____ of its law abiding citizens.
※ 반영 : reflection

Q. Do most people in your country abide by the law?
A. I would say, yes, most people in my country abide by the law. Korea is considered a safe country, which is a reflection of its law abiding citizens.

PART 2

Talk about a new law you would implement where you live to make it a better place.

You should say:
   what law it would be
   how easy it would be to introduce such a law
   how popular it would be
and explain what the benefits of such a new law would be.

당신이 사는 곳을 더 좋은 곳으로 만들기 위해 시행하고 싶은 새로운 법에 대해서 말해보세요.

당신은 반드시 말해야 합니다.
   어떤 법인지
   그런 새로운 법을 도입하는 것이 얼마나 쉬울 것인지
   그 법은 얼마나 인기가 있을 것인지
그리고 그런 새로운 법의 이익은 무엇일지 설명하세요.

※ 절대로 지금 시행되고 있는 법에 대해서 말하면 안 된다. 내가 영어로 아카데믹하게 잘 설명할 수 있는 주제를 골라서, 그 주제와 관련된 법을 상상해 보자. 여기서는 교통과 환경 문제를 바탕으로 새로운 법을 정했다.

주어지는 1분을 어떻게 활용할 것인가? (How to Use Your 1 Minute Preparation Time)

1. 질문 파악 새로운 법 묘사에 초점을 맞추는 문제이다.	내가 영어로 잘 설명할 수 있는 법을 떠올린다.
2. 묘사 대상 결정하기 영어로 가장 자신 있게 묘사할 수 있는 법을 떠올린다.	새로운 법을 선정해야 하기 때문에 이미 시행되고 있는 법을 이야기 해서는 안 된다. 다소 허무맹랑하더라도 내가 잘 아는 분야를 선정해서 그럴싸한 논리를 더해서 시행하고 싶은 법을 떠올리자.
3. 하위 질문 확인 + 스토리 작성 하위 질문의 개수를 확인하고, 각각에 대한 답을 적는다.	sub-questions는 3개처럼 보이지만, 마지막 문장의 'and explain what the benefits of such a new law would be'를 포함해서 4개이다. 반드시 4개의 질문에 모두 답하되, 답의 길이는 똑같지 않아도 상관없다.
4. 주제 관련 아카데믹 표현 사용 법과 관련해서 학습한 아카데믹한 표현들을 떠올린다.	implement, in a household, public transportation, more than adequate, convenient, a huge contributing factor, polluting the planet, introduce such a law, owning cars as status symbols, come into effect, incredibly unpopular, environmentalists, approve of the law, in the long term, the amount of carbon emissions, inspire, follow suit
5. 주의해야 할 문법 문제의 시제 및 인칭 대명사 등을 확인한다.	상황을 가정하면서 설명하는 문제이기 때문에, would 라는 조동사를 적극적으로 활용하자.

Brainstorming

Sub-question 1 what law it would be	한 가구에서 오직 한 대의 차량을 소유하는 법
Sub-question 2 how easy it would be to introduce such a law	자동차 소유를 사회적 신분의 상징으로써 여기기 때문에 매우 어려울 것임
Sub-question 3 how popular it would be	믿기 힘들 정도로 인기가 없을 것임
Sub-question 4 and explain what the benefits of such a new law would be	장기적으로 지구에 이로울 것임, 한국에서 생산되는 탄소 배출량을 극적으로 줄일 것이고 다른 나라들이 따르도록 격려할 것임

✏️ 다음 불법포인트를 참고해서 영어 문장을 완성해 보자. (주어와 시제, 품사와 단복수 등을 고려할 것!)

❶ 지금 나는 나의 도시에서 시행하고 싶은 새로운 법을 묘사하고 싶습니다.
Now, I would like to describe a new law I would _____ in my city.
※ 시행하다 : implement

❷ 내가 선택한 법은 한 가구에서 오직 한 대의 차량을 소유하는 것입니다. 내가 서울에서 살기 때문에 나는 대중 교통이 도시를 돌아다니는데 아주 적당하다고 말할 수 있습니다. 자동차를 소유하는 것은 매우 편리할 수 있는 반면, 또한 지구를 오염시키는 커다란 기여 요소입니다. 한 집에서 사는 가족들이 1대 이상 자동차를 소유할 필요는 없는 것 같습니다.
The law that I've chosen is having only one car in a _____ . Since I live in Seoul, I can say that public transportation is more than _____ for people to get around the city. While having a car can be very convenient, it is also _____ to polluting the planet. _____ for a family living in one house to have more than one car.
※ 가구, 가정 : household / 적당한 : adequate / 커다란 기여 요소 : a huge contributing factor
　~할 필요는 없는 거 같다 : it doesn't seem necessary

❸ 사람들이 자동차를 소유하는 것을 사회적 신분의 상징으로 여기기 때문에 이런 법을 도입하는 것은 매우 어려울 것입니다.
It would be very difficult to introduce such a law since people consider owning cars a _____ .
※ 신분의 상징 : status symbol

❹ 그러므로, 만약 이 법률이 시행 된다면, 믿기 힘들 정도로 인기가 없을 것입니다.
Therefore, if this law were to _____ , it would be incredibly unpopular.
※ 시행되다 : come into effect

❺ 하지만 환경주의자들은 이 법에 찬성할 것이고 이것은 장기적으로 지구에 이로울 것입니다. 이것은 한국에서 생산되는 탄소 배출량을 극적으로 줄일 것이고 다른 나라들이 따르도록 격려할 것입니다.
However, _____ would _____ of the law and it would be beneficial for the planet _____ . It would dramatically reduce _____ _____ produced by South Korea and might inspire other countries to _____ .
※ 환경주의자 : environmentalist / 찬성하다 : approve / 장기적으로 : in the long term
　탄소 배출량 : the amount of carbon emissions / (선례를) 따르다 : follow suit

Sample Answer

> Talk about a new law you would implement where you live to make it a better place.
>
> You should say :
>   what law it would be
>   how easy it would be to introduce such a law
>   how popular it would be
> and explain what the benefits of such a new law would be.

Now, I would like to describe a new law I would implement in my city.

The law that I've chosen is having only one car in a household. Since I live in Seoul, I can say that public transportation is more than adequate for people to get around the city. While having a car can be very convenient, it is also a huge contributing factor to polluting the planet. It doesn't seem necessary for a family living in one house to have more than one car.

It would be very difficult to introduce such a law since people consider owning cars a status symbol.

Therefore, if this law were to come into effect, it would be incredibly unpopular.

However, environmentalists would approve of the law and it would be beneficial for the planet in the long term. It would dramatically reduce the amount of carbon emissions produced by South Korea and might inspire other countries to follow suit.

That's all from me, thank you very much for your attention.

PART 3

1) Are lawyers respected in your country? [Why?/Why not?]
당신의 나라에서는 변호사들이 존경을 받아요? [왜?/왜 아닌지?]

Brainstorming	Direct Answer	피해자를 대변하기 때문에 상당히 존경 받음
	Supporting Sentence 1	존경 받는 직업이고 보수가 좋아서 변호사 되기를 열망함
	Supporting Sentence 2	시간, 에너지 그리고 재정적인 투자가 필요함

✏️ 다음 불법포인트를 참고해서 영어 문장을 완성해 보자. (주어와 시제, 품사와 단복수 등을 고려할 것!)

❶ 네, 변호사들은 우리나라에서 꽤 존경을 받는데, 법률적 지식이 없는 피해자들을 대변하기 때문입니다.
Yes, lawyers are well _____ in my country because they _____ who do not have knowledge in the law.
※ 존경하다 : respect / 피해자들을 대변하다 : speak for victims

❷ 많은 사람들은 이것이 존경 받는 직업이고 변호사가 보통 보수가 좋기 때문에 변호사가 되기를 열망합니다.
Many people _____ to be lawyers as it is a respected _____ and they are usually _____ .
※ 열망하다 : aspire / 직업 : profession / 보수가 좋은 : well paid

❸ 그러나 변호사가 되는 것은 쉽지 않는데, 이것은 시간, 에너지 그리고 재정적인 면에 막대한 투자가 필요하기 때문입니다.
However, becoming a lawyer is not easy because it needs a significant _____ in time, energy and finances.
※ 투자 : investment

Q. Are lawyers respected in your country? [Why?/Why not?]
A. Yes, lawyers are well respected in my country because they speak for victims who do not have knowledge in the law. Many people aspire to be lawyers as it is a respected profession and they are usually well paid. However, becoming a lawyer is not easy because it needs a significant investment in time, energy and finances.

2) In your opinion is it fair that lawyers are paid very well?
당신 생각에 변호사들이 보수가 아주 좋다는 것은 공정해요?

Brainstorming	Direct Answer	공부량과 책임감을 고려하면 공정함
	Supporting Sentence 1	모든 변호사의 보수가 좋은 것은 아님
	Supporting Sentence 2	정부의 공익 서비스로 일하는 변호사들은 보수가 더 적음

✏️ 다음 불법포인트를 참고해서 영어 문장을 완성해 보자. (주어와 시제, 품사와 단복수 등을 고려할 것!)

❶ 사람들이 변호사가 되기 위해서 쏟아야만 하는 공부량과 이 직업이 짊어진 책임의 양을 고려하면, 이것은 공정합니다.
Considering the amount of work that people have to _____ become a lawyer and the amount of _____ that the job carries, it is fair.
※ 쏟다, 넣다 : put in to / 책임 : responsibility

❷ 하지만, 모든 변호사들이 보수가 아주 좋은 건 아니라는 것을 인식하는 것이 중요합니다.
However, it is important to be _____ that not all lawyers are paid very well.
※ 인식하는 : aware

❸ 정부의 공익 서비스로 일하는 변호사들이 있는데 우리가 일반적인 변호사에게 기대하는 것 보다 상대적으로 보수를 적게 받습니다.
There are lawyers who work in _____ for the government, who are paid considerably less than what we usually expect of lawyers.
※ 공익 서비스 : public service

Q. In your opinion is it fair that lawyers are paid very well?
A. Considering the amount of work that people have to put in to become a lawyer and the amount of responsibility that the job carries, it is fair. However, it is important to be aware that not all lawyers are paid very well. There are lawyers who work in public service for the government, who are paid considerably less than what we usually expect of lawyers.

3) **Do you think that being a police officer is a good career choice? What are some of the advantages of this profession?**
당신은 경찰관이 되는 것은 좋은 직업 선택이라고 생각해요? 이 직업의 몇 가지 장점들은 무엇이에요?

Brainstorming	Direct Answer	좋은 직업 선택
	Supporting Sentence 1	생활 보장 제공
	Supporting Sentence 2	다양성과 도전을 즐기는 사람들에게 이상적임
	Supporting Sentence 3	모든 사람들이 주당 40시간 동안 책상에 앉아 있는 것을 좋아하는 건 아님

✏️ 다음 불법포인트를 참고해서 영어 문장을 완성해 보자. (주어와 시제, 품사와 단복수 등을 고려할 것!)

❶ 경찰관은 상당히 존경을 받기에 이것은 좋은 직업 선택입니다.
Police officers are well respected and therefore it is a good _____.
※ 직업 선택 : career choice

❷ 이 직업의 한 가지 장점은 은퇴 후 많은 연금뿐만 아니라 많은 급여와 복지혜택으로 생활 보장을 제공한다는 것입니다.
One advantage of the job is that it offers _____, with good pay and benefits as well as a good _____ after _____.
※ 생활 보장 : life security / 연금 : pension / 은퇴 : retirement

❸ 또한 형사사법 분야에서 일하는 것은 다양성과 도전을 즐기는 사람들에게 이상적입니다.
Also, working in the field of _____ is ideal for people who enjoy variety and a _____.
※ 형사사법 : criminal justice / 도전 : challenge

❹ 모든 사람들이 사무실에서 일주일에 40시간 동안 책상에 앉아 있는 것을 좋아하는 것은 아닙니다.
Not everyone likes to _____ for 40 hours a week in an office.
※ 책상에 앉다 : sit behind a desk

Q. Do you think that being a police officer is a good career choice? What are some of the advantages of this profession?

A. Police officers are well respected and therefore it is a good career choice. One advantage of the job is that it offers life security, with good pay and benefits as well as a good pension after retirement. Also, working in the field of criminal justice is ideal for people who enjoy variety and a challenge. Not everyone likes to sit behind a desk for 40 hours a week in an office.

4) **Do you agree that all police officers should have guns?**
당신은 모든 경찰관들이 총을 소지해야 한다는 것에 동의해요?

Brainstorming	Direct Answer	나라와 업무에 따라 다름
	Supporting Sentence 1	폭력으로 악명 높은 곳에서는 총을 소지
	Supporting Sentence 2	작고 안전한 지역, 단순한 거리 순찰에는 총을 휴대할 필요 없음

✏️ 다음 **불법포인트**를 참고해서 영어 문장을 완성해 보자. (주어와 시제, 품사와 단복수 등을 고려할 것!)

❶ 이것은 경찰관이 어느 나라에서 일하고 그들의 구체적인 일이 어떤 책임을 포함하고 있는지에 따라 다릅니다.
_____ which country the police officer works in and what responsibilities their specific job involves.
※ 이것은 ~에 따라 다르다 : it depends on

❷ 폭력으로 악명 높은 곳에서는 일반인들을 보호할뿐 만 아니라 그들 자신의 보호를 위해서 경찰들은 무장하는 것이 필요합니다.
In places which are _____ violent, it is necessary for the police to _____ , for their own _____ as well as the protection of the public.
※ 악명 높게 : notoriously / 무장하다, 무기를 소지하다 : be armed / 보호 : protection

❸ 하지만 더 작고 더 안전한 지역이거나 단순한 거리 순찰과 같은 경찰관이 총을 휴대할 필요가 없는 상황들이 많이 있습니다.
However, there are many _____ where police do not need to _____ such as in smaller, safer areas or if they are simply _____ .
※ 상황 : situation / 총을 휴대하다 : carry guns / 거리를 순찰하다 : patrol the streets

Q. Do you agree that all police officers should have guns?
A. It depends on which country the police officer works in and what responsibilities their specific job involves. In places which are notoriously violent, it is necessary for the police to be armed, for their own protection as well as the protection of the public. However, there are many situations where police do not need to carry guns such as in smaller, safer areas or if they are simply patrolling the streets.

Day 18 The Government & Law 불법포인트 정리

법적 나이, 법정 연령	the legal age	찬성하다	approve
각각	respectively	장기적으로	in the long term
표	vote	탄소 배출량	the amount of carbon emissions
개인적으로	personally	(선례를) 따르다	follow suit
결혼하다	get married	존경하다	respect
투표, 선거	voting	피해자들을 대변하다	speak for victims
법을 도입하다	introduce a law	열망하다	aspire
많은 스트레스	a lot of stress	직업	profession
경찰관	a police officer	보수가 좋은	well paid
지원하다	apply for	투자	investment
법을 준수하는	law abiding	쏟다, 넣다	put in to
필요한	necessary	책임	responsibility
논리적인	logical	인식하는	aware
갖추다, 소유하다	possess	공익 서비스	public service
토론 기술	debating skills	직업 선택	career choice
보호	protection	생활 보장	life security
주의를 기울이다	pay attention to	연금	pension
곤란해지다 문제가 생기다	get into trouble	은퇴	retirement
법을 준수하다	abide by the law	형사사법	criminal justice
반영	reflection	도전	challenge
시행하다	implement	책상에 앉다	sit behind a desk
가구, 가정	household	이것은 ~에 따라 다르다	it depends on
적당한	adequate	악명 높게	notoriously
커다란 기여 요소	a huge contributing factor	무장하다, 무기를 소지하다	be armed
~할 필요는 없는 거 같다	it doesn't seem necessary	보호	protection
신분의 상징	status symbol	상황	situation
시행되다	come into effect	총을 휴대하다	carry guns
환경주의자	environmentalist	거리를 순찰하다	patrol the streets

Day 19 Mass Media, Movie & Play
대중매체, 영화와 연극

PART 1

1) Do you prefer to buy books or borrow them?
2) What book would you take on a long journey?
3) Have you given up reading a book recently?
4) How often do you go to the cinema?
5) What is the advantage of seeing a film at the cinema?
6) Do you usually watch films alone or with others?
7) Which actor or actress would you like to play you in a film?

PART 2

Describe a TV drama that you enjoy.

You should say :
- what type of drama it is
- who the main actor or actress is
- how popular it is with other people in your country

and explain why you like it.

PART 3

1) How have television programmes changed since you were a child?
2) Do you think governments should control what TV programmes show?
3) What is the difference between men and women when choosing what to read?
4) What is the difference between reading and watching TV?

보이는 Speaking QR 코드

PART 1

1) Do you prefer to buy books or borrow them?
당신은 책을 사는 것을 더 좋아해요? 아니면 책을 빌리는 것을 더 좋아해요?

Brainstorming	Direct Answer	사는 것, 내 집에 큰 도서관을 갖는 것이 꿈
	Additional Information	소유한 책의 수를 늘리고 있음

✏️ 다음 불법포인트를 참고해서 영어 문장을 완성해 보자. (주어와 시제, 품사와 단복수 등을 고려할 것!)

> ❶ 나는 책을 사는 것을 더 좋아하고 나는 언젠가 내 집에 큰 도서관을 갖는 것을 꿈꿉니다.
> I prefer to _____ books and I _____ having a vast library in my house some day.　　※ 구매하다 : purchase / ~을 꿈꾸다 : dream of
>
> ❷ 그래서 나는 내가 소유한 책의 수를 늘리고 있습니다.
> So I am _____ the number of books that I own.
> ※ 쌓아 올리다 : build up

Q. Do you prefer to buy books or borrow them?
A. I prefer to purchase books and I dream of having a vast library in my house some day. So I am building up the number of books that I own.

2) What book would you take on a long journey? 당신은 긴 여행을 갈 때 어떤 책을 가져갈 거예요?

Brainstorming	Direct Answer	코헬료의 영어판 연금술사
	Additional Information	흥미진진한 소설, 내 영어 수준도 확인할 수 있음

✏️ 다음 불법포인트를 참고해서 영어 문장을 완성해 보자. (주어와 시제, 품사와 단복수 등을 고려할 것!)

> ❶ 나는 파블로 코헬료의 연금술사 영문판 한 권을 가져갈 것입니다.
> I would take an _____ of The Alchemist by Pablo Coelho with me.
> ※ 영문판 : English language copy
>
> ❷ 이 책은 여행하는 동안 읽기에 흥미진진한 소설이고 나는 내 영어 수준도 확인할 수 있습니다.
> It is a _____ to read while travelling and I would also be able to check _____ .
> ※ 흥미진진한 소설 : fascinating novel / 내 영어 수준 : my level of English

Q. What book would you take on a long journey?
A. I would take an English language copy of The Alchemist by Pablo Coelho with me. It is a fascinating novel to read while travelling and I would also be able to check my level of English.

3) **Have you given up reading a book recently?** 당신은 최근에 책을 읽는 것을 포기한 적이 있어요?

Brainstorming	Direct Answer	포기한 적이 없음
	Additional Information	항상 책 한 권을 다 읽으려고 노력함

✏️ 다음 **불법포인트**를 참고해서 영어 문장을 완성해 보자. (주어와 시제, 품사와 단복수 등을 고려할 것!)

❶ 아니요, 나는 책을 읽는 것을 포기해본 적이 없습니다.
No, I haven't ever _____ reading a book.
  ※ 포기하다 : give up

❷ 나는 책을 반쯤 읽다가 이야기에 흥미를 잃더라도 항상 책을 다 읽으려고 노력을 합니다.
I always _____ finishing books even if I _____ a story halfway through reading it.
  ※ 전념하다 : commit to / 흥미를 잃다 : lose interest in

Q. **Have you given up reading a book recently?**

A. No, I haven't ever given up reading a book. I always commit to finishing books even if I lose interest in a story halfway through reading it.

4) **How often do you go to the cinema?** 당신은 얼마나 자주 영화관에 가요?

Brainstorming	Direct Answer	적어도 일주일에 한 번
	Additional Information	할리우드 블록버스터 영화에 관심 있음

✏️ 다음 **불법포인트**를 참고해서 영어 문장을 완성해 보자. (주어와 시제, 품사와 단복수 등을 고려할 것!)

❶ 나는 영화광이어서 적어도 일주일에 한번 영화관에 갑니다.
I am a moviegoer, so I _____ at least once a week.
  ※ 영화 보러 가다 : go to the cinema

❷ 나는 할리우드 대작 블록버스터 영화를 보는 것에 매우 관심 있습니다.
I _____ watching big Hollywood blockbusters.
  ※ ~에 매우 관심 있다 : be very interested in

Q. **How often do you go to the cinema?**

A. I am a moviegoer, so I go to the cinema at least once a week. I am very interested in watching big Hollywood blockbusters.

5) What is the advantage of seeing a film at the cinema?
영화관에서 영화를 보는 것의 장점은 무엇이에요?

Brainstorming	Direction Answer	분위기
	Additional Information	입체 음향과 대형 화면으로 보는 느낌은 강렬함

✏️ 다음 **불법포인트**를 참고해서 영어 문장을 완성해 보자. (주어와 시제, 품사와 단복수 등을 고려할 것!)

❶ 영화관에서 영화를 보는 주된 장점은 분위기입니다.
The main advantage of _____ at the cinema is the _____ .
※ 영화를 보다 : watch a movie(=see a film) / 분위기 : atmosphere

❷ 인상적인 입체 음향과 함께 대형 화면으로 영화를 보는 느낌은 정말 강렬합니다.
The effect of seeing a film on a huge screen with _____ is very powerful. ※ 인상적인 입체 음향 : impressive surround sound

Q. What is the advantage of seeing a film at the cinema?
A. The main advantage of watching a movie at the cinema is the atmosphere. The effect of seeing a film on a huge screen with impressive surround sound is very powerful.

6) Do you usually watch films alone or with others?
당신은 보통 혼자 영화를 봐요? 아니면 다른 사람들과 봐요?

Brainstorming	Direct Answer	친구들과 함께 영화 보는 것을 더 좋아함
	Additional Information	치킨과 맥주를 먹으면서 영화에 대해 이야기하는 것을 좋아함

✏️ 다음 **불법포인트**를 참고해서 영어 문장을 완성해 보자. (주어와 시제, 품사와 단복수 등을 고려할 것!)

❶ 나는 친구들과 함께 영화를 보는 것을 더 좋아하는데 이것은 그들과 소중한 시간을 보내는 좋은 방법이기 때문입니다.
I prefer to watch a movie with friends because it is a great way to spend _____ with them.
※ 소중한 시간 : quality time

❷ 나는 또한 우리가 치킨과 맥주를 먹으면서 영화에 대해 이야기하는 것을 아주 좋아합니다.
Also I love talking about the movie _____ while we have chicken and beer.
※ 나중에, 그 뒤에 : afterwards

Q. Do you usually watch films alone or with others?
A. I prefer to watch a movie with friends because it is a great way to spend quality time with them. Also I love talking about the movie afterwards while we have chicken and beer.

7) Which actor or actress would you like to play you in a film?
당신은 영화에서 어떤 배우가 당신의 역할을 했으면 좋겠어요?

Brainstorming	Direct Answer	키이라 나이틀리
	Additional Information	내가 가장 좋아하는 여배우, 다재다능함

✏️ 다음 불법포인트를 참고해서 영어 문장을 완성해 보자. (주어와 시제, 품사와 단복수 등을 고려할 것!)

❶ 나는 영화에서 내 역할을 키이라 나이틀리가 했으면 좋겠는데, 그녀는 매우 사랑스럽게 보이고 그녀의 영국 악센트는 지적으로 들립니다.
I would like Keira Knightley to play me in a film because she looks so _____ and her British accent sounds _____ .
※ 사랑스러운 : lovely / 지적인 : intelligent

❷ 그녀는 내가 가장 좋아하는 여배우이고 아주 다재다능합니다.
She is my favourite actress and very _____ .
※ 다재다능한 : versatile

Q. Which actor or actress would you like to play you in a film?
A. I would like Keira Knightley to play me in a film because she looks so lovely and her British accent sounds intelligent. She is my favourite actress and very versatile.

PART 2

Describe a TV drama that you enjoy.

You should say:
- what type of drama it is
- who the main actor or actress is
- how popular it is with other people in your country

and explain why you like it.

당신이 즐겨보는 TV 드라마에 대해 묘사하세요.

당신은 반드시 말해야 합니다.
- 그것이 어떤 유형의 드라마인지
- 누가 남녀 주인공인지
- 당신의 나라에서 다른 사람들에게는 얼마나 인기가 있는지

그리고 당신이 왜 이 드라마를 좋아하는지 설명하세요.

※ 어떠한 TV 드라마를 선정해야 할까? 당연히 한국 드라마보다는 외화, 특히 영어권에서 만든 드라마가 영어로 답하기 쉽다. 시험관도 알만한 외화를 선정해서 대답한다면 시험관의 호응도도 높아질 것이다.

주어지는 1분을 어떻게 활용할 것인가? (How to Use Your 1 Minute Preparation Time)

1. 질문 파악 TV 드라마 묘사에 초점을 맞추는 문제이다.	내가 영어로 잘 설명할 수 있는 TV 드라마를 떠올린다.
2. 묘사 대상 결정하기 영어로 가장 자신 있게 묘사할 수 있는 TV 드라마를 떠올린다.	한국 드라마보다는 외화, 특히 영어권에서 만든 드라마가 영어로 답하기 쉽고, 시험관도 알만한 외화를 선정해서 대답한다면 시험관의 호응도도 높을 것이다.
3. 하위 질문 확인 + 스토리 작성 하위 질문의 개수를 확인하고, 각각에 대한 답을 적는다.	sub-questions는 3개처럼 보이지만, 마지막 문장의 'and explain why you like it'을 포함해서 4개이다. 반드시 4개의 질문에 모두 답하되, 답의 길이는 똑같지 않아도 상관없다.
4. 주제 관련 아카데믹 표현 사용 TV 드라마와 관련해서 학습한 아카데믹한 표현들을 떠올린다.	my favourite TV programme, a British TV drama, created by the BBC, an updated version, the character and stories, originally written by, season, episodes, a feature-length film, extremely popular actors, busy filming schedules, the TV drama, as a big fan of, show
5. 주의해야 할 문법 문제의 시제 및 인칭 대명사 등을 확인한다.	드라마를 묘사하는 문제로 현재 시제를 주로 쓴다.

Brainstorming

Sub-question 1 what type of drama it is	셜록, BBC에 의해 제작된 영국의 TV 드라마, 아서 코난 도일의 소설
Sub-question 2 who the main actor or actress is	두 명의 주인공들, 베네딕트 컴버배치와 마틴 프리먼
Sub-question 3 how popular it is with other people in your country	영국뿐만 아니라 해외에서도 매우 인기 있음
Sub-question 4 and explain why you like it	나는 열광적인 베네딕트 컴버배치의 팬, 내 영어 실력을 향상시키기 위한 아주 좋은 방법

✏️ 다음 불법포인트를 참고해서 영어 문장을 완성해 보자. (주어와 시제, 품사와 단복수 등을 고려할 것!)

❶ 지금 나는 내가 정말 좋아하는 TV 프로그램에 대해 이야기하고 싶습니다.
Now, I would like to talk about my _____ TV programme.
※ 가장 좋아하는 : favourite

❷ 내가 선택한 TV 드라마는 셜록이라고 불립니다. 이것은 BBC에 의해 제작된 영국의 오락물 입니다. 그리고 원래 아서 코난 도일이 쓴 셜록 홈즈의 등장인물과 이야기의 최신 버전입니다. 각 시즌은 오직 3개의 에피소드로 구성되어 있지만 이것은 약 1시간 30분 분량인 장편 영화의 길이입니다.
The TV drama that I've chosen _____ Sherlock. It is a British show, created by the BBC. It is an updated version of the character and stories of Sherlock Holmes, originally written by Arthur Conan Doyle. Each season only _____ three episodes but they are about an hour and a half long, which is the length of a _____ !
※ ~라고 불리다 : be called / ~로 구성되다 : consist of / 장편 영화 : feature-length film

❸ 지금까지 3개의 시즌이 있었습니다. 하지만 두 명의 주인공들, 베네딕트 컴버배치와 마틴 프리먼은 지금 엄청나게 인기가 있어서 그들의 바쁜 촬영 일정 때문에 시청자들은 시즌들 사이를 수년간 기다려야만 합니다.
There have been three seasons _____ . But because the two _____ , Benedict Cumberbatch and Martin Freeman, are extremely popular now, viewers have to wait years between seasons due to their busy filming schedules.
※ 지금까지 : so far / 주인공 : main actor

❹ 셜록은 영국뿐 만 아니라 해외에서도 매우 성공적입니다. 예를 들면, 한국의 많은 사람들은 이 드라마를 좋아하고 많은 소녀들이 베네딕트 컴버배치를 사랑합니다.
Sherlock has been not only very successful in the UK but also _____ as well. For example, many people in South Korea enjoy this drama and a lot of girls love Benedict Cumberbatch!
※ 해외에 : abroad

❺ 나는 열광적인 베네딕트 컴버배치의 팬으로서 나는 그의 모든 드라마와 영화를 보려고 노력합니다. 이것은 또한 내 영어 실력을 향상시키기 위한 아주 좋은 방법입니다.
As _____ Benedict Cumberbatch myself, I try to watch all his dramas and movies. It is a great way for me to _____ my English skills too!
※ ~의 열광적인 팬 : a big fan of / 향상시키다 : improve

Sample Answer

> Describe a TV drama that you enjoy.
>
> You should say :
>   what type of drama it is
>   who the main actor or actress is
>   how popular it is with other people in your country
> and explain why you like it.

Now, I would like to talk about my favourite TV programme.

The TV drama that I've chosen is called Sherlock. It is a British show, created by the BBC. It is an updated version of the character and stories of Sherlock Holmes, originally written by Arthur Conan Doyle. Each season only consists of three episodes but they are about an hour and a half long, which is the length of a feature-length film!

There have been three seasons so far. But because the two main actors, Benedict Cumberbatch and Martin Freeman, are extremely popular now, viewers have to wait years between seasons due to their busy filming schedules.

Sherlock has been not only very successful in the UK but also abroad as well. For example, many people in South Korea enjoy this drama and a lot of girls love Benedict Cumberbatch!

As a big fan of Benedict Cumberbatch myself, I try to watch all his dramas and movies. It is a great way for me to improve my English skills too!

That's all from me, thank you very much for your attention.

PART 3

1) How have television programmes changed since you were a child?
당신이 아이였을 때 이후로 TV 프로그램들은 어떻게 변했어요?

Brainstorming	Direct Answer	채널 선택권이 거의 없었음
	Supporting Sentence 1	인기 드라마, 연속극, 뉴스뿐이었음
	Supporting Sentence 2	오늘날 케이블 채널에서 인기 있는 리얼리티 탤런트 쇼도 없었음

✏️ 다음 불법포인트를 참고해서 영어 문장을 완성해 보자. (주어와 시제, 품사와 단복수 등을 고려할 것!)

❶ 내가 아이였을 땐, 오늘날 있는 것들과 비교하면 볼 만한 채널 선택권이 더 거의 없었습니다.
When I was a child, there were far fewer channel options to watch _____ what there are today.
※ ~와 비교해서 : compared to

❷ 텔레비전에 등장했던 대부분의 프로그램들은 인기 드라마와 연속극 그리고 뉴스로 제한되었습니다.
Most programmes featured on television were limited to popular dramas, _____ and the news.
※ 연속극 : soap opera

❸ 오늘날 케이블 채널에서 가장 인기 있는 어떤 리얼리티 TV 탤런트 쇼도 없었습니다.
There weren't any _____ , which are the most popular offerings on cable channels today.
※ 리얼리티 TV 탤런트 쇼 : reality TV talent show(슈퍼스타K와 같은 오디션 프로그램)

Q. How have television programmes changed since you were a child?
A. When I was a child, there were far fewer channel options to watch compared to what there are today. Most programmes featured on television were limited to popular dramas, soap operas and the news. There weren't any reality TV talent shows, which are the most popular offerings on cable channels today.

2) Do you think governments should control what TV programmes show?
당신은 정부가 TV 프로그램들이 보여주는 것을 통제해야 한다고 생각해요?

Brainstorming	Direct Answer	정부의 역할이 아님
	Supporting Sentence 1	TV 방송국에 달려있음
	Supporting Sentence 2	정부에 의한 미디어 검열은 내 자유를 침해하는 행위임

✏️ 다음 **불법포인트**를 참고해서 영어 문장을 완성해 보자. (주어와 시제, 품사와 단복수 등을 고려할 것!)

❶ 아닙니다. 나는 TV 프로그램의 내용과 그들이 무엇을 보여줄 수 있는지를 좌우하는 것이 정부의 역할이라고 생각하지 않습니다.
No, I don't think that it is the government's role to _____ the contents of TV programmes and what they are able to show.
※ 좌우하다, 지시하다 : dictate

❷ 대중이 무엇에 관심 있고 어느 범위까지 밀고 나갈 수 있고 어느 것을 할 수 없는지를 판단하고 결정하는 것은 TV방송국에 달려있습니다.
It is up to television networks to decide what _____ are interested in and to _____ which boundaries they can push and which they cannot.
※ 대중들 : the public / 판단하다 : gauge

❸ 만약 정부에 의한 미디어 검열같은 것이 있다면, 나는 이것을 내 자유를 침해하는 행위라고 여길 것입니다.
I would consider it an _____ of my liberty if there was that kind of _____ by the government.
※ 침해 : infringement / 미디어 검열 : media censorship

Q. Do you think governments should control what TV programmes show?
A. No, I don't think that it is the government's role to dictate the contents of TV programmes and what they are able to show. It is up to television networks to decide what the public are interested in and to gauge which boundaries they can push and which they cannot. I would consider it an infringement of my liberty if there was that kind of media censorship by the government.

3) What is the difference between men and women when choosing what to read?
무엇을 읽을 건지 선택할 때 남성과 여성 사이에 차이점은 무엇이에요?

Brainstorming	Direct Answer	성별에 따른 차이가 없음
	Supporting Sentence 1	어떤 사람들은 여자는 소설과 패션 잡지, 남자는 경제 서적과 시사 주간지를 읽을 것이라고 생각함
	Supporting Sentence 2	나는 개인의 개성과 관심에 달려있다고 생각함

✏️ 다음 불법포인트를 참고해서 영어 문장을 완성해 보자. (주어와 시제, 품사와 단복수 등을 고려할 것!)

❶ 나는 무엇을 읽을 건지 선택하는 데 있어 차이는 성별로 설명된다고 생각하지 않습니다.
I don't think the difference in choosing what to read _____ gender.
※ ~로 설명되다 : come down to

❷ 어떤 사람들은 여자들은 소설이나 패션 잡지를 선택할 가능성이 높은 반면, 남자들은 경제 서적이나 시사 주간지에 끌린다고 주장할지도 모릅니다.
Some people might argue that women are more likely to select novels and fashion magazines, _____ many men are attracted to _____ and _____ _____ .
※ 반면에 : whereas / 경제 서적 : economic book / 시사 주간지 : weekly news magazine

❸ 개인적으로 나는 이것은 개인의 개성과 관심에 달려 있다고 생각합니다.
Personally, I think it depends on the individual's _____ and interests.
※ 개성, 성격 : personality

Q. What is the difference between men and women when choosing what to read?
A. I don't think the difference in choosing what to read comes down to gender. Some people might argue that women are more likely to select novels and fashion magazines, whereas many men are attracted to economic books and weekly news magazines. Personally, I think it depends on the individual's personality and interests.

4) What is the difference between reading and watching TV?
독서와 TV 시청 사이의 차이점은 무엇이에요?

Brainstorming	Direct Answer	사람들이 상상력을 발휘해야 하는 양
	Supporting Sentence 1	TV 시청은 시청자의 상상력이 필요 없음
	Supporting Sentence 2	독서는 독자의 상상력이 필요함

✏️ 다음 **불법포인트**를 참고해서 영어 문장을 완성해 보자. (주어와 시제, 품사와 단복수 등을 고려할 것!)

❶ 독서와 TV 시청 사이의 가장 큰 다른 점은 사람들이 그들의 상상력을 얼마나 많이 발휘해야 하는가입니다.
The main difference between reading and watching TV is how much people must _____ .
※ 상상력을 발휘하다 : use one's imagination

❷ TV 시청은 시간을 보내는데 즐거운 방법이지만 시청자는 그들에게 보여지는 것을 상상할 필요가 없습니다.
Watching TV is a pleasant way to _____ , but the viewer does not have to _____ what is being presented to the audience.
※ 시간을 보내다 : pass the time / 상상하다, 마음속으로 그리다 : visualise

❸ 어떤 사람이 책을 읽을 땐, 훨씬 더 독자의 상상력을 발휘하는 것이 필요한데 그들은 그들 앞에 펼쳐지는 어떠한 장면도 볼 수 없기 때문입니다.
When someone is reading, they need to use their own imagination much more because they cannot see any _____ in front of them.
※ 장면 : scene

Q. What is the difference between reading and watching TV?
A. The main difference between reading and watching TV is how much people must use their imagination. Watching TV is a pleasant way to pass the time, but the viewer does not have to visualise what is being presented to the audience. When someone is reading, they need to use their own imagination much more because they cannot see any scenes in front of them.

Day 19 Mass Media, Movie & Play 불법포인트 정리

구매하다	purchase	지금까지	so far
~을 꿈꾸다	dream of	주인공	main actor
쌓아 올리다	build up	해외에	abroad
영문판	English language copy	~의 열광적인 팬	a big fan of
흥미진진한 소설	fascinating novel	향상시키다	improve
내 영어 수준	my level of English	와 비교해서	compared to
포기하다	give up	연속극	soap opera
전념하다	commit to	리얼리티 TV 탤런트 쇼	reality TV talent show
흥미를 잃다	lose interest in	좌우하다, 지시하다	dictate
영화 보러 가다	go to the cinema	대중들	the public
~에 매우 관심 있다	be very interested in	판단하다	gauge
영화를 보다	watch a movie / see a film	침해	infringement
분위기	atmosphere	미디어 검열	media censorship
인상적인 입체 음향	impressive surround sound	~로 설명되다	come down to
소중한 시간	quality time	반면에	whereas
나중에, 그 뒤에	afterwards	경제 서적	economic book
사랑스러운	lovely	시사 주간지	weekly news magazine
지적인	intelligent	개성, 성격	personality
다재다능한	versatile	상상력을 발휘하다	use one's imagination
가장 좋아하는	favourite	시간을 보내다	pass the time
~라고 불리다	be called	상상하다, 마음속으로 그리다	visualise
~로 구성되다	consist of	장면	scene
장편 영화	feature-length film		

Day 20 ▸ Art 예술

PART 1

1) Do you like music?
2) What is your favourite musical instrument?
3) Are you learning a musical instrument at the moment?
4) Is live music popular in your country?
5) Do you think art is an important part of life?
6) How important do you think art is in the lives of people?
7) Why do you think people like to have paintings in their homes?

PART 2

Describe your favourite photograph.

You should say :
    what the photo shows
    who took it
    where it is kept now
and explain how you feel when you look at this photo.

PART 3

1) What are the pros and cons of digital photography?
2) Why do some people post their photographs online?
3) When can an image be worth a thousand words?
4) Is a photograph a reliable form of identification?

보이는 Speaking QR 코드

PART 1

1) Do you like music? 당신은 음악을 좋아해요?

Brainstorming	Direct Answer	음악을 좋아함
	Additional Information	항상 집에서 음악을 들음

✏️ 다음 불법포인트를 참고해서 영어 문장을 완성해 보자. (주어와 시제, 품사와 단복수 등을 고려할 것!)

❶ 네, 나는 음악을 좋아합니다.
Yes, I _____ music.
※ ~을 좋아하다 : be fond of

❷ 나는 항상 집에서 음악을 듣습니다.
I always _____ at home.
※ 음악을 듣다 : listen to music

Q. Do you like music?
A. Yes, I am fond of music. I always listen to music at home.

2) What is your favourite musical instrument? 당신이 가장 좋아하는 악기는 무엇이에요?

Brainstorming	Direct Answer	피아노
	Additional Information	클래식 피아노 연주를 좋아하고 최근에 조성진의 CD를 샀음

✏️ 다음 불법포인트를 참고해서 영어 문장을 완성해 보자. (주어와 시제, 품사와 단복수 등을 고려할 것!)

❶ 내가 가장 좋아하는 악기는 피아노입니다.
My favourite _____ is the piano.
※ 악기 : musical instrument

❷ 나는 클래식 피아노 작품들을 듣는 것을 정말 좋아하고 최근에 조성진의 CD를 샀습니다. 그는 폴란드의 수도인 바르샤바에서 열린 권위 있는 제 17회 국제 프레데릭 쇼팽 피아노 콩쿠르에서 우승한 사람입니다.
I love listening to classical piano pieces and I recently bought Seongjin Cho's CD. He is the one who won the _____ 17th international Frederic Chopin piano _____ in the Polish capital, Warsaw.
※ 권위 있는 : prestigious / 콩쿠르, 대회 : competition

Q. What is your favourite musical instrument?
A. My favourite musical instrument is the piano. I love listening to classical piano pieces and I recently bought Seongjin Cho's CD. He is the one who won the prestigious 17th international Frederic Chopin piano competition in the Polish capital, Warsaw.

3) Are you learning a musical instrument at the moment? 당신은 지금 악기를 배우고 있어요?

Brainstorming	Direct Answer	지금은 일 때문에 바빠서 연습을 할 수 없음
	Additional Information	예전에는 클라리넷을 연주했고 언젠가 다시 하고 싶음

✏️ 다음 **불법포인트**를 참고해서 영어 문장을 완성해 보자. (주어와 시제, 품사와 단복수 등을 고려할 것!)

❶ 나는 일 때문에 너무 바빠서 연습을 할 수 없기 때문에 지금은 악기를 배우고 있지 않습니다.
I am not learning an instrument _____ since I am too busy with work to _____ .
※ 지금 : at the moment / 연습하다 : practice

❷ 하지만 나는 클라리넷을 연주하곤 했고 언젠가 다시 연주를 계속하고 싶습니다.
But I used to play the clarinet and would like to _____ it _____ again some day.
※ ~을 계속하다 : take ~ up

Q. Are you learning a musical instrument at the moment?
A. I am not learning an instrument at the moment since I am too busy with work to practice. But I used to play the clarinet and would like to take it up again some day.

4) Is live music popular in your country? 당신의 나라에서 라이브 음악은 인기 있어요?

Brainstorming	Direct Answer	인기가 있음
	Additional Information	국제적인 스타들이 공연을 위해 방문함

✏️ 다음 **불법포인트**를 참고해서 영어 문장을 완성해 보자. (주어와 시제, 품사와 단복수 등을 고려할 것!)

❶ 라이브 음악 콘서트는 한국에서 꽤 인기가 있습니다.
Live music concerts are quite _____ in Korea.
※ 인기 있는 : popular

❷ 우리는 많은 관객이 참석하는 라이브쇼를 공연하기 위해 방문하는 니요나 마룬 파이브 같은 많은 국제적인 스타들을 확보하고 있습니다.
We get a lot of international stars like Ne-Yo and Maroon 5 coming to _____ live shows which _____ .
※ 공연하다 : perform / 관람객이(참석자가) 많다 : be well attended

Q. Is live music popular in your country?
A. Live music concerts are quite popular in Korea. We get a lot of international stars like Ne-Yo and Maroon 5 coming to perform live shows which are well attended.

5) Do you think art is an important part of life? 당신은 예술이 삶의 중요한 부분이라고 생각해요?

Brainstorming	Direction Answer	예술은 삶의 중요한 부분임
	Additional Information	사람들에게 영감을 불어넣고 세상을 아름답게 함

✏️ 다음 불법포인트를 참고해서 영어 문장을 완성해 보자. (주어와 시제, 품사와 단복수 등을 고려할 것!)

❶ 나는 내 자신을 상당히 창의적인 사람이라고 생각하기에, 네, 나는 예술이 삶의 중요한 부분이라고 생각합니다.
I consider myself quite a _____ so yes, I do think that art is an important part of life.
※ 창의적인 사람 : creative person

❷ 예술은 사람들에게 영감을 불어넣는 힘을 가지고 있고 세상을 아름답게 합니다.
It has the power to inspire people and _____ to the world.
※ 아름답게 하다 : add beauty

Q. Do you think art is an important part of life?
A. I consider myself quite a creative person so yes, I do think that art is an important part of life. It has the power to inspire people and adds beauty to the world.

6) How important do you think art is in the lives of people?
당신은 사람들의 삶에서 예술이 얼마나 중요하다고 생각해요?

Brainstorming	Direct Answer	모든 사람들에게 영향을 미침
	Additional Information	동기 부여, 스트레스 완화, 기분도 좋게 함

✏️ 다음 불법포인트를 참고해서 영어 문장을 완성해 보자. (주어와 시제, 품사와 단복수 등을 고려할 것!)

❶ 나는 비록 잠재적이더라도 예술은 모든 사람들에게 영향을 미친다고 생각합니다.
I believe that art _____ everyone, even if it is _____ .
※ ~에 영향을 미치다 : have an effect on / 잠재의식적인 : subconscious

❷ 예술은 사람들에게 동기를 부여할 수 있고 스트레스 완화를 제공하고 단순히 그들의 기분도 좋게 합니다.
Art can motivate people, provide _____ or simply improve their mood.
※ 스트레스 완화 : stress relief

Q. How important do you think art is in the lives of people?
A. I believe that art has an effect on everyone, even if it is subconscious. Art can motivate people, provide stress relief or simply improve their mood.

7) Why do you think people like to have paintings in their homes?
당신은 왜 사람들이 그들의 집에 그림을 소유하는 것을 좋아한다고 생각해요?

Brainstorming	Direct Answer	방을 더 매력적이고, 아늑하고 편안한 분위기로 만들기 위함
	Additional Information	그림은 최고의 신분 상징임

✏️ 다음 불법포인트를 참고해서 영어 문장을 완성해 보자. (주어와 시제, 품사와 단복수 등을 고려할 것!)

❶ 대부분의 사람들은 방을 더 매력적으로 보이게 하고 아늑하고 편안한 분위기를 조성하기 위해서 벽에 그림을 걸어 놓습니다.

Most people _____ to make a room look more attractive and create a _____ , comfortable atmosphere.

※ 벽에 그림을 걸다 : hang paintings up on the wall / 아늑한 : homely

❷ 또한 그림은 현대 사회에서 최고의 신분의 상징이 될 수 있습니다.

Also paintings can be an _____ in modern society.

※ 최고의 신분의 상징 : ultimate status symbol

Q. Why do you think people like to have paintings in their homes?

A. Most people hang paintings up on the wall to make a room look more attractive and create a homely, comfortable atmosphere. Also paintings can be an ultimate status symbol in modern society.

PART 2

Describe your favourite photograph.

You should say :
- what the photo shows
- who took it
- where it is kept now

and explain how you feel when you look at this photo.

당신이 가장 좋아하는 사진에 대해서 묘사하세요.

당신은 반드시 말해야 합니다.
- 이 사진이 무엇을 보여주는지
- 이것을 누가 찍었는지
- 지금 이것을 어디에 보관하는지

그리고 당신이 이 사진을 볼 때 어떤 느낌이 드는지 설명하세요.

※ 사진 묘사는 정말 자주 출제되는 문제 중의 하나이다. 관련된 주제들, 친구에 대한 묘사나 흥미로웠던 여행 등을 준비하며 공부했던 단어들을 떠올리면서 가상의 사진을 만들어 보자.

주어지는 1분을 어떻게 활용할 것인가? (How to Use Your 1 Minute Preparation Time)

1. 질문 파악 내가 좋아하는 사진 묘사에 초점을 맞추는 문제이다.	내가 영어로 잘 설명할 수 있는 사진을 떠올린다.
2. 묘사 대상 결정하기 영어로 가장 자신 있게 묘사할 수 있는 사진을 떠올린다.	갑자기 떠오르는 사진이 없다면 내가 잘 아는 친구나 가족 혹은 유명인과 찍은 사진을 설정하고 스토리를 이어간다.
3. 하위 질문 확인 + 스토리 작성 하위 질문의 개수를 확인하고, 각각에 대한 답을 적는다.	sub-questions는 3개처럼 보이지만, 마지막 문장의 'and explain how you feel when you look at this photo'를 포함해서 4개이다. 반드시 4개의 질문에 모두 답하되, 답의 길이는 똑같지 않아도 상관없다.
4. 주제 관련 아카데믹 표현 사용 사진과 관련해서 학습한 아카데믹한 표현들을 떠올린다.	my favourite photograph, the photo, a picture of my best friend, on holiday in Spain, come on holiday, take a photograph, frame, as a birthday present, that year, look at, it reminds me of happy memories, in my childhood, as a photographer
5. 주의해야 할 문법 문제의 시제 및 인칭 대명사 등을 확인한다.	사진은 photograph, photo, picture, 내 친구는 my best friend, my friend, Taeho, he 등으로 다양한 동의어를 사용해 보자.

Brainstorming

Sub-question 1 what the photo shows	11살 때 가장 친한 친구 태호와 스페인에서 찍은 사진
Sub-question 2 who took it	우리 엄마
Sub-question 3 where it is kept now	내 침대 옆 테이블
Sub-question 4 and explain how you feel when you look at this photo	내 유년 시절의 행복한 기억이 생각남, 태호가 보고 싶음

✏️ 다음 **불법포인트**를 참고해서 영어 문장을 완성해 보자. (주어와 시제, 품사와 단복수 등을 고려할 것!)

❶ 지금 나는 내가 가장 좋아하는 사진에 대해 이야기하고 싶습니다.
Now, I would like to talk about my favourite _____.
※ 사진 : photograph(=photo / picture)

❷ 내가 선택한 사진은 나랑 가장 친한 친구인 태호와 내가 아이였을 때 찍은 사진입니다. 우리가 11살이었을 때, 우리가 함께한 첫 번째 휴가인 스페인 휴가 중에 찍은 우리의 사진입니다. 우리는 그 당시 단지 1년 정도만 서로 알고 있었지만, 나의 부모님은 내가 우리 가족과 여행갈 때 친구 한 명을 초대할 수 있게 해주셔서 나는 그를 초대했습니다. 재미있는 건 이 사진에서 우리 모두 눈을 감았습니다.
The photo that I've chosen is a picture of my best friend Taeho and I as children. It is a photo of us _____ in Spain, which was our first holiday together, taken when we were 11 years old. We had only known each other for about a year at the time but my parents let me _____ a friend to travel with us so I invited him. The funny thing is both of us closed our eyes for the photo.
※ 휴가 중에 : on holiday / 초대하다 : invite

❸ 나의 어머니가 이 사진을 찍고 그 해 나를 위해 생일 선물로 사진을 액자에 넣어 주었습니다.
My mother took the photograph and _____ it for me as a birthday present _____.
※ 액자에 넣다 : frame / 그 해 : that year

❹ 이것은 여전히 내 침대 옆 테이블 위에 놓여있습니다.
It still _____ my _____.
※ ~에 올려놓다 : sit on / 침대 옆 테이블 : bedside table

❺ 나는 사진을 볼 때마다 이 사진은 나의 유년 시절의 행복한 기억들을 생각나게 합니다. 그는 지금 사진 작가로 영국에 살고 있어서 우리는 단지 2년에 한 번만 서로 만납니다. 나는 태호가 몹시 보고 싶습니다.
Whenever I look at it, it _____ me _____ happy memories in my childhood.
My friend now lives in England as a _____ so we only see each other _____. I miss Taeho terribly.
※ A로 하여금 B를 생각나게 하다 : remind A of B / 사진 작가 : photographer
2년에 한 번 : once every couple of years

Sample Answer

> Describe your favourite photograph.
>
> You should say:
>   what the photo shows
>   who took it
>   where it is kept now
> and explain how you feel when you look at this photo.

Now, I would like to talk about my favourite photograph.

The photo that I've chosen is a picture of my best friend Taeho and I as children. It is a photo of us on holiday in Spain, which was our first holiday together, taken when we were 11 years old. We had only known each other for about a year at the time but my parents let me invite a friend to travel with us so I invited him. The funny thing is both of us closed our eyes for the photo.

My mother took the photograph and framed it for me as a birthday present that year.

It still sits on my bedside table.

Whenever I look at it, it reminds me of happy memories in my childhood. My friend now lives in England as a photographer so we only see each other once every couple of years. I miss Taeho terribly.

That's all from me, thank you very much for your attention.

PART 3

1) What are the pros and cons of digital photography? 디지털 사진 촬영의 장점과 단점은 무엇이에요?

Brainstorming		
	Direct Answer	장점은 필름의 낭비 없이 실수를 허용하는 것
	Supporting Sentence 1	쉽게 지우고 다시 찍을 수 있음
	Supporting Sentence 2	사진 현상에서 얻어지는 어떤 예술적 특징을 가질 수 없음

✎ 다음 불법포인트를 참고해서 영어 문장을 완성해 보자. (주어와 시제, 품사와 단복수 등을 고려할 것!)

❶ 디지털 사진 촬영의 가장 큰 이점은 필름 낭비 없이 실수를 허용한다는 것입니다.
The biggest advantage of digital _____ is that it allows for mistakes without wasting film.
※ 사진 촬영, 사진술 : photography

❷ 디지털 사진 촬영으로 만약 사용자들이 실수를 하거나 어떤 사진이 맘에 들지 않는다고 결정을 하면, 쉽게 지우고 다시 찍을 수 있습니다.
With digital photography, if users _____ or decide that they don't like a shot, it can easily be deleted and taken again.
※ 실수하다 : make a mistake

❸ 하지만 디지털 사진 촬영은 필름에서 사진들을 현상하는 오래된 방식에서 얻어지는 어떤 예술적 특징이 부족합니다.
However, digital photography lacks a certain _____ gained through the _____ process of _____ from film.
※ 예술적 특징 : artistic quality / 오래된, 구식의 : old-fashioned / 사진을 현상하다 : develop photographs

Q. What are the pros and cons of digital photography?

A. The biggest advantage of digital photography is that it allows for mistakes without wasting film. With digital photography, if users make a mistake or decide that they don't like a shot, it can easily be deleted and taken again. However, digital photography lacks a certain artistic quality gained through the old-fashioned process of developing photographs from film.

2) Why do some people post their photographs online?
왜 어떤 사람들은 온라인에 그들의 사진을 올려요?

Brainstorming	Direct Answer	친구들과 연락을 취하는 방법
	Supporting Sentence 1	친구들에게 그들이 어디에 있고 무엇을 하는지 볼 수 있게 함
	Supporting Sentence 2	더 많은 팔로워를 확보하는 좋은 자기 홍보 수단임

✏️ 다음 불법포인트를 참고해서 영어 문장을 완성해 보자. (주어와 시제, 품사와 단복수 등을 고려할 것!)

❶ 어떤 사람들은 친구들과 연락하는 방법으로써 소셜미디어 사이트들에 그들의 사진을 올립니다.
Some people post their photos on social media sites as a way of _____ friends.
※ ~와 연락하다 : keep in contact with(=keep in touch with)

❷ 페이스북 페이지나 인스타그램에 사진들을 올리는 것은 친구들에게 그들이 어디에 있는지 그들이 무엇을 하고 있는 중인지 볼 수 있게 합니다.
Posting photographs on a Facebook page or Instagram _____ friends _____ see where they are and what they have been doing.
※ A로 하여금 B하게 하다 : allow A to B

❸ 또한 이것은 더 많은 팔로워(추종자)들을 확보하기 위한 좋은 자기 홍보 수단입니다.
Also it is a great _____ to have more followers.
※ 자기 홍보 수단 : self-promotional tool

Q. Why do some people post their photographs online?
A. Some people post their photos on social media sites as a way of keeping in contact with friends. Posting photographs on a Facebook page or Instagram allows friends to see where they are and what they have been doing. Also it is a great self-promotional tool to have more followers.

3) When can an image be worth a thousand words?
언제 사진 한 장이 천 마디 말의 가치가 될 수 있어요?

Brainstorming		
	Direct Answer	전쟁 지역의 사진들이 잡지나 신문에 실렸을 때
	Supporting Sentence 1	사람들에게 비극과 테러를 생각나게 함
	Supporting Sentence 2	소개팅 할 때 데이트 상대의 사진은 주선자의 설명보다 가치 있음

✏️ 다음 불법포인트를 참고해서 영어 문장을 완성해 보자. (주어와 시제, 품사와 단복수 등을 고려할 것!)

❶ 이 표현은 종종 전쟁 지역의 사진들이 잡지나 신문에 실렸을 때 특히 정확합니다.
This _____ is often particularly accurate when pictures from _____ are printed in magazines or newspapers.
※ 표현 : expression / 전쟁 지역 : war zone

❷ 이러한 사진들은 사람들에게 한 나라가 겪고 있는 비극과 테러를 생각나게 합니다.
These photos remind people of the _____ and terror a country is _____ .
※ 비극 : tragedy / 겪다 : go through

❸ 또한 사람들이 소개팅 할 때, 데이트 상대의 사진은 주선자의 자세한 설명보다 훨씬 더 가치가 있습니다.
Also when people _____ , a picture of their date is much worthier than a matchmaker's detailed explanations.
※ 소개팅 하다 : go on a blind date

Q. When can an image be worth a thousand words?
A. This expression is often particularly accurate when pictures from war zones are printed in magazines or newspapers. These photos remind people of the tragedy and terror a country is going through. Also when people go on a blind date, a picture of their date is much worthier than a matchmaker's detailed explanations.

4) Is a photograph a reliable form of identification? 사진은 신원확인의 신뢰할만한 형태인가요?

Brainstorming	Direct Answer	더 이상 신뢰할만한 형태가 아님
	Supporting Sentence 1	포토샵을 이용함
	Supporting Sentence 2	성형수술의 일반화

✏️ 다음 불법포인트를 참고해서 영어 문장을 완성해 보자. (주어와 시제, 품사와 단복수 등을 고려할 것!)

❶ 아니요, 나는 사진이 더 이상 신원확인의 신뢰할만한 형태라고 생각하지 않습니다.
No, I don't think that a photograph is a reliable form of _____ any more.
※ 신원확인 : identification

❷ 발달된 기술 때문에, 많은 사람들은 실제 사진보다 더 멋지고 더 날씬하게 보이도록 만들기 위해 그들의 사진에 포토샵을 이용합니다.
Due to _____ , many people use Photoshop to make their pictures look better and slimmer than the original ones.
※ 발달된 기술 : advanced technology

❸ 또한 성형 수술을 받는 것이 일반화되면서 이러한 수술을 받은 사람의 사진이 최근에 찍은 것이 아니라면 신원을 확인하는 것이 어려울 수 있습니다.
Also, as _____ has become normalised, it could be challenging to _____ someone who has undergone such a procedure _____ their photograph was recently taken.
※ 성형 수술을 받다 : get plastic surgery / 식별하다 : identify / 만약 ~가 아니라면 : unless(=if ~ not)

Q. Is a photograph a reliable form of identification?
A. No, I don't think that a photograph is a reliable form of identification any more. Due to advanced technology, many people use Photoshop to make their pictures look better and slimmer than the original ones. Also, as getting plastic surgery has become normalised, it could be challenging to identify someone who has undergone such a procedure unless their photograph was recently taken.

Day 20 Art 불법포인트 정리

~을 좋아하다	be fond of	~에 올려놓다	sit on
음악을 듣다	listen to music	침대 옆 테이블	bedside table
악기	musical instrument	A로 하여금 B를 생각나게 하다	remind A of B
권위 있는	prestigious	사진 작가	photographer
콩쿠르, 대회	competition	2년에 한 번	once every couple of years
지금	at the moment	사진 촬영, 사진술	photography
연습하다	practice	실수하다	make a mistake
~을 계속하다	take ~ up	예술적 특징	artistic quality
인기 있는	popular	오래된, 구식의	old-fashioned
공연하다	perform	사진을 현상하다	develop photographs
관람객이(참석자가) 많다	be well attended	~와 연락하다	keep in contact with / keep in touch with
창의적인 사람	creative person	A로 하여금 B하게 하다	allow A to B
아름답게 하다	add beauty	자기 홍보 수단	self-promotional tool
~에 영향을 미치다	have an effect on	표현	expression
잠재의식적인	subconscious	전쟁 지역	war zone
스트레스 완화	stress relief	비극	tragedy
벽에 그림을 걸다	hang paintings up on the wall	겪다	go through
아늑한	homely	소개팅 하다	go on a blind date
최고의 신분의 상징	ultimate status symbol	신원확인	identification
사진	photograph / photo / picture	발달된 기술	advanced technology
휴가 중에	on holiday	성형 수술을 받다	get plastic surgery
초대하다	invite	식별하다	identify
액자에 넣다	frame	만약 ~가 아니라면	unless / if ~ not
그 해	that year		

Your journey starts here.

주한영국문화원 IELTS  영국문화원 IELTS ⊕

Telephone.   02 3702 0601   Website.   https://www.britishcouncil.kr/exam/ielts

E-mail.   exams@britishcouncil.or.kr

Address.   서울특별시 중구 서소문로 11길 19 (정동 34-5 배재정동빌딩B동) 2층
주한영국문화원 (우)04516

아이엘츠 & 유학 준비는
유학 1위 기업과 함께!

종로유학원
Chongro Overseas Educational Institute

대한민국 1등 안심유학

언론사, 소비자, 전문가들이 선정하는 최고 권위의 브랜드 대상에서
수년간 유학부문 1위를 지키며 명실공히 국가대표 유학원임을 인정받고 있습니다.

올해의 브랜드 대상
16년 연속 수상
주관 | 한국경제신문, 한국소비자포럼

대한민국 국가브랜드 선정
유학원 최초 고기브랜드 선정
주최 | 중앙일보, 후원 | 지식경제부

대학생 선호도 1위 기업
12년 연속 수상
주최 | 한국대학신문

국제교육&박람회 전문가 그룹
ICEF 인증

EnglishUSA
파트너 맴버(2023 ~)

대한민국 대표브랜드 대상
교육/유학부분 1위 수상

문의 | 1577 - 5682

시원스쿨LAB × 줄리정 인강

IELTS 불변의 법칙
줄리정 프리패스

베스트셀러 1위 저자 줄리정
대한민국 아이엘츠의 전설!

아이엘츠 대표 **스타강사 줄리정 전 강의 포함**	아이엘츠 불변의 법칙 **베스트셀러 1위 저자 직강**	최신 경향 완벽 반영 **캠브릿지 공식 교재 + 강의 포함**

전 모듈 대비 **기초~실전까지 한 번에**	기적의 비법노트 **줄리정 VOCA 비법노트 무료**	6.5 미달성 시 **수강기간 무한연장**

지금 시원스쿨 아이엘츠(ielts.siwonschool.com)에서 유료로 수강 가능합니다.

* [1위] 줄리정's IELTS 불변의 법칙 | 2017.01.14 YES24 > IELTS 주간 베스트셀러 1위

시원스쿨 IELTS